Tai Kang

MW01705216

CANADIAN

Macroeconomics
PROBLEMS AND POLICIES

Microeconomics
PROBLEMS AND POLICIES

T•h•i•r•d e•d•i•t•i•o•n

BRIAN LYONS

STUDY GUIDE AND WORKBOOK

K.D. Munt
J.W. Mackintosh
D.B. Kennedy
J.A. Rink
Red River College

Prentice-Hall Canada Inc., Scarborough, Ontario

Canadian Cataloguing in Publication Data

Main entry under title:

Canadian macroeconomics/ microeconomics:
Problems and policies, third edition. Study guide and workbook

Supplement to : Lyons, Brian. Canadian macroeconomics. 3rd ed.
Supplement to : Lyons, Brian. Canadian microeconomics. 3rd ed.
ISBN 0 - 13 -117680-3

1. Macroeconomics - Problems, exercises, etc.
2. Microeconomics-Problems, exercises, etc.
2. Canada - Economic conditions – 1971 – –
Problems, exercises, etc. *
I. Munt, K.D. (Kris Daniel), 1948-
II. Lyons, Brian. Canadian macroeconomics. 3rd ed.
III. Lyons, Brian. Canadian microeconomics. 3rd ed.

HB172.5.L962 1991 338.5'0971 C90-095813-8

Prentice-Hall, Inc., Englewood Cliffs, New Jersey
Prentice-Hall International, Inc., London
Prentice-Hall of Australia, Pty., Ltd ., Sydney
Prentice-Hall of India Pvt., Ltd., New Delhi
Prentice-Hall of Japan, Inc., Tokyo
Prentice-Hall of Southeast Asia (Pte.) Ltd., Singapore
Editora Prentice-Hall do Brasil Ltda., Rio de Janeiro
Prentice-Hall Hispanoamericana, S.A., Mexico

ISBN 0 - 13 - 117680-3

Copy Editor: Chelsea Donaldson
Production Editor: Amy Lui-Ma
Production Coordinator: Lisa Kreuch

2 3 4 5 AP 95 94 93 92

Printed and bound in Canada by Alger Press Limited

CONTENTS

MACROECONOMICS

Chapter

MICROECONOMICS

To the student

The purpose of this study guide and workbook is to assist you in learning the material in the macroeconomics and microeconomics textbooks which the guide accompanies. Since each chapter of these texts contains a summary and a listing of important terms, there is no reason to repeat them here. However, this study guide does contain a brief review of the central theme of each chapter, together with those concepts that are the most difficult for students.

This study guide contains numerous specific learning objectives which match the written material in the texts and the corresponding self-test questions in this guide. If you prepare answers to these objectives, you will have a stronger understanding of the material.

An important component of this study guide is the self-tests. By doing the self-tests, you can check your understanding of the basic concepts in each chapter. The self-tests consist of various types of questions (true-false, multiple-choice, fill-in-the-blanks, short written answers, problems and case studies). While doing the self-tests will check your understanding of the basics of each chapter, you should also refer back to the specific learning objectives of each chapter, and assure yourself that you are able to demonstrate the level of comprehension demanded of you in any of the objectives in this guide. Your instructor will likely test you on them.

To make the most effective use of the texts and this study guide, the following approach is suggested:

(i) Read the chapter in the text, including the definitions of new terms and the summary, making notes or highlighting key sections as you wish. You will notice as you use the text that the key terms have already been highlighted for you. This highlighting provides a convenient guide to the main ideas of a chapter. This study guide does not test you in detail on the many new terms that you will be exposed to throughout the tests. You are expected to master these terms on your own.

(ii) Read the review of the chapter in the study guide.

(iii) Do the study guide's self-test questions for that chapter, checking the answers for correctness and referring back to the text when necessary.

(iv) Prepare answers to the learning objectives in the study guide, again referring back to the text as necessary.

(v) Prepare answers to the questions at the end of each chapter in the texts.

Chapter 1

WHAT IS ECONOMICS?

This short chapter deals with introductory matters such as the definition of economics and the nature of the subject, which ranges from technical analysis to value judgements concerning practical policy choices, to broad philosophical issues. It points out that much so-called economic "knowledge" consists largely of myths, and that an important objective of introductory economics courses is to replace these myths with logical economic analysis. While such economic analysis does not automatically make policy decisions for government, it clarifies the economic consequences of each policy choice under consideration, and thus assists in the decision-making process. For purposes of studying economics, the subject is divided into two sections: macroeconomics, which deals with the overall operation of the economy, and microeconomics, which focuses on particular aspects of the economic system.

General Learning Objective

Consider the scope, the purpose, and the approaches to the study of economics.

Specific Learning Objectives

	Self-Test Reference
1. Develop a definition of economics	# 1-2
2. Examine some of the myths related to economic reality	# 3
3. Consider the limitations of economic analysis	# 4-6
4. Distinguish between "micro" and "macro" economics	# 7-8

Self-Test

1. "Economics" as the term is used in its broadest sense, deals with

   (a) decisions made by society concerning the production of goods.

   (b) decisions made by society concerning the distribution of goods.

   (c) how a society satisfies the material needs and wants of its people.

   (d) all of the above.

2. Economics (is/is not) a precise science like mathematics because________________________

____

____.

3. Identify which of the following statements are false with respect to Canada's economy:

____ 1. Poverty would be eliminated if only the minimum wage rate were increased.

____ 2. Even the most carefully thought out government policies could not eliminate unemployment and inflation.

____ 3. Lower interest rates would reduce the level of inflation.

____ 4. A balanced government budget is always desirable.

____ 5. A lower international value for the Canadian dollar would damage our economy.

4. Which is correct? Economic analysis of a policy issue:

(a) will provide the government with a decision as to which policy choice it should make.

(b) will help to clarify the economic consequences of various possible policies available to government, while still leaving it up to government to make the final choice.

5. **TRUE** or **FALSE?** The disagreement which is so common among economists shows that the field of economics is so inconclusive and contradictory that the analysis and recommendations of economists cannot be taken seriously.

6. **TRUE** or **FALSE?** The study of economics emphasizes "what ought to be" rather than "what is" or "what could be." Explain.

____

____

____

____

____

7. "Macroeconomics" deals with ______________________________

____

____

8. "Microeconomics" deals with ______________________________

____

____

Chapter 2

THE ECONOMIC PROBLEM

Human wants are endless. Resources available to any society for satisfying human wants are limited or scarce. For these two reasons no society, no matter how rich, is capable of fulfilling all the material wants of its people. This is the essence of the economic problem: scarcity. No simple solution exists for this problem. However, some economists have suggested that it is just a matter of increasing efficiency, using resources more fully, acquiring more resources, or limiting our wants.

The economic problem of scarcity gives rise to three important issues facing any economy: what goods to produce, how to produce them and for whom to produce. Answers to these questions demand that choices be made by society. Such choices often involve "opportunity costs."

General Learning Objective

Recognize the finite nature of any society's resources, along with the infinite nature of human wants, as being the fundamental economic problem.

Specific Learning Objectives

	Self-Test Reference
1. Identify the three types of resources and their characteristics	# 1-5
2. Recognize the universality of the economic problem	# 6-9
3. Illustrate the economic problem by use of a production-possibilities curve	# 17a
4. Develop the concept of ''opportunity cost''	# 11-12
5. Examine the role of an economic system in developing answers to the three basic economic questions	# 10, 13-16
6. Apply the concept of opportunity cost to a business problem	#17 b-m

Self-Test

1. Besides the physical ability to do work, the labor input includes________________________

____

____.

2. Capital equipment is particularly important because______________________________

____

____.

3. The land resource includes

   (a) any product manufactured from a natural element such as iron.

   (b) forests, fields and streams.

   (c) energy sources provided by nature.

   (d) (b) and (c) above.

4. In a "resource rich" country such as Canada

   (a) land provides such an unlimited supply of materials that it could not be described as "scarce."

   (b) labor is abundant, rather than scarce, as is demonstrated by the high unemployment figures.

   (c) capital is the most abundant of all three resources.

   (d) all resources would still be described by economists as being "scarce."

5. While some of the earth's resources become depleted, other resources are being created through____ .

6 Basic human needs (i.e., those material things necessary to sustain life) are

   (a) limited. (c) abundant.
   (b) infinite. (d) scarce.

7. Human wants are

   (a) endless, since people everywhere appear to desire more goods than are available.

   (b) limited, due to the finite nature of resources.

   (c) always short of what society is capable of producing.

   (d) proportionate to human needs.

8. What is meant by the statement that every economic system (such as socialism, capitalism, communism) faces the fact of scarcity?

   (a) All economies have depressions during which scarcities exist.

   (b) There are times when some products can be had only by paying high prices.

   (c) There are insufficient productive resources to satisfy all the wants of a society's people.

   (d) In the beginning, every society faces shortages, but a mature economy such as our own overcomes scarcity in time.

   (e) None of the above.

9. The economic problem facing any society would be less serious if

   (a) human wants were limited.

   (b) resources were more abundant.

   (c) technology advanced at a more rapid pace.

   (d) all of the above.

10. The "what" problem in economics means that

    (a) goods and services should be produced as efficiently as possible.

    (b) economists have a responsibility to tell us what goods to produce.

    (c) every society should produce only those goods which it can produce most efficiently.

    (d) government must direct our productive efforts.

    (e) every society must in some way decide what goods it will produce (and not produce).

11. The "opportunity cost" of a $150 000 house is

(a) the other products that could have been obtained instead of the house.

(b) the annual interest payable on the money borrowed to buy the house.

(c) not a serious consideration in the decision whether to buy the house.

(d) the $150 000 spent on the house.

12. If all resources in one country were useful only for the production of diamonds, then

(a) the opportunity cost of producing the diamonds would be extremely high.

(b) there would be zero opportunity cost of producing diamonds.

(c) the opportunity cost of producing gold would be zero.

(d) opportunity cost is unaffected by resource usefulness.

13. "How to produce" would not be a problem for society if

(a) technology were to improve in all areas.

(b) natural resources were in no danger of being depleted.

(c) only one mix of inputs were possible in the production of any product.

(d) all resources were equally scarce.

14. The fact that capital is used extensively on Canadian farms whereas labor is used extensively in South East Asia implies that

(a) Canadian farms are economically more efficient than farms in South East Asia.

(b) production is higher on a given land area in Canada than in South East Asia.

(c) production costs per ton of wheat are lower in South East Asia than in Canada.

(d) no implication may be drawn about the relative efficiency of farming in South East Asia as compared with Canada.

15. A nation which chooses to allocate more of its resources to the production of capital goods rather than consumer goods is likely to ______________________________ than a nation that does not.

16. In economics, the question of "for whom" to produce goods and services means

(a) how much should be exported and how much should be kept inside the country.

(b) how society should divide up its total output of goods and services among the population.

(c) businesses must research the market for particular products before they produce and market them.

(d) the more society produces of one product, the less it can produce of other products.

(e) poor people buy macaroni; rich people buy steak.

17. Bob Shaftoe, a small regional retailer, wanted to expand his business interests, so he decided to acquire a manufacturing enterprise from one of his local suppliers. He reasoned that if he could fully employ the business' existing resources he would be able to produce one or a combination of two products for his customers according to the following table.

Production Possibilities	Product A	Product B
A	52	0
B	49	8
C	45	15
D	40	21
E	34	26
F	27	30
G	19	33
H	10	35
I	0	36

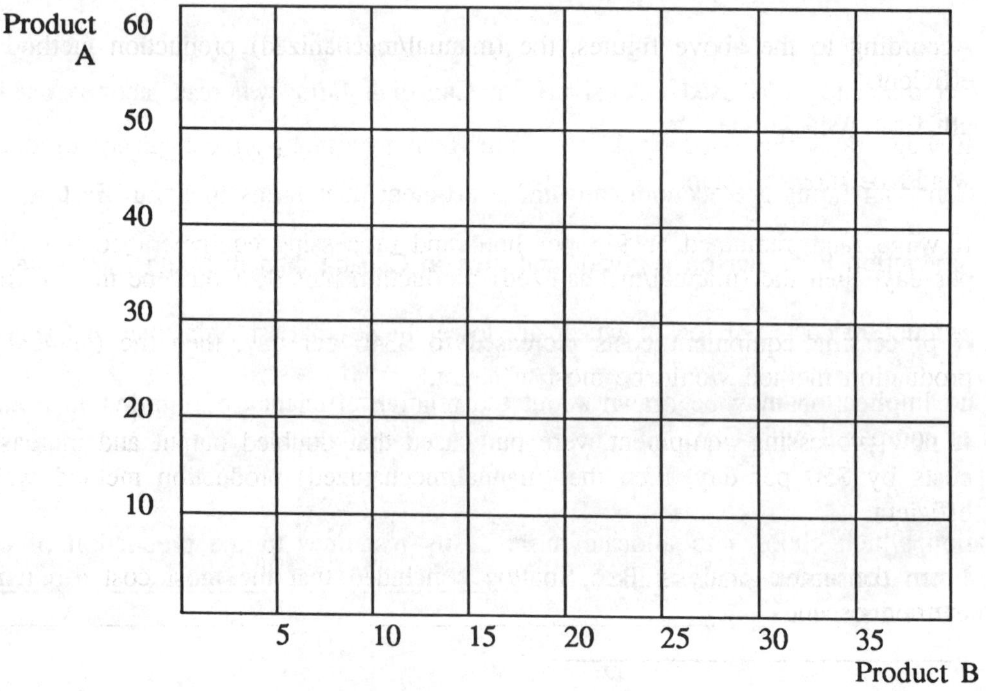

(a) Sketch the production possibility curve on the above axes.

(b) If Bob allocated all of the resources of his new business to the production of product A, the business would produce ______ units of A.

(c) If he chose to produce 26 units of product B, the business would have to give up producing ______ units of A.

(d) If the opportunity cost of the first 8 units of B is 3 units of product A, then the opportunity cost of producing the 36th unit of B is ______ units of product A.

(e) If the business could only produce 26 units of product A and 24 units of product B, Mr. Shaftoe may have reason to conclude that the resources of his business are being ______ ____.

(f) What change would occur in the production possibilities table if Bob could purchase better machinery, hire more staff, acquire more supplies or increase the productivity of his labor force?

____

____

(g) If Bob could manage a more efficient way of producing more of product A, the opportunity cost of producing product B would (increase/ decrease/ remain the same).

Upon further investigation, Bob determined that the business could produce product B using either of two production methods: manual or mechanical. Manual production requires 4 employees, working 8 hours per day at $15 per hour. Mechanized production requires only 2 employees and processing equipment which cost $290 per day to operate. Either method will produce 25 units of product B per day. Overhead costs for each method are $70 per day, and material costs are $10 per unit of output.

(h) According to the above figures, the (manual/mechanized) production method is the most efficient.

(i) If wage rates increased by $5 per hour, then the (manual/mechanized) production method would be most efficient.

(j) If wage rates remained at $15 per hour and processing equipment costs declined by $60 per day, then the (manual/mechanized) production method would be most efficient.

(k) If processing equipment costs increased to $340 per day, then the (manual/mechanized) production method would be most efficient.

(l) If new processing equipment were purchased that doubled output and increased operating costs by $50 per day, then the (manual/mechanized) production method would be most efficient.

(m) From the above analysis Bob Shaftoe concluded that the most cost efficient production method depends on ________________________, ________________________, and ___ ______________________________.

Chapter 3

TYPES OF ECONOMIC SYSTEMS

Chapter 3 introduces the two basic types of economic systems — "command" and "market" — and reviews the strengths and weaknesses of each. Particular emphasis is placed on the role of profits in the operation of the market system, because many people have exaggerated and erroneous ideas about profits. In reality, there is no such thing as a "pure" command or market system, and Canada's mixed free enterprise system contains substantial elements of both private free markets and government influence.

General Learning Objective

Compare the command system and market system as alternate solutions to the economic problem.

Specific Learning Objectives

		Self-Test Reference
1.	Identify the major characteristics of the command, market and mixed economies	# 1-17
2.	Define the concept of "profit" and confirm the importance of profit in a market economy	# 18-22
3.	Assess the role that "competition" plays in an ideal market economy	# 23
4.	Compare the method and the effectiveness of economic decision-making in the command and market economies	# 24
5.	Recognize the element of command and market forces in a modern mixed economy	# 25

Self-Test

1. In a command economy, the decisions regarding **what** to produce, **how** to produce it, and **for whom** to produce it are basically made by ____________________________

____.

2. Which of the following statements concerning a command type of economic system are **TRUE,** and which are **FALSE?**

____ (a) work incentives are less strong than in free-enterprise systems.

____ (b) there is a tendency to overproduce some goods while underproducing others.

____ (c) there are serious planning problems due to the size and complexity of the economy.

____ (d) the level of capital investment tends to be inadequate, so that economic growth is slow.

____ (e) production methods tend to be more efficient than in free-enterprise systems.

____ (f) consumer goods are often inferior in quality and in scarce supply.

3. As part of its "perestroika" (= "restructuring") programs the Soviet Union has in recent years introduced a number of economic reforms, which include:

1. ______________________________

2. ______________________________

3. ______________________________

4. What do you consider to be the likely consequence for the U.S.S.R.'s command system of the reforms listed in question 3?

____

____

____

5. In a market system, decisions regarding what to produce are made for the most part by______

______________________________.

6. The interaction between buyers and sellers in the market for "reemicycles" results in the establishment of:

(a) prices of reemicycles but not the quantity traded.

(b) the quantity of reemicycles traded, but not the price.

(c) neither price nor quantity of reemicycles being traded.

(d) both prices and quantity of reemicycles being traded.

7. The market type of economic system would correct a **shortage** of a product by:

(a) lowering the price of the product and the profits of the business firms causing the shortage.

(b) lowering the price of the product but increasing profits and output of the product by means of a government subsidy.

(c) government instructions to producers to increase production of the product.

(d) raising the price of the product and the profits of its producers.

(e) doing none of the above.

8. A market system type of economy would correct a **surplus** (oversupply) of a product by ____

____

____.

9. In a market system type of economy, decisions regarding how to produce things are made most basically by ____

____

____.

10. In a market system type of economy, the "for whom" question is basically decided by

(a) the way in which total incomes are divided up among individuals and groups.

(b) the marketing departments of businesses.

(c) the social status of individuals and groups.

(d) the government.

(e) economists.

11. Suppose a society discovers the following three production possibility choices as to what goods and services to produce.

	Consumer Goods	Capital Goods	Military Goods
Choice A	5	5	20
Choice B	10	10	10
Choice C	20	5	5

(a) If the governing authorities (i.e., the federal government) decide on choice A, this is known as a

(i) traditional economic system.
(ii) market economy.
(iii) command economy.
(iv) mixed economy.

(b) Suppose another society ends up with choice C. This is a result of the federal government deciding on one-third of the use of resources and private sector decisions accounting for the remaining two-thirds. From the choices in Question (a), this is known as a (i), (ii), (iii), or (iv).

12. Based on the principles of a market-type economy, a third society assumes choice B of Question 11. As a result of this choice, the economy encounters the following:

(a) an **excess** of wheat grains;

(b) a **shortage** of apartments, especially one-bedroom units;

(c) a **surplus** of consumer audio goods;

(d) **too many** computer analysts.

From this set of circumstances, (a) to (d), determine the effects of choice B on each of the following sectors of the economy and provide a **reason** for your answer.

	Effects On	**Reasons**
(i)	Apartment rents ____________________.	(i)
(ii)	Employment of labor in audio-goods production ____________________.	(ii)
(iii)	Wages and salaries of audio-goods employees ____________________.	(iii)
(iv)	Salaries of computer analysts ____________________.	(iv)

(v) Apartment contractors & construction trades ______________________________. (v)

(vi) Price of wheat ______________________________ (vi)
______________________________.

(vii) Incomes of wheat farmers ______________________________ (vii)
______________________________.

13. Place each of the following choices in the appropriate category of the table at the end of this question.

(a) Auto manufacturers install robots to enhance the profits of the shareholders.

(b) Physicians receive high relative incomes based on the limited supply of medical doctors and the high demand for their services.

(c) A production target of 10 000 generators is set for the electrical products industry.

(d) Vladimir Myshkoff is a professional hockey player who played for the Soviet Army Team receiving the standard lieutenant's salary of 20 000 rubles ($25 000).

(e) In 1986, Vladimir played in the Canadian National Hockey League and received a **negotiated** salary with bonuses of $450 000.

(f) Economists are to receive three times the salary of lawyers.

(g) Consumers switch from movie-going to movie rentals for VCRs.

(h) The government requires that retailers use computerized cash registers.

COMPLETE THE TABLE:

Type of Economy	What to Produce	How to Produce	For Whom
Command System			
Market System			

14. "Canadians are a mixed-up people with no sense of ethical values. Everyone knows that hockey is far less necessary than steel; yet hockey players are paid far more than steelworkers." Why is this so?

(a) Hockey players are really entertainers rather than producers.

(b) There are fewer professional hockey players than steelworkers.

(c) Hockey players are more skilled than persons who get less pay.

(d) The demand for hockey players is greater than for steelworkers.

(e) Good hockey players are more scarce, as compared to the demand for their services, than are steelworkers.

15. In a market type of economic system, the questions of **what** to produce, **how** to produce it, and **for whom** to produce are basically decided by

(a) the government.

(b) tradition.

(c) the people, working consciously for the social good rather than for their own interests.

(d) the free decisions of households and businesses, made out of self- interest.

(e) economists.

16. Which best describes how a traditional economic system decides **what** to produce, **how** to produce it, and **for whom** to produce?

(a) An elected government makes these decisions.

(b) People in effect inherit their economic roles, production methods and status from their parents.

(c) Businesses and households make these decisions by producing and selling and buying goods and services.

(d) A king, who by tradition inherits the monarchy from his father, makes these decisions.

(e) None of the above.

17. Which of the following statements regarding the market system type of economy are **TRUE**, and which are **FALSE**?

____ (a) It is a consumer-oriented production system.

____ (b) It provides strong work incentives for people.

____ (c) It grows steadily, and is not prone to economic fluctuations and crises, such as recessions or depressions.

____ (d) It tends to generate a high material standard of living.

____ (e) It tends to result in a quite equal distribution of economic benefits among various groups and individuals.

____ (f) Its production methods tend to be less efficient than those of other systems.

____ (g) Private economic power groups are unable to become established and enrich themselves at the expense of less powerful groups.

____ (h) It tends to create economic insecurity, particularly due to periodic increases in unemployment.

18. Generally, manufacturers' after-tax profits per dollar of sales amount to about _____ cents.

19. These after-tax profits are available for two uses:

(a) ____;

(b) ____.

20. If Beverley owns $12 000 of stock of Consolidated Freebles Ltd., and receives annual dividends of $720, the "rate of return" on her investment (before tax) is ______%.

21. State whether each of the following statements regarding business profits is **TRUE** or **FALSE**.

____ (a) They provide strong incentives for businesses to produce what the consumers want.

____ (b) They provide strong incentives for businesses to produce goods and services as efficiently as possible.

____ (c) They are considerably larger than the general public supposes them to be.

____ (d) They are an important source of funds for capital investment, which increases prosperity.

22. Mary Jones invested $60 000 of her savings in her own word processing business. The business attained sales of $100 000 in the first year of operation and total costs came to $95 000. Thus, Mary was left with $5000. Of the $5000, $1250 was paid in taxes on profits; $2750 was spent on new word processing software and Mary put aside $1000 for her personal use.

Determine:

(a) Profits (before tax) ____________

(b) Profits (after tax) ____________

(c) Mary's before-tax rate of return on her investment is _________

(d) The profits are composed of (fill-in the blanks)

Taxes + New Investment + Payments To Owners = Total Profit

____ + ___________ + _____________ = _________

(e) Suppose that in addition to the $5 000 profit earned by the business Mary also paid herself a salary of $30 000 but in her first year in business turned down a salaried position for $35 000. Thus, Mary's opportunity cost regarding salary is ______. Now, the economist would measure total profits as ______.

23. Which of the following statements are true, regarding the decision by a monopolist (with a great deal of market power) to raise prices?

____ (a) The higher prices will have no effect on resource allocation in this industry.

____ (b) Consumer wishes will not be affected, since they can always refrain from buying the higher priced product.

____ (c) In order to maintain prices at the higher level, the monopolist may deliberately restrict the output of this product.

____ (d) "Consumer sovereignty" in the market place is restricted in the sense that the higher prices do not reflect the consumers' desire for more output, but rather they reflect the monopolist's power to increase profits.

24. Suppose you were employed in the central planning offices of a command economy in which there was practically no unemployment. You were asked to re-schedule for a 20% increase in the production of blue jeans. What are the implications for each of the following industries?

1. Agriculture:

(a) raw cotton production ______________________________

____

(b) grain and forage crops ______________________________

____

(c) livestock production ______________________________

____

2. Textiles:

(a) cotton fabrics ______________________________

____

3. Garment industry:

(a) blue jean production ______________________________

____

(b) woolens ______________________________

____

4. Capital goods industries (e.g., machinery, tools, specialized equipment, etc.) __________

____

25. List five areas in which government gets involved in economic decision making in a mixed economy such as Canada's:

1. ______________________________

____

2. ______________________________

____

3. ______________________________

____

4. ______________________________

____

5. ______________________________

____

Chapter 4

MEASURING THE PERFORMANCE OF THE ECONOMY

This chapter introduces some of the terms and concepts used to measure the performance of the economy with respect to output and prices. While the concepts of GDP and the CPI are basically simple, it is important to remember that these are statistical estimates rather than precise measures of output and prices, respectively. Nonetheless, they provide useful information regarding our economic performance especially in determining total production, types of production and inflation. Regrettably, GDP figures have not reflected the true costs of production, in that they have put no dollar cost on the deterioration of our environment caused by industrial processes. Since the terms introduced in this chapter will be used repeatedly throughout the text, it is important to understand them and their significance thoroughly.

This chapter also explains the terms **labor force** and **unemployment**. Unemployment rates are identified and several criteria are presented which are used to determine the number of people who are unemployed.

General Learning Objective

Measure the performance of Canada's economy, using statistics relating to GDP, employment, and the C.P.I.

Specific Learning Objectives

		Self-Test
1.	Define "Gross National Product" (GNP) and describe its four major components	# 1-6
2.	Demonstrate the equality of the "expenditures flow" and the "income flow" .	# 7
3.	Distinguish between GNP and GDP	# 8, 9
4.	Distinguish "money GDP" from "real GDP"	# 10-12, 15
5.	Consider the limitations of GDP statistics with respect to (a) omissions (b) living standards (c) quality of life	# 13, 14
6.	Use the Consumer Price Index (CPI) to measure the rate of inflation	# 16-20
7.	Calculate unemployment rates	# 21-23

Self-Test

1. Gross National Product (GNP) is defined as The Market value of the total annual output of final goods & services produced in the Nation.

2. Iron ore is sold to a steel mill for $80 000 to be made into steel. That steel is sold to a filing cabinet manufacturer for $180 000, and is made into filing cabinets that are sold for $260 000. The actual addition to GNP arising from these transactions by using the expenditure approach is $ 260,000.

3. The four major components of GNP are

   (a) consumption (C);

   (b) Investment (I);

   (c) Government (G);

   (d) Net exports (X-M).

4. Match the major components of GNP with the following statements.

   G (a) The Government of Canada builds a new technology centre.

   M (b) A Canadian family take a summer vacation to Wally World, USA.

   I (c) An entrepreneur purchases equipment for a new business.

   X (d) Americans buy cedar shingles from British Columbia.

   I (e) Canada Construction builds 100 homes for sale to senior citizens.

   C (f) A student purchases a computer to assist her in her studies.

   M (g) An American executive attends a convention in Halifax.

   I (h) A retailer orders next fall's inventory.

5. If consumption spending is $100 billion, investment spending is $40 billion, government spending is $60 billion, exports are $80 billion, and imports are $60 billion, GNP will be $220 billion.

6. If GNP = 430, C = 200, G = 150, I = 60, X = 50; then M = 30.

7. Total incomes generated from the spending components in question 6 will amount to $430.

8. Suppose that Canada's GNP for a certain year totals $500 billion. This figure includes $10 billion earned by Canadians on investments made in foreign countries, but excludes $32 billion earned by foreigners on investments they have made in Canada. Canada's GDP would be $522

9. The fact that Canada's GDP normally exceeds its GNP indicates that foreign investment in Canada is (greater, smaller) than investments by Canadians in foreign countries.

10. Money GDP (current GDP) is calculated in terms of prices that were stable during the year in which the GDP was measured.

11. Real GDP (constant GDP) differs from the above definition in that real GDP is measured using stable prices of the base year.

12. Historically, money GDP has risen faster than real GDP because Price increases were greater than the real output.

13. Three things not measured by GDP are Quality of life, standard of living and underground Market.

14. The best method of comparing living standards over a period of time would be to compare:

(a) real GNP

(b) money GDP

(c) either GNP or GDP per capita

(d) real disposable income per capita

15.

Year	Money GDP (Billions)	Real GDP (Billions)	GDP Deflator
1981	356	356	100.0
1982	374	---	108.4
1983	406	355	114.4
1984	445	378	---
1985	479	395	121.3
1986	506	---	124.0
1987	---	424	129.7
1988	602	448	134.4

The GDP deflator is a price index for all goods and services produced.

The relationship between "money" GDP and "real" GDP is given by the following equation:

$$\text{REAL GDP} = \text{MONEY GDP X} \frac{100}{\text{GDP DEFLATOR}}$$

(a) The real GDP for 1982 is $345 and for 1986 is 408 Billions

(b) The money GDP for 1987 is $550 billion

(c) The GDP deflator for 1984 is 117.7 .

(d) Money GDP includes changes due to changes in price levels and output levels. While money GDP rose by approximately 69.1% between 1981 and 1988, real output rose by 25.8 % and prices rose by 34.4 %, for the same period.

(e) Between 1981 and 1982, money GDP grew by 5.1 %, while real GDP decreased by 3.09 %.

16. Inflation is defined as The annual rate of increase in the general price level
________________.

17. Inflation is measured by Refers to consumer Price Index the annual increase in the C.P.I.
________________.

18. The Consumer Price Index is defined as A weighted average of the Prices of a "basket" of goods and services purchased by a typical urban family.

19. If the CPI rises from 138.2 to 143.8 over a period of one year, the rate of inflation for that year is 4.1%.

20. If the CPI at the beginning of the year is 127.2 and the rate of inflation during that year is 4%, the CPI at the end of that year would be 132.3.

21. The unemployment rate expresses The percentage of the labour force that is unemployed.

22. If the number of employed people is 12 000 000 and the number of unemployed people is 1 167 000, the unemployment rate is 8.86%

23.

Year	Real GNP $(billions)	Labor Force (millions)	Employed (millions)	Unemployment Rate %
81	136.6	11.9	11.0	7.5
82	130.1	12.0	10.6	10.0
83	134.4	12.2	10.7	11.9

In 1983, employment was up, but so was the unemployment rate. Why? The labour force grew faster than Job opportunities.

Chapter 5

SOURCES OF ECONOMIC PROSPERITY: THE SUPPLY SIDE

With the introductory chapters now complete, we begin our analysis of the operation of the economy. Essentially, we will conclude that economic prosperity is the result of a balanced interaction between the two sides of the economy:

(a) the supply side--the economy must have the ability ("productivity") to produce goods and services effectively, and

(b) the demand side--there must be sufficient demand for the economy's goods and services to enable the economy to actually operate at its potential level of output and productivity.

Chapter 5 deals with the **supply side** of the economy; consideration of the **demand side** begins in Chapter 7. The key concept on the supply side is **productivity**: Chapter 5 discusses several important factors which affect productivity, emphasizing the consumption/saving/investment relationship. How a society chooses to allocate its economic resources between **consumption** (for present enjoyment) and **saving and investment** (for future prosperity) is the most fundamental factor influencing its economic performance. These are some of the most basic and most important concepts in the field of economics, and they are relevant not only to the early stages of an economy's growth (when investment is essential), but also to today's situation. Many observers believe that excessive emphasis on current consumption (and therefore neglect of capital investment) during much of the 1960's and 1970's underlies recent problems such as the productivity slowdown and "stagflation." Only recently have governments begun to place more emphasis on managing the supply side of the economy, or what economists commonly refer to as aggregate supply (AS). Chapter 5 ends with a discussion of AS graphically illustrated as a supply curve. The reasons for its shape and the underlying causes for shifts in its position are also presented.

General Learning Objective

Examine those factors that can influence an economy's ability (potential) to produce goods and services.

Specific Learning Objectives

		Self-Test Reference
1.	Define "productivity"	# 1
2.	Identify the primary source of increased productivity for an economy	# 2, 3
3.	Examine the real costs and benefits of capital investment to society	# 4-10
4.	Identify five secondary sources of increased productivity for an economy	# 11-15
5.	Consider the effects of the productivity slowdown in Canada commencing in the mid 1970's	# 16-19
6.	Identify the probable causes of the productivity slowdown of the mid 1970's and 1980's	# 20
7.	Develop the concept of "aggregate supply"	# 21-27

Self-Test

1. The most commonly-used definition of "productivity" is

   (a) the total output (GDP) of a nation.

   (b) the total number of worker-hours worked per year.

   (c) profit per unit of output.

   (d) output per worker per hour.

   (e) none of the above.

2. The most important source of increased productivity is generally considered to be

   ____

   ____

3. The basic difference between capital and consumer goods is that

   (a) capital goods cost more money than consumer goods.

(b) the production of capital goods is the end goal of all economic activity.

(c) capital goods are used to produce more goods, while consumer goods are intended to be used up by consumers.

(d) capital goods are used up (depreciate) over a period of time.

(e) capital goods are purchased by governments.

4. The meaning of "investment" as a basic economic concept is

(a) using society's productive resources to produce consumer goods.

(b) putting money in the bank.

(c) using money to make money.

(d) using society's productive resources to produce capital goods.

5. To an economist, the basic meaning of the concept of "saving" is

(a) forgoing present consumption so as to free resources for possible investment.

(b) hoarding money.

(c) putting money in the bank.

(d) storing consumer goods (e.g., food) for use in the future.

(e) hoarding goods.

6. Is it true that a society must save if it is to be able to have investment?

(a) No, because capital goods production and consumer goods production are not in any way connected.

(b) No, because you can borrow money to invest it — it need not be saved.

(c) Yes, because the productive resources used to produce capital goods could have been used to produce consumer goods.

(d) Yes, because investment involves the accumulation of consumer goods for future use.

7. If a nation places great emphasis on capital investment, in the short run the levels of consumption enjoyed by its people will be (lower/higher) than they could have been, and in the long run they could be (lower/ higher) than they would have been.

8. The primary cost of capital investment to an economy is

(a) a decrease in leisure time.

(b) the forgone production of future goods.

(c) an increase in the standard of living of its citizens.

(d) the forgone present enjoyment of consumer goods and services.

(e) none of the above.

9. Explain the reasoning behind this statement:

"For an advanced, wealthy nation, economic growth is easy; but for underdeveloped nations with a very low standard of living, economic progress is extremely difficult, if not impossible."

____

____

____

____

10. Industrialization requires vast amounts of **investment**, and a correspondingly large amount of **saving**. Explain how such high levels of saving were achieved in

(a) Great Britain during the Industrial Revolution ______________________

____

____

____.

(b) the Soviet Union after 1917 ______________________

____

____

____.

11. In addition to capital investment five possible sources of productivity are:

(a) ______________________________

(b) ______________________________

(c) ______________________________

(d) ______________________________

(e) ______________________________

12. Suppose that, as a result of teaching night school, a college instructor's income increases by $1 600. If he pays an additional $400 of income tax due to this extra income, his "marginal tax rate" is ______%.

13. Carol Markotic earns $24 000 per year, on which she pays income taxes of $5 000. If she works in the evenings and increases her income to $32 000, her income taxes will increase to $7 000. The "marginal tax rate" paid by Carol will be ________%. The "average tax rate" paid by Carol is 20.8% on an income of $24 000. The average tax rate on the $32 000 income will be _______%.

How would a significant increase in either of these tax rates probably affect Carol's incentive to work and save?

____

____

14. "Economies of scale" are defined as ______________________________

____

______________________________.

15. The small size of the Canadian market relative to other nations is generally considered to

(a) be no obstacle to increasing productivity, because it is large enough to allow economies of scale.

(b) restrict the growth of productivity due to the small size of many Canadian manufacturing plants.

(c) restrict the growth of productivity due to the short production runs arising from the fact that one plant must often produce several different products.

(d) (b) and (c) together.

(e) be the major source of the "productivity slowdown" of recent years.

16. During the 1977-82 period, real output per worker employed in Canada

    (a) increased more rapidly than in previous years.

    (b) generally failed to increase as in previous years, falling in some years and stagnating over the period in question.

    (c) increased considerably, but less rapidly than in previous years.

    (d) declined steadily.

    (e) none of the above.

17. Low productivity generally leads to:

    (a) higher costs and prices.

    (b) lost sales and jobs.

    (c) higher real income earned by workers.

    (d) (a) and (b) above.

18. The declining rate of productivity gains in Canada during the 1980's:

    (a) threatens jobs in Canada's export industries.

    (b) reduces Canada's ability to compete effectively with the U.S. under the Free Trade Agreement.

    (c) results in an increase in the demand for labor in Canada's industry.

    (d) (a) and (b) above.

19. What is the effect of a slowdown in worker productivity?

    (a) a decline in the purchasing power of wage earners' incomes.

    (b) a decline in living standards.

    (c) a failure of wage increases to keep up with the inflation rate.

    (d) all of the above.

20. How has each of the following factors contributed to the productivity slowdown experienced in Canada during the late 1970's and early 1980's?

(a) Recession of 1981-82: ______________________________

____

____

(b) Demographics: ______________________________

____

____

(c) Interest rate levels: ______________________________

____

____

(d) Changing composition of Canada's industries: ______________________________

____

____

(e) Production technology: ______________________________

____

____

(f) Foreign ownership: ______________________________

____

____

21. "Aggregate supply" is defined as ______________________________

____

______________________________.

22.

Cost Per Unit of Output	Volume of Output
$ 2	10
2	20
2	50
3	60
4	70
5	80
6	90
7	100
8	100
10	100

Using the above data plot an aggregate supply curve on the graph below.

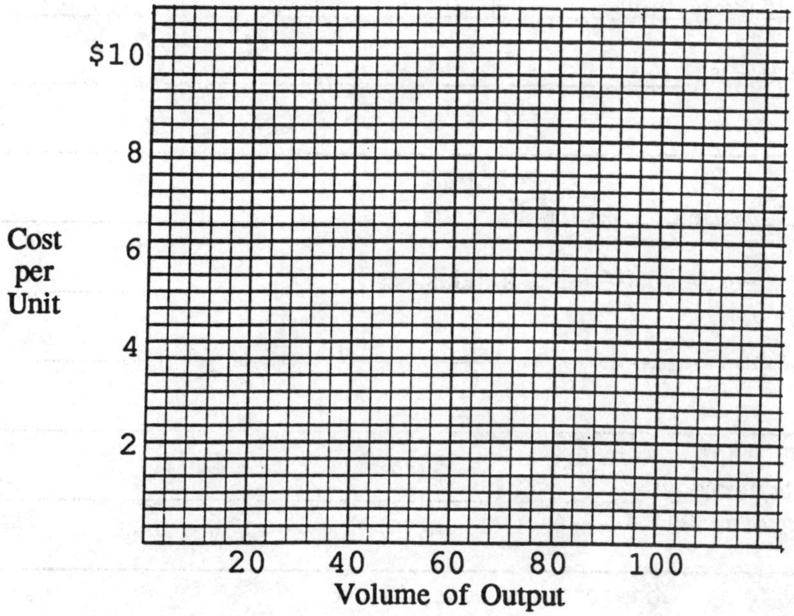

23. State whether each of the following statements concerning aggregate supply is **TRUE** or **FALSE.**

____ (a) The most basic cause of a decrease in aggregate supply is a rise in the cost of producing goods and services.

____ (b) Supply side economists generally advocate policies that encourage households to work, save and invest.

____ (c) A decrease in aggregate supply will generally benefit the country.

____ (d) An increase in aggregate supply will increase the volume of output and decrease cost levels.

____ (e) The aggregate supply curve shows the total quantity of goods and services that will be produced (supplied) at different cost levels.

24. The rising portion of an AS curve indicates that

(a) production costs are rising.

(b) increases in output are accompanied by increases in costs per unit.

(c) some industries may be experiencing production "bottlenecks."

(d) all of the above.

(e) none of the above.

25. The AS curve will likely shift to the right if

(a) factor input costs decline.

(b) efficiency has improved.

(c) an economy's resource base has increased.

(d) all of the above.

(e) (b) and (c) above.

26. The AS curve will shift upward to the left if

(a) the government makes available a tax incentive.

(b) new entrants to the labor force are better trained.

(c) worker productivity decreases.

(d) production costs per unit decrease.

(e) none of the above.

27. If the average wage rate throughout the economy were to decline,

(a) production costs would increase per unit of output.

(b) producers would raise prices.

(c) production would decline.

(d) none of the above.

(e) (a) and (c) above.

Chapter 6

CONSUMPTION, SAVING AND INVESTMENT IN THE CANADIAN ECONOMY

This chapter profiles the basic concepts of saving and investment introduced in Chapter 5. It emphasizes the importance of capital investment (and therefore saving) to the Canadian economy in the past and in the future, when major investment in the manufacturing and energy sectors will be crucial. It is important to note that, although Canadians accumulate considerable personal savings, and business investment was strong as the 1980's came to a close, even more emphasis on capital investment (and thus sacrifices of current consumption) will be necessary during the 1990's. Much of the 1960's and 1970's are now widely regarded as a period in which high consumption was achieved in part at the expense of capital investment, while the 1980's are viewed as a period in which capital investment (and saving) had to be emphasized if serious economic difficulties were to be avoided. These fundamentally important "supply-side" matters of resource allocation have been neglected by economists and government policy-makers for many years, and have attracted increased attention and concern only recently.

General Learning Objective

Distinguish consumption spending from investment spending, and explain the rationale for capital investment with regard to long-term economic growth.

Specific Learning Objectives

	Self-Test Reference
1. Recognize the significance of consumption spending as a component of GDP	# 1, 2
2. Establish the major determinant of consumption spending	# 3
3. Consider the various factors that determine the level of personal savings	# 4-9
4. Indicate the significance of investment spending to Canada's economy	# 10
5. Identify the major determinants of investment spending	# 11-13

6. Establish the relationship between investment, potential prosperity and actual prosperity of a nation . . . . # 14-15

Self-Test

1. "Consumption" includes spending by households on

   (a) consumer non-durable goods, durable goods and services.

   (b) consumer non-durable goods only.

   (c) consumer non-durable goods and durable goods only.

   (d) consumer non-durable goods, durable goods, services and stocks and bonds.

   (e) none of the above.

2. The proportion of total output represented by consumer goods and services is about more than half 63 %.

3. The major factor upon which the level of total consumption spending in the economy depends is

   (a) the level of consumer indebtedness.

   (b) the stock of liquid assets (e.g., bank accounts) on hand.

   (c) the level of personal income.

   (d) the level of personal disposable income.

   (e) none of the above.

4. List five factors which have an impact on personal savings decisions:

   (a) Interest Rates

   (b) level of disposable income

   (c) consumer expectations

   (d) Gov't incentives

   (e) habits

5. As personal disposable income rises, consumption spending ___↑___ and saving ___↑___.

6. Ed's take-home pay is $2 000 per month. Of this, he spends $1 400 on consumer goods and services, puts $100 into a trust company account, and uses $500 to invest in stocks. Thus, each month, Ed's "saving" is $___60___.

7. Which of the following would be classified as "saving"?

____ (a) interest paid on mortgages.

__✓__ (b) repayment of principal on mortgages.

__✓__ (c) contributions to pension plans made by payroll deductions.

__✓__ (d) purchases of stocks and bonds of corporations.

____ (e) payment of premiums for property insurance.

__✓__ (f) purchases of government bonds.

__✓__ (g) putting money into a trust company account to finance a summer vacation.

8. During the late 1980's, the percentage of disposable income saved by Canadians was about ___9___ %.

9. State whether each of the following would be classified as consumption, real investment, or saving and financial investment.

__C__ (a) Fred Framish buys a stove for his home.

__SI__ (b) Fred Framish buys $500 of corporate shares.

__I__ (c) Fred Framish buys an air conditioner for his restaurant.

__SI__ (d) $50 monthly is deducted from Ben Stockton's paycheque to provide for a pension (the money to be invested in stocks, bonds, and other securities).

__C__ (e) Ben uses $100 of his savings to buy a suit.

__I__ (f) Bill Bigelow builds an extra bedroom on his bungalow.

10. Generally, investment by private business has amounted to roughly 15-19% of GDP.

11. The most important factor in deciding the level of investment spending by business is

(a) development of improved technology.

(b) the amount of undistributed profits on hand.

(c) trends in consumer spending.

(d) the rate of interest.

(e) business expectations regarding future profits from investment projects.

12. An increase in interest rates should cause the level of business investment spending to ↓ ________.

13. The three main sources of funds for capital investment in Canada have been:

(a) foreign savings.

(b) business savings.

(c) personal savings.

14. Higher levels of real investment by a society in the present

(a) guarantee greater economic prosperity in the future.

(b) are not related in any known way to future levels of economic prosperity.

(c) make possible greater economic prosperity in the future.

(d) reduce consumption levels in both the present and the future.

(e) reduce consumption levels in the present and do not affect potential future prosperity in any known way.

15. Explain how investment affects the availability of consumer products and economic prosperity in the short run and the long run. In short run I makes capital good hence less consumer goods but in long run I capital can ∴ make more consumer goods + services

Chapter 7

SOURCES OF ECONOMIC PROSPERITY: THE DEMAND SIDE

In this chapter, our focus shifts from the **supply side** of the economy to the **demand side**. The key concept on the demand side is "aggregate demand," or total spending on goods and services. Prosperity requires a balanced interaction between the supply side and the demand side of the economy, with aggregate demand neither too low nor too high relative to the economy's ability to produce goods and services.

If aggregate demand is too low, the result will be classic "recession," with output, employment and prices all depressed. If aggregate demand is excessively high, the economy will suffer from classic "inflation," as high demand generates not only high levels of output and employment, but also rapidly rising prices. Thus, ideally, aggregate demand would be high enough to generate high levels of output and employment, but not so high as to generate too rapid inflation: this would represent the balanced interaction between the supply side and the demand side of the economy referred to in the preceding paragraph.

Chapter 7 inevitably creates some confusion among students with regard to the role of **saving** in the economy. Chapter 5 presents saving as a good thing, essential to investment and prosperity. Now, Chapter 7 seems to suggest that saving is a bad thing, because it reduces aggregate demand, and thus could cause a recession. Which is correct? Would the economy benefit from **more** saving or less? There is no simple answer to this question, as it depends on the balance between **saving** and **investment**. An increase in saving that was not offset by higher investment would not only depress aggregate demand, but also would contribute to lower future productivity and prosperity. Thus, the economy needs a balance between consumption and saving and investment: there should be enough **consumption** to purchase the output which the economy can currently produce (and thus avoid a recession today), as well as enough **saving** to finance capital **investment** (and thus increase future prosperity).

General Learning Objective

To explore the importance of total spending (i.e., the ''demand side'') as a determinant of economic prosperity.

Specific Learning Objectives

		Self-Test Reference
1.	Recognize the components of aggregrate demand	# 1, 2
2.	Demonstrate the equality of GDP and total incomes	# 3
3.	Recognize the threat to the economy posed by savings	# 4, 5
4.	Consider the means by which the leakage effect of savings may be offset	# 6
5.	Examine the "paradox of thrift"	# 7
6.	Describe the conditions that result in GDP being at equilibrium	# 8
7.	Assess the effect on GDP when planned savings is either less than or greater than planned investment	# 9-12
8.	Demonstrate the effect on GDP of other leakages and injections	# 13, 14
9.	Demonstrate how the interaction of aggregate demand and aggregate supply affect the performance of the economy	# 15-19

Self-Test

1. "Aggregate demand" is defined as ______________________________________

   ______________________________________, and consists of four components:

   ______________________________, ______________________________,

   ____________________, and ______________________________________.

2. The largest component of aggregate demand in Canada is ____________________ and the smallest is ____________________.

3. Consider the following statements:

   (a) "Aggregate demand can never be sufficient to purchase all the goods and services an economy is capable of producing, since total income payments will fall short of the value of production".

   (b) "Aggregate demand is always sufficient to purchase all goods and services an economy is capable of producing, since total income payments will be equal to the value of production".

Are either of the above quotations correct? Explain:

____

____

____

____

4. "Saving" is a possible source of economic difficulties because

   (a) too much saving causes inflation.

   (b) savings lead to speculation in the stock market.

   (c) the rich people who save a great deal get richer due to their investment income.

   (d) it can cause an economic slowdown due to inadequate demand for goods and services.

   (e) none of the above.

5. The problem referred to in the previous question will not occur if

   (a) money that is saved is invested in the stock market.

   (b) money that is saved is deposited in banks.

   (c) money that is saved is transferred to businesses and used to purchase capital goods.

   (d) the government places a tax on savings.

   (e) none of the above.

6. Saving can actually help the economic system to grow, if ______________________________

   ____

   ____.

7. If all the spenders in an economy simultaneously try to save more, the resulting change in national income will pull savings (up/down).
   This prediction is commonly referred to as the ______________________________.

8. If planned investment is **equal** to planned savings, GDP and total income will tend to ______

____.

9. If planned investment is **less** than planned savings, GDP and total income will tend to ______

____.

10. The effect described in the previous question will occur because

    (a) output is depressed.

    (b) prices are depressed and output remains stable.

    (c) output rises.

    (d) prices and output rise.

    (e) prices and/or output are depressed.

11. If planned investment is **greater** than planned savings, GDP and total incomes will tend to __

____.

12. The effect described in the previous question will occur because

    (a) prices and output are depressed.

    (b) prices and/or output rise.

    (c) prices rise and output remains stable.

    (d) output is depressed.

    (e) output rises.

13. If all other things remain constant:

    (a) an increase in taxes will cause GDP to ______________________________;

    (b) a decrease in taxes will cause GDP to ______________________________;

    (c) a decrease in government spending will cause GDP to tend to ______________

    ____.

(d) an increase in investment spending will cause GDP to ______________________________

____.

14. Fill in the blanks:

(a) If leakages exceed injections, then AD, output, employment and prices will ____________ ______________________________ and the economy will likely ______________________________;

(b) If (I + G + X) > (S + T + M) then AD will ______________________________ and the economy will ____________________;

(c) If leakages ____________________ injections then the economy will likely remain stable.

15.

AD		AD'	
Price Level	Volume Output	Price Level	Volume Output
$8	50%	$10	70%
6	60	8	80
4	70	6	90
2	80	4	100
2	90		

Using the above data, plot two aggregate demand curves (AD & AD') on the graph below.

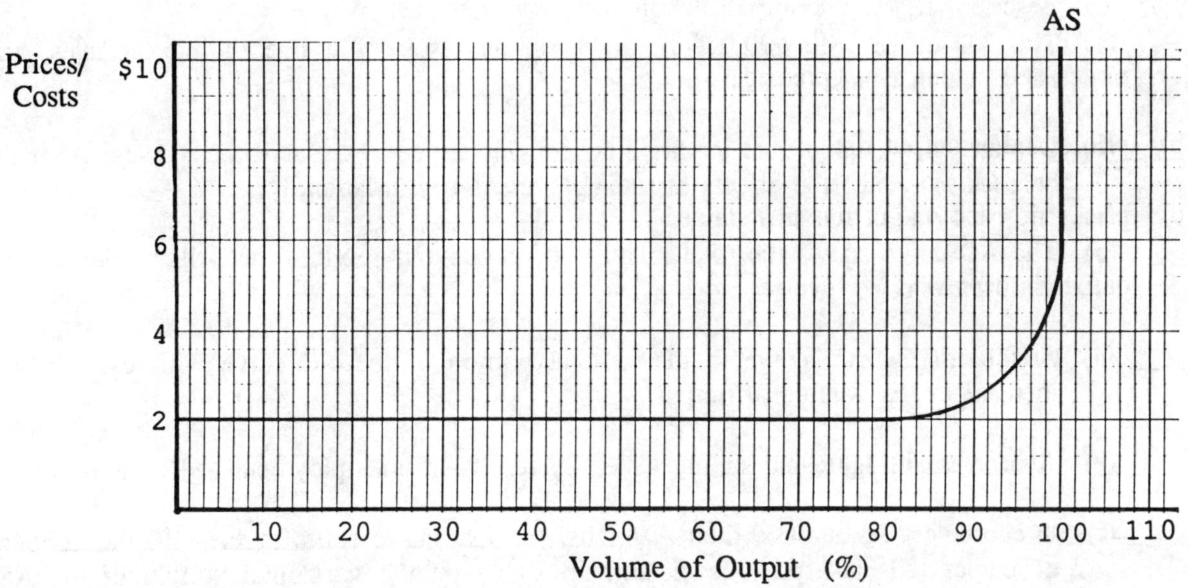

The resulting shift in the above AD curve (AD to AD[1]) is likely to

(a) (increase/decrease) price levels.

(b) (increase/decrease) real GDP.

(c) (increase/decrease) unemployment.

(d) (increase/decrease) incomes.

(e) (increase/decrease) interest rates.

(f) (increase/decrease) consumption.

16. Explain or illustrate on the graph in Question 15 how inflation (rising prices) caused by an increase in AD might have been reduced or avoided.

____

____

____

____

17. State whether each of the following is **TRUE** or **FALSE**.

____ (a) The AD curve will shift to the right as the result of a rise in interest rates, all things being equal.

____ (b) Demand management and supply side policies aimed at influencing AD and AS can be used to reduce the effects of unemployment and inflation.

____ (c) The AD curve shows the total quantity of goods and services that will be demanded at different price levels.

____ (d) A shift in the AD curve in the vertical portion of the AS curve will result in an increase in the volume of output.

____ (e) A decrease in aggregate supply generally results in unemployment and inflation.

____ (f) If consumers spend less, then AD falls, the AD curve shifts to the left, the volume of output falls and price levels remain stable on the horizontal portion of the AS curve.

18. During a recession,

(a) aggregate demand is depressed, causing output, employment and prices to be depressed.

(b) aggregate demand is depressed and output and employment rise, causing prices to fall.

(c) aggregate demand is depressed, causing output and employment to be depressed and prices to rise.

(d) prices fall, causing aggregate demand to rise and output and employment to rise.

(e) prices rise, causing output, employment and aggregate demand to fall.

19. During an economic boom,

(a) prices rise, causing aggregate demand, output and employment to fall.

(b) prices fall, causing output, employment and aggregate demand to rise.

(c) aggregate demand rises, causing output and employment to rise, which causes prices to fall.

(d) aggregate demand rises and output and employment fall, causing prices to rise.

(e) aggregate demand rises, causing output, employment and prices to rise.

Chapter 8

THE PROBLEM OF ECONOMIC INSTABILITY

Chapter 8 examines a long-standing problem associated with market economies: fluctuations in economic activity (business cycles), in which the economy alternates between periods of rapid expansion and recessions. These business cycles arise from fluctuations in aggregate demand, which in turn generate fluctuations in output, employment and price levels.

These fluctuations in aggregate demand arise from various factors, which are identified as fluctuations in investment spending, the "multiplier effect," the "accelerator effect" and fluctuations in export demand. While these factors can be separated for purposes of analysis, the separation is in reality quite artificial. Acutally, it is the dynamic interaction of all of these factors which generates business cycles. For instance, in any recession, depressed investment spending and depressed consumption spending are each partly the **cause** and partly the **result** of the recession: through the "multiplier" and "accelerator" effects, each is related to the other, partly as a cause and partly as a result.

Chapter 8 places particular emphasis on the recession side of business cycles, leaving the problem of inflation to be examined in Chapter 12. Also, in order to present the problem of business cycles as simply and clearly as possible, Chapter 8 omits any reference to the government sector of the economy and the government's likely responses to economic downturns. The role of the government in dealing with business cycles will be covered in Chapters 9 and 11, as our coverage of the operation of the economy becomes more complete.

General Learning Objective

Consider the reasons for fluctuations in economic activity.

Specific Learning Objectives

	Self-Test Reference
1. Recognize the four phases of the business cycle	#1, 2
2. Review the development of business cycle theories and recognize the importance of aggregate demand as a source of cyclical fluctuations	# 3
3. Account for the instability of investment spending	# 4-6

4. Develop the theory of the multiplier, demonstrate its contribution to economic instability, and identify the size of the Canadian multiplier . . . . # 7-13

5. Consider the "accelerator effect" as a cause of cyclical swings, and demonstrate the effect of a combined accelerator-multiplier reaction . . . . # 14-23

6. Profile an economic boom and an economic recession . . . . # 24-28

7. Examine the approaches to economic forecasting . . . . # 29

Self-Test

1. Identify the phase of the business cycle indicated by each of the following:

Contraction (a) Unemployment is rising, consumer spending is at comparatively low levels.

expansion (b) Both employment and real investment are rising.

Peak (c) Inflation is at its highest level and output is considered to be at maximum.

Trough (d) Unemployment has peaked, economic activity is at its slowest, and prices are depressed but stable.

2. The sequence "expansion — peak — contraction — trough":

(a) Indicates four distinct business cycles.

(b) Indicates four distinct phases of a single business cycle.

(c) Indicates two distinct business cycles — an upswing and a downswing.

(d) Indicates four phases of four business cycles.

3. The most likely cause of business cycles is Fluctuations in aggregate Demand (Total demand in the economy).

4. Investment spending tends to be the most variable of the components of aggregate demand since:

(a) residential construction activity changes substantially between periods of economic expansion and recession.

(b) investment spending decisions are based on business expectations of future sales and profits.

(c) businesses attempt to reduce their inventory investment when recessions are expected.

(d) inventory levels increase during boom periods.

(e) all of the above.

5. Which of the following components of business investment is considered to be the most variable?

(a) production of equipment.

(b) construction.

(c) additions to business inventories.

(d) no single component is more variable than any other.

6. Which of the following best describes the effect of changes in business investment on the economy?

(a) The leakage of saving in fairly steady, and fluctuations in investment can mean that leakages are not matched by injections, causing economic activity to fluctuate.

(b) Although business investment is an injection, leakages of the same magnitude can be expected to offset the injections, resulting in economic stability.

(c) An increase in investment will automatically cause savings to increase, thereby resulting in a decline in economic activity.

7. The size of the multiplier depends on The fraction of changes in income which is re-spent. ______.

8. The greater the "leakages" from re-spending, the smaller the multiplier effect. The three leakages from re-spending are imports, Taxes, and savings.

9. If 40% of increases in income are re-spent, the size of the multiplier will be ______

1.67 ______.

10. The multiplier effect tends to

(a) smooth out upswings and downswings in business activity.

(b) cause a small change in investment to result in a considerably larger change in GDP and total incomes.

(c) slow down the growth of the economy.

(d) make price levels more stable.

(e) operate more strongly in economic upswings than in downswings.

11. A multiplier of 3 implies that when

(a) investment increases by $3, GDP and total incomes increase by $1.

(b) investment increases by $1, GDP and total incomes increase by $3.

(c) investment increases by $1, consumption increases by $3.

(d) consumption increases by $3, investment increases by $1.

(e) consumption increases by $1, investment increases by $3.

12. The best estimate of the Canadian multiplier for a one year period is 1.6 ______.

13. Because of the pure water and the transportation access, a company builds a distillery in rural Manitoba. In the first year of operation, the company employs two hundred local people and pays out a total wage and salary bill of $6 million. After personal saving, taxes and the purchase of imports, the distillery workers spend $2 million on domestic consumer goods and services.

(a) The multiplier is 1.5 ______.

(b) Suppose the owners of the business invest $9 million in new machinery and equipment for the distillery. Over time, what is the total effect on the area's income? Also, show the first 3 stages of the multiplier effect.

Initial investment spending $ 9 ______

Stage 1 of respending $ 3 ______

Stage 2 of respending $1 million
TOTAL CHANGE IN INCOME
(End of Stage 2): $13 " "
TOTAL CHANGE IN INCOME
(End of Series): $13.5 " "

(c) If the multiplier had been 2.5, then the total change in income in part (b) would be $22.5 million

14. The "accelerator effect" refers to a situation in which

(a) a fall in the demand for capital goods will cause the demand for consumer goods to fall.

(b) without increased government spending, the economy will collapse.

(c) increases in incomes are partially re-spent, causing larger increases in GDP and total incomes.

(d) an increase in the demand for consumer goods causes an increase in the demand for capital goods.

(e) none of the above.

15. The condition that must exist if the accelerator effect is to operate is that The economy must be at or near capacity output.

16. "Induced investment" refers to Capital investment spending undertaken by business in response to increases in sales that have brought production to near-capacity levels that are expected to continue.

17. For the level of induced investment to be maintained, consumer spending must keep rising.

18. If consumer spending rises more slowly than in the past, induced investment will drop.

19. Suppose a company maintains $3 of capital for every $1 of sales. If current sales are $1 million, the desired level of capital is 3. If sales rise to $3 million, desired capital is 9. Ignoring the effects of capital consumption, this mean that new investment for this company is 6.

20. The effect of the accelerator on the economy is to

(a) make the demand for capital goods more stable.

(b) reduce consumer spending.

(c) ensure that the economy will continue to grow steadily.

(d) smooth out the economic fluctuations associated with the business cycle.

(e) make the demand for capital goods even more unstable.

21. Economists estimate that when the multiplier effect and the accelerator effect are combined, an increase in investment spending of $80 million can cause GDP and total incomes to rise between $ 160 million and $ 240.

22. Suppose that the distillery described in Question 13 has the following levels of sales. The owners wish to maintain a constant capital to sales ratio.

Year	Sales	Capital	Investment
1987	$12 million	$30 million	
1988	$15 million	________	________
1989	$20 million	________	________

Answer parts (a) and (b) to fill in the table.

(a) Assuming no lags in investment spending, determine the desired level of capital for the years 1988 and 1989.

(b) As a result of the new capital requirements, what is the level of investment spending (excluding depreciation of existing capital) for the years 1988 and 1989?

(c) In 1990, distillery sales remained at $20 million. Determine the following:

Required capital for this level of sales 50 million

New investment required 0.

(d) Based on Questions (a) through (c), determine the expansion years and the recession years.

1988 expansion

1989 expansion

1990 Recession

23. The previous question demonstrated the accelerated effects of investment spending in response to increased yearly sales. We must remember that the multiplier is still to be considered in this analysis as strengthening the expansionary phases of the business cycle of 1988 and 1989 and adding to the recessionary tendencies of 1990.

Assuming a multiplier of 2, complete the following table using the investment spending from Question 22 to confirm the interaction of accelerator and multiplier.

Year	Investment Spending	Change in Income
1988	7.5	15
1989	12.5	25
1990	0	0

24. During recessions, which is most likely to decline sharply?

(a) household spending on consumer goods.

(b) government spending on goods and services.

(c) consumer spending on services.

(d) business spending on capital goods.

(e) municipal government spending.

25. Which of the following are likely to happen during a typical economic boom?

Yes (a) Housing sales increase rapidly.

Yes (b) Capital investment spending by business increases more rapidly than usual.

Yes (c) The prices of goods and services in general increase more rapidly than usual.

Yes (d) Automobile sales increase rapidly.

NO (e) Interest rates decline.

26. Which of the following are likely to happen during a typical economic recession?

Yes (a) Automobile sales decrease.

Yes (b) Interest rates decline.

Yes (c) Housing sales are depressed.

Yes (d) The prices of goods and services in general increase more rapidly than usual.

No (e) Unemployment increases.

27. During a recession, which one of the following would most likely experience unemployment?

(a) teachers
(b) brewers
(c) managers
(d) lawyers
(e) bricklayers

28. Describe the effect of the 1981-82 recession on each of the following:

(a) Industrial capacity utilization rate ______________________________

______________________________.

(b) Consumer spending ______________________________

______________________________.

(c) Corporate profits ______________________________

______________________________.

(d) Real business investment spending ______________________________

______________________________.

(e) Employment ______________________________

______________________________.

(f) Unemployment rate ______________________________

______________________________.

29. Briefly describe two approaches used to prepare economic forecasts:

(1) ______________________________

______________________________.

(2) ______________________________

______________________________.

Chapter 9

STABILIZING THE ECONOMY: GOVERNMENT FISCAL POLICY

This chapter introduces the concept that the performance of the entire economy can be influenced by government policies which affect the level of aggregate demand. In particular, "fiscal policy" uses budget deficits to stimulate aggregate demand in order to combat recessions; budget surpluses are used as an anti-inflationary policy to dampen aggregate demand. Chapter 9 emphasizes the use of budget deficits to stimulate the economy, leaving anti-inflation policies to a later chapter.

To finance its budget deficits, the government normally borrows funds through bond issues, thereby incurring a "National Debt." Properly managed deficits and debt can have beneficial effects on the economy, and have become an accepted part of government economic policy. However, both economic theory and recent experience suggest that **excessively large** budget deficits can harm the economy's performance. If such deficits are financed by "printing money" on a large scale, it is obvious that severe inflation will result. A more subtle problem can occur if such deficits are financed by borrowing--the result of this can be economic **stagnation**, as the economy, productivity and living standards fail to grow. This seems to contradict everything that we have said about budget deficits, which are supposed to **stimulate** aggregate demand and the economy. However, the problem with excessive government deficits and borrowing occurs on the supply side of the economy. The economy only generates a certain volume of saving in any given year, so if government borrowing absorbs too much of these savings, fewer funds will be available for capital investment by private business, which can be "crowded out" by government borrowing. In effect, then, **excessive** government borrowing for spending on consumption purposes (tax cuts, social welfare programs and so on) can shift the allocation of society's economic resources away from investment and toward consumption, and thus increase current prosperity at the expense of future prosperity. While such excessive government budget deficits may stimulate the **demand side** of the economy, they can undermine capital investment (the **supply side**), stagnating growth. Since the mid-1970's and into the 1990's there have been concerns that this could be a problem in the Canadian economy, as the federal government's commitments regarding its taxation and expenditure programs have resulted in persistently large budget deficits and massive borrowing.

General Learning Objective

Examine the use of fiscal policy to stimulate economic activity and growth.

Specific Learning Objectives

		Self-Test Reference
1.	Assess the effect of Keynesian thought on the traditional role of government in the economy	# 1-3
2.	Define "fiscal policy"	# 4
3.	Apply fiscal policy to stimulate the economy	# 5-14
4.	Demonstrate the reinforcement made to fiscal policy by the multiplier and accelerator effects	# 15-17
5.	Consider the choices government may make with respect to financing a deficit budget	# 18-19
6.	Define the National Debt and establish the reasons for its accumulation	# 20-22
7.	Examine the record and the causes of federal deficits and rising National Debt since 1975	# 23-25
8.	Establish the major concerns which massive federal deficits and a mounting National Debt have given rise to since 1975	# 26-30
9.	Consider the alternatives by which the federal government's budget may be reduced during the 1990's	# 31-34

Self-Test

1. Prior to the 1930's, economists believed that the economy would

   (a) always fail to generate "full employment."

   (b) occasionally generate "full employment", but only with government intervention.

   (c) periodically fail to generate "full employment", which would be self-correcting.

   (d) tend to remain in a recession over an extended time period.

2. As a result of the belief described in the preceding question, the advice of economists to governments regarding their budget was to ________________________________

   ____

   ____.

3. During the Great Depression of the 1930's, John Maynard Keynes advised governments to use budget ________________, which could improve the economic situation by ______________

____

____.

4. "Fiscal policy" refers to:

   (a) the printing of additional money during economic recessions.

   (b) the use of government expenditures and tax revenues to influence the performance of the economy.

   (c) the use of budget deficits to combat recessions.

   (d) the use of budget surpluses to combat inflation.

   (e) (b) and (c) and (d) together.

5. When there is a government budget deficit, government spending is

   (a) rising.

   (b) less than tax revenues.

   (c) equal to tax revenues.

   (d) greater than tax revenues.

   (e) falling.

6. A government budget deficit will tend to ________________ aggregate demand, GDP and total incomes.

7. When there is a government budget surplus, government spending is

   (a) falling.

   (b) greater than tax revenues.

   (c) rising.

   (d) equal to tax revenues.

   (e) less than tax revenues.

8. A government budget surplus will tend to ________________ aggregate demand, GDP and total incomes.

9. When government's budget is balanced, government spending is

(a) less than tax revenues.

(b) equal to tax revenues.

(c) rising.

(d) greater than tax revenues.

(e) falling.

10. A balanced government budget will have a ________________ effect on GDP and total incomes.

11. Which of the following policies should be used by the federal government during an economic recession?

____ (a) Postponement of a program aimed at encouraging provincial highway construction.

____ (b) Increases in social welfare payments to individuals.

____ (c) Reduction of subsidies to farmers and other forms of transfer payments (such as unemployment insurance).

____ (d) Reduction of federal tax rates on personal and corporate income.

____ (e) Controls on government spending designed to produce a federal budget surplus.

____ (f) Increased depreciation allowances (capital cost allowances) for corporations.

____ (g) Increases in government spending on public works.

12. During an economic recession, the federal budget should be

(a) set so that government spending is less than tax revenues.

(b) set so that government spending equals tax revenues.

(c) designed to enable the government to reduce the National Debt.

(d) set so that government spending is greater than tax revenues.

(e) reduced.

13. Explain briefly how ''counter cyclical fiscal policy'' can be used to reduce the level of economic fluctuations:

____

____

____.

14. Which of the following are examples of automatic stabilizers?

____ (a) the Unemployment Insurance Plan.

____ (b) increased hiring of unemployed people by various government departments.

____ (c) public works projects such as roads and parks construction.

____ (d) the Personal Income Tax system.

15. If the size of the multiplier is 1.6 and government spending is increased by $70 million (without any change in taxes), GDP will ______________________________

____.

16. The concept of "pump priming" is that ______________________________

____

____.

17. Explain briefly why the following statement is **TRUE** or **FALSE**. "Creating jobs merely means more government hiring of unemployed people, at the taxpayers' expense."

____

____

____

____.

18. Which of the following is generally considered to be the most appropriate way to finance federal budget deficits?

(a) Print as much money as necessary to finance the deficit.

(b) Borrow the money by selling bonds.

(c) Borrow the money from the World Bank.

(d) Borrow from other nations.

(e) None of the above.

19. If the government finances budget deficits by excessive printing of more money, the result will be ____

____

____.

20. The "National Debt" is defined as ____________________________

____

____.

21. How is the National Debt related to federal government budget deficits?

____

____

____.

22. Which of the following are considered to be legitimate economic reasons for government borrowing:

____ (a) to finance budget deficits for the purpose of combatting economic recessions.

____ (b) to finance the government's operating expenses, such as payroll.

____ (c) to finance the deficits of Crown corporations such as the Post Office.

____ (d) to finance production of transportation facilities, such as roads, airports, and harbours.

____ (e) to finance wartime government expenditures.

23. State whether each of the following statements concerning government budget deficits and the National Debt is **TRUE** or **FALSE**.

____ (a) Government budget deficits and debt are evidence of economic mismanagement on the part of the government.

____ (b) The National Debt need never be paid off.

____ (c) Interest payments on government debt represent a heavy burden on Canadians as a group.

____ (d) Budget deficits are proof of inefficiency in the operation of government departments and services.

____ (e) Excessive budget deficits can contribute to inflation.

____ (f) Budget deficits and government debt inevitably impose economic burdens on future generations.

____ (g) The National Debt is owed mainly to Canadians.

____ (h) Excessive budget deficits can depress capital investment and economic growth.

____ (i) The National Debt as a percentage of GNP has risen steadily since 1950.

____ (j) Government budget deficits are not comparable to business losses.

____ (k) Large government budget deficits can cause higher interest rates.

24. State whether each of the following statements concerning the budget deficits of Canada's federal government since 1975 is **TRUE** or **FALSE**.

____ (a) The deficits were exceptionally large in dollar terms, but not as a percentage of GDP.

____ (b) The deficits were exceptionally large both in dollar terms and as a percentage of GDP.

____ (c) The deficits shrank to insignificant amounts when the economy was growing.

____ (d) The deficits became "structural," as the federal government decided to increase spending while holding down its taxation revenues.

____ (e) Indexing of federal transfer payments resulted in reduced federal deficits.

____ (f) "Indexing" provisions of the personal income tax assessment resulted in federal tax revenues being lower than they would have been.

____ (g) By the end of the 1980's, federal budget deficits had risen to the $25 to $30 billion range.

25. During the decade from 1975 to 1985, Canada's National Debt

(a) increased more than eight-fold, but declined as a percent of GDP.

(b) increased in both dollar amounts and as a percent of GDP.

(c) rose less quickly in percentage terms than did GDP.

(d) decreased slightly as foreign borrowing supplied extra funds.

26. As a consequence of massive federal deficits during the 1980's, capital investment by business may be depressed due to:

(1) ____

____.

(2) ____

____.

27. The "crowding out" of capital investment by government borrowing to pay for current expenses means that

(a) present generations enjoy greater consumption, but at the expense of future generations.

(b) present generations are impoverished as interest charges on the National Debt escalate.

(c) future generations will be better off, as investment opportunities will be greater.

(d) neither present nor future generations can suffer any economic consequences.

28. The impact of a rising proportion of our National Debt being held by foreigners is that

(a) this represents a rising external burden on Canada's economy.

(b) future generations will be burdened by higher interest payments.

(c) future generations will be burdened by having to pay off the foreign debt.

(d) all of the above.

29. The large federal government deficits of the mid-1980s

(a) resulted in less flexibility in government actions to reduce unemployment.

(b) gave rise to concerns that severe inflation could result.

(c) increased the value of the Canadian dollar.

(d) (a) and (b) above.

30. Higher federal government deficits exert an (upward, downward) influence on interest rates, since the federal government's consequent borrowing will (increase, decrease) the demand for money. In turn, the (higher, lower) interest rates will cause a(n) (increase, decrease) in the size of the government's deficit, since interest charges are now a (major, minor) budget item. If the government has to increase its borrowing in order to finance rising interest costs, the result can be compared to a (compound, simple) interest calculation.

31. Approximately 75% of the federal government's total spending is on:

(a) agriculture and defense.

(b) energy and transportation.

(c) pensions and health care.

(d) social development and interest payments.

32. On the expenditure side, federal government deficit reduction is very difficult since:

(1) ____ and

(2) ____.

33. The generally accepted view of government deficits is that

(a) it would be more desirable for governments to balance their budget at all times.

(b) they should be reduced when the country enters into a recession.

(c) they are an appropriate policy for dealing with economic recession.

(d) their presence indicates fiscal irresponsibility by governments.

34. Which action will (a) result in a greater impact on GDP, and (b) create a greater deficit: a $30-per-capita increase in government spending or a $30-per-capita cut in personal income taxes? Explain your answer.

____

____

____

____.

Chapter 10

MONEY AND THE ECONOMIC SYSTEM

This chapter deals with money: what it is and how it is created. In Canada, coins, bank notes and bank deposits are used as money, with the vast majority of money taking the form of bank deposits, which are transferred between people and businesses by cheques. These deposits are created through the lending activities of the banking system, which is able to create large volumes of bank deposits on the basis of relatively small cash reserves.

Since Chapter 7, we have stressed the importance of the level of aggregate demand to the performance of the economy. Obviously, the volume of money in circulation (the "money supply") strongly influences the level of aggregate demand, making it essential that neither too little nor too much money be created, which could cause recession or inflation, respectively. Unfortunately, it is not easy to define and measure the money supply as precisely as we would like, because there are different definitions of "money" and thus different measures of the money supply. **M1** includes only immediately spendable funds, while **M2** and **M2+** include various types of savings deposits, which could be converted into immediately spendable deposits on quite short notice, thus adding greatly to the level of aggregate demand. Consequently, while there is general agreement on the importance of the money supply to the level of aggregate demand and the performance of the economy, there is disagreement on how to actually measure the money supply.

General Learning Objective

Describe the origin and role of money in today's economy.

Specific Learning Objectives

		Self-Test Reference
1.	List the major functions and characteristics of money	# 1-6
2.	State the role played by precious metals, bank notes, cheques and credit cards in the evolution of money	# 7-10
3.	Define and give examples of money and "near money"	# 11
4.	Distinguish between M1, M2 and M2+	# 12-18

5. Explain how the banking system is able to create money by multiple amounts through loan and deposit expansion . . . . # 19-20

6. Calculate the maximum possible deposit expansion by a banking system, given the reserve ratio and available cash resources . . . . # 21-25

7. Explain how Canada's privately owned banking system can contribute to economic instability . . . . # 26-30

Self-Test

1. The volume of money in circulation ("money supply") is important to the performance of the economy because it influences the level of Aggregate Demand
____
____.

2. If the money supply is too small, the result will be recession, while an excessively large money supply will cause inflation.

3. The three functions of money are:

   (a) medium of exchange;

   (b) store of value;

   (c) a standard of value.

4. Each of the following transactions demonstrates a particular function of money. Match a function from the previous question with a transaction.

   (a) a hairstylist adds up her gratuities for the day a store of value.

   (b) M. and Mme. Laframboise purchase an Inuit carving medium of exchange

   (c) Bobby puts one half of his weekly allowance in his piggy bank a store of value

   (d) a homemaker buys $150 worth of groceries a week medium of exchange

   (e) Reza works for a fast food outlet for minimum wage after school and on weekends A Standard of value.

5. The basic requirement of "money" is that it be

   (a) authorized by the central government as legal tender.

(b) backed by precious metals.

(c) generally accepted as a medium of exchange.

(d) some sort of credit or debt.

6. It is also desirable that money be Portable, durable, and divisible.

7. State whether each of the following statements concerning precious metals is **TRUE** or **FALSE**.

T (a) Gold is a precious metal.

T (b) Debased coinage will cause inflation.

F (c) Coins are exchanged for their intrinsic value rather than their face value.

F (d) Debasing coinage increases its purchasing power.

T (e) A 1956 Canadian silver dollar has an intrinsic value that exceeds its face value.

8. State whether each of the following statements concerning bank notes in Canada is **TRUE** or **FALSE**.

T (a) They are issued by the Bank of Canada, which is a federal government agency.

F (b) They are backed by gold.

F (c) They represent a promise by the government to pay money to the holder of the note.

T (d) They declare the notes to be legal tender.

F (e) They comprise more than half of Canada's money supply.

9. State whether each of the following statements concerning demand deposits in Canada is **TRUE** or **FALSE**.

F (a) They represent the deposits of cash (notes and coins) made into depositors' accounts and held on their behalf by the bank.

T (b) They are transferred between depositors' accounts according to instructions written on cheques.

T (c) They represent the largest single form of money.

F (d) They are not really money.

F (e) They are money, but represent a small proportion of the money supply.

10. Cheques are

(a) the means by which approximately 90% of the volume of money is transacted.

(b) instructions to banks to transfer money (bank deposits) from one person to another.

(c) a separate form of money from cash (notes and coins).

(d) (a) and (b) above

(e) all of the above

11. State whether each of the following is regarded as money, near money or neither.

(a) a department store credit card neither

(b) a corporate bond neither

(c) a $20 Bank of Canada bank note money

(d) a gold coin money

(e) a $500 Canada Savings Bond neither

(f) a chequable bank deposit money

(g) a Government of Canada family allowance cheque neither

(h) $10 worth of pennies money

(i) a work of art neither

(j) a savings account near money

(k) a share of Bank of Montreal stock neither

12. Canada's money supply consists of approximately 10 % cash (bank notes and coins) and 90 % book entries (deposits).

13. State whether each of the following statements concerning **M1** is **TRUE** or **FALSE.**

T (a) It is the narrowest definition of the money supply.

T (b) It includes currency (notes and coins) outside the banking system.

T (c) It includes demand deposits (current chequing accounts).

F (d) It includes chequable personal savings deposits.

T (e) It was the official measure of the money supply used by the federal government from 1975 to 1982.

14. **M1** includes currency outside the banks plus demand deposits.

15. **M2** includes M1 plus

(a) deposits backed by gold.

(b) fiat money held by foreigners.

(c) non-personal notice deposits.

(d) term deposits.

(e) none of the above [circled]

16. **M2+** includes M2 plus deposits at trust mortgage loan companies, credit union.

17. From the data below, calculate:

(a) M1 25 (b) M2 105 (c) M3 150

Foreign currency deposits	$2 billion
Demand deposits	15 billion
Deposits at trust and mortgage loan companies	30 billion
Personal savings deposits	50 billion
Non-personal notice deposits	30 billion
Cash in bank safes	3 billion
Currency outside banks	10 billion
Deposits in credit unions and caisses populaires	15 billion

18. Canada's money supply is backed

(a) dollar for dollar by gold.

(b) by 8 cents of gold per dollar.

(c) by silver as well as gold.

(d) by the nation's ability to compete in international markets.

(e) by people's faith in its purchasing power.

19. The domestic value of Canada's currency will (rise/fall) as prices (rise/fall) in general, because its purchasing power will (rise/fall).

20. The vast majority of Canada's money supply consists of Bank Deposits which are created by the lending activities of the banking system.

21. Banks are able to operate safely with their deposits far in excess of their cash reserves because

(a) they are owned by the federal government.

(b) their cash withdrawals tend to be offset by cash deposits.

(c) most financial transactions are by cheque, and require no withdrawals of cash from the banks.

(d) (b) and (c) above.

(e) (a) and (b) above.

22. If a bank has $10 million in total reserves and must hold $8.1 million as required reserves, then it can lend out 1.9 million.

23. If the required cash reserve ratio on demand deposits were to increase from 5% to 10%, then the money supply will Decrease.

24. If the cash reserve ratio is 5% and the cash reserves of the banking system are $18 billion, total bank deposits

(a) will be $360 billion.

(b) could be as large as $360 billion.

(c) will be $36 billion.

(d) could be as large as $90 billion.

(e) will be $0.90 billion.

25. A deposit of $20 000 in cash into a chequing account of a bank with a required reserve ratio of 10% will increase the bank's required reserves by $ 2000 and its excess reserves by $ 18 000. If the bank is willing and able to lend out all of its new excess reserves and the proceeds are deposited into another bank, then this second bank's required reserves increase by $ 1800 and its excess reserves (increase/~~decrease~~) by $ 16,200. If this process is repeated until all excess reserves have been eliminated, then the result beginning with the initial $20 000 cash deposit, will have (increased/~~decreased~~) the money supply by $ 200,000.

26. What happens to Canada's money supply when

(a) cash is deposited into a bank remains the same

(b) a loan is paid off Decreases

(c) a transfer is made between bank accounts remains the same

(d) cash is withdrawn from a savings account remains the same

(e) a bank lends money increases

(f) a Canada Savings Bond is redeemed for cash increases

27. Canada's chartered banks are

(a) privately owned corporations (owned by stockholders).

(b) owned and operated by the federal government.

(c) regulated by the federal government, particularly with respect to their lending activities.

(d) (a) and (c) above.

(e) owned and operated by the provincial governments in accordance with federal regulations.

28. Government regulation of the banking system is intended to

(a) limit the profits of the banks.

(b) promote increased lending and more rapid increases in the money supply during periods of recession.

(c) avoid excessive increases in lending and the money supply which could generate inflation.

(d) (b) and (c) above.

(e) all of the above.

29. Explain how a privately owned banking system can contribute to the problem of economic instability. In good times banks lend more money to increase the money supply, which may result in too much money and Cause Inflation. In bad times banks lend less money to decrease the money supply which results in less consumption and higher Unemployment.

30. In times of high inflation should the money supply be increased? decreased? What about during periods of high unemployment? __________

Chapter 11

STABILIZING THE ECONOMY: GOVERNMENT POLICIES TO CONTROL THE MONEY SUPPLY

The previous chapter established the importance of the money supply to the level of aggregate demand and thus to the performance of the economy. Chapter 11 deals with how the government, through the Bank of Canada, exercises control over the size and the rate of growth of the money supply. This "monetary policy" is directed toward the same objectives as the "fiscal policy" discussed in Chapter 9 — influencing the level of aggregate demand so as to influence the performance of the economy.

One source of difficulty in Chapter 11 tends to be the "open-market" operations of the Bank of Canada. In studying this it can be helpful to focus first on Bank of Canada purchases of bonds from and sales of bonds to the chartered banks. When the bonds are paid for, the transactions have a direct effect on the banks' deposits (reserves) at the Bank of Canada, and thus on their lending activities. In the more complex case of bond purchases from and sales to the public, the final result is the same: the complexity arises from the fact that there are more steps in between. The key thing to remember here is that the public does not deal directly with the Bank of Canada; rather, the chartered banks act as an intermediary in these transactions. Thus, in Figure 11-3, the Bank of Canada's cheques to the public are honored by the banks, and the Bank of Canada compensates the banks by increasing their deposits (= reserves) at the Bank of Canada. Similarly, in Figure 11-4, when a private individual writes cheques to the Bank of Canada the funds do not go directly from the individual's account to the Bank of Canada; rather, they go from the private account to the banks, with the banks' deposits (= reserves) at the Bank of Canada being reduced by the same amount to compensate. The net result is a flow of funds from the public through the banks, to the Bank of Canada, and lower cash reserves for the banks.

The other major difficult concept in this chapter is the financing of federal budget deficits by the "printing" of money by the Bank of Canada, or, more correctly, by increasing the money supply. The basic concept is simple: the Bank of Canada creates new "book entry" money in the government's account to pay for the bonds it must buy from the government. The problem is that many students seem to want the Bank of Canada to **resell** the bonds to the public to raise the funds for its bond purchase. This leads to the wholly incorrect conclusion that this operation acts like a "tight money" policy, with bond sales by the Bank of Canada reducing the banks' reserves and the money supply, rather than increasing the money supply. It can be helpful to compare the financing of government budget deficits by selling bonds to the Bank of Canada ("printing money") to the practice of debasing the currency which was described in Chapter 10.

Finally, while there has been an increased emphasis in recent years on the importance of the money supply and monetary policy, there remains the serious problems raised in Chapter 10 of how to actually define and measure the money supply. For a long time the Bank of Canada used **M1** as the official measure of the money supply, but critics argued that some of the savings deposits included in **M2** and **M2+** should also be counted as money. By 1980, M1 was no longer viewed as a reliable measure of the money supply. New types of deposits were created, most notably daily interest chequing deposits — the classification **M2** includes these deposits, whereas **M1** does not. Today, most observers would now include daily interest chequing deposits (**M2**) in their definition of money.

General Learning Objective

Distinguish different tools of monetary policy and explain how these tools would be used under different economic conditions.

Specific Learning Objectives

		Self-Test Reference
1.	Recognize the nature of regulation of the banking system	# 1-7
2.	Explain the fundamental nature of the Bank of Canada	# 8
3.	Identify the tools used by the Bank of Canada	# 9-10
4.	Understand the appropriate use of monetary policy under varying economic conditions	# 11-16
5.	Understand the complementary nature of monetary and fiscal policy	# 17-24

Self-Test

1. The danger of a privately owned banking system that is not regulated by the government is that

   (a) banks will generally tend to lose money due to poor lending policies.

   (b) it will operate less efficiently than a government-operated system.

   (c) it will generally not make enough loans to keep the economy moving.

   (d) it will worsen the problem of economic instability by making too many loans during periods of inflation and too few loans during recessions.

   (e) none of the above.

2. State whether it is **TRUE** or **FALSE** that the federal government regulates the Canadian banking system in each of the following ways:

T (a) The ability of the chartered banks to make a loan is controlled by the Bank of Canada.

T (b) All banks are required to provide insurance on deposits.

T (c) There are special requirements which must be met before a new chartered bank can be formed.

F (d) The chartered banks are owned and operated by the federal government, through the Bank of Canada.

T (e) The chartered banks are required to keep a certain amount of cash reserves against their deposits.

F (f) There are limits on the profits which banks may earn.

F (g) There are limits on the fees which the banks may charge the public for their services (e.g., cheque charges).

3. A chartered bank is A Privately owned financial institution which is under Parliament laws & regulations.

4. The required cash reserve ratios for notice deposits and demand deposits are 3 % and 10 % respectively. However cash reserve requirements generally average about 4 % of all deposits.

5. Of the total cash reserves held by the banking system, about 33 to 50 % consists of actual cash. The remainder consists of Bank of canada ______.

6. Banks are also required to keep secondary reserves consisting mainly of Treasury Bills Bank of canada, which are ______. Secondary reserves are required to be 4 % of all deposits.

7. Canada's money supply is controlled by

(a) the provincial governments.

(b) the International Monetary Fund.

(c) the federal government, through the Bank of Canada.

(d) Parliament.

(e) the chartered banks.

8. The Bank of Canada is owned by The federal govt;
its basic role is to regulate money supply + interest rates.

9. The four approaches to exercising monetary policy are:

Approach	Description
(a) open market operations	Buying + selling Bonds on the open market
(b) Bank rate	changing the rate of interest at which chartered banks can borrow from the Bank of canada.
(c) secondary reserve ratio	changing the amount of total deposits which chartered Banks are to hold as short assets
(d) Moral suasion	attempting to persuade chartered banks to follow Policies of Bank of canada

10. Of the approaches identified in the previous question, the most effective alternative appears to be open market operations.

11. If the Bank of Canada sells $20 million in government bonds to the public, the cash reserves of the banks will fall by $ 20m, their lending activities will decline, interest rates will rise and the money supply will decline by $ 20m. If the bonds are sold to the chartered banks the money supply will Be same.

12. If the secondary reserve ratio were increased,

(a) an increase in the money supply would be possible.

(b) the money supply would tend to fall.

(c) the money supply would certainly rise.

(d) the money supply would not be affected.

(e) interest rates would decline.

13. An increase in the Central Bank Rate is generally considered to be an indication that monetary policy is becoming tighter.

14. Under a "floating" Bank Rate, the Bank Rate changes every week, being set at a level of ______________________________

15. To stimulate economic recovery, the Bank of Canada could adopt a(n) easy money policy which would increase the money supply, which would tend to reduce interest rates.

16. The action taken by the Bank of Canada, as identified in the previous question, could be accomplished by (selling/buying) bonds in the open market, (raising/lowering) the Bank Rate, or by transferring Government of Canada deposits (into/out of) the chartered banks.

17. During a recession, the appropriate monetary and fiscal policies are

(a) tight money and a budget surplus.

(b) tight money and a budget deficit.

(c) easy money and a budget surplus.

(d) easy money and a budget deficit.

18. During a period of inflation, the appropriate monetary and fiscal policies are

(a) tight money and a budget deficit.

(b) tight money and a budget surplus.

(c) easy money and a budget deficit.

(d) easy money and a budget surplus.

19. A tight money policy tends to have a particularly severe effect on the sales of

(a) the food industry.

(b) the housing industry.

(c) the gasoline industry.

(d) the clothing industry.

(e) the entertainment industry.

20. Suppose the federal government finances large budget deficits by selling government bonds to the Bank of Canada. The Bank of Canada will pay the federal government for these bonds by increase federal govt deposits at the Bank of Canada
______________________________.

21. As a result of the situation described in the previous question, the nation's money supply will increase, and the rate of inflation will increase. However, if a budget deficit is financed by selling bonds to the public the nation's money supply will same and the rate of inflation will same.

22. During the first half of the 1970's,

(a) Canada's money supply grew relatively slowly, causing an economic slowdown.

(b) monetary policy was primarily concerned with restraining inflation.

(c) (a) and (b) above.

(d) Canada's money supply increased unusually rapidly, generating severe inflation.

(e) none of the above.

23. State whether each of the following statements concerning the monetary situation in Canada since the mid-1970's is **TRUE or FALSE.**

T (a) There has been widespread agreement on the importance of controlling the growth of the money supply.

T (b) The Bank of Canada undertook from 1975 to 1982 to keep the growth of the money supply within publicly announced limits.

T (c) Canada's monetary policy has been more influenced by "monetarism" than it was earlier in the decade.

T (d) The Bank of Canada's policies have contributed to high interest rates.

T (e) The Bank of Canada used **M1** as the official measure of the money supply from 1975 to 1982.

24. State whether each of the following statements is **TRUE** or **FALSE.**

T (a) Monetary policy is more effective in fighting inflation than unemployment.

T (b) The Bank of Canada is ultimately accountable to the Government of Canada.

F (c) The Prime Rate is generally 1 to 2 percentage points lower than the Bank Rate.

F (d) If a $1000 Treasury Bill sells for $960 and yields $40 in interest, the Bank Rate will be set at 10.40%.

T (e) For an easy money policy to have an impact on output levels, lenders and borrowers must lend and borrow.

T (f) When the Bank of Canada buys bonds in the open market the price of bonds increases and interest rates decrease.

F (g) When the Government of Canada transfers its deposits held with the Bank of Canada to a chartered bank, the money supply increases.

T (h) The aim of monetary policy is to achieve economic stability (full employment without inflation).

T (i) Changes in the Bank Rate affect private sector profits.

T (j) If the prime rate falls, all other factors being constant, the quantity of money demanded falls.

T (k) Recent developments in the Canadian banking industry point to more competition and less regulation.

Chapter 12

THE NATURE AND CAUSES OF INFLATION

This is a very important chapter, as it deals with the dominant economic problem and policy issue of the early eighties. In view of the confusion concerning the causes of inflation, it is important to remember that the overwhelming majority of economists agree that the most fundamental cause of inflation is excess aggregate demand. Students sometimes get the impression that "cost-push" factors are the basic cause of inflation, partly because they are more visible than excess demand, and partly because "cost-push" factors have been unusually strong in recent years. In this context, it is important to remember that these "cost-push" forces were generated by a period of severe "demand-pull" inflation in the first half of the 1970's.

It is an established fact that periods of severe inflation are associated with rapid increases in the money supply, and that excessive increases in the money supply will generate inflation of a demand-pull nature. A more difficult concept is that such rapid increases in the money supply could be the result of cost-push pressures as well. That is, if economically powerful corporations and strong labor unions increase their prices and wages sufficiently rapidly to force the general level of prices upwards, an increase in the level of aggregate demand will be required just to maintain the present level of output and employment (at the new, higher price level). The government is presented with a policy dilemma: if it does not speed up the growth of the money supply, there will be insufficient aggregate demand and higher unemployment, while if it does speed up the growth of the money supply sufficiently to maintain output and employment, the result will be increasingly severe inflationary pressures. Thus, according to this theory, cost-push pressures on prices and wages from strong unions and large corporations can actually become a source of pressure on the government to increase the money supply excessively rapidly. Since the mid-1970's, unusually strong cost-push pressures appear to have been present in the Canadian economy. However, the "inflation psychology" which generated these cost-push pressures was itself the result of exceptionally severe demand-pull inflation during the 1972-75 period, reinforcing the argument that excessive aggregate demand is the **most fundamental** source of inflation.

In discussing the causes of inflation, it is worth emphasizing that high interest rates are much more a **result** of inflation than a **cause** of inflation. If there is to be any economic incentive to save during periods when the real value of money is being reduced by inflation, interest rates must be sufficiently high to offset inflation.

The last section, called "The Causes of Inflation in Review" attempts to broaden the discussion of inflation, presenting inflation as the result of excessive expectations of people generally — as workers, consumers, business owners and government leaders — regarding the capabilities of the economy to satisfy our wants. On the broadest level, inflation is how economic reality asserts itself against our unrealistic expectations; it is the economy's way of telling us "no," that it cannot achieve what we are demanding of it. The excessive pressures which we place upon it take the form of frustrating price increases rather than the increase in output, employment and living standards that we intended.

General Learning Objective

Examine the fundamental causes of inflation, with respect to the demand and supply sides of the economy.

Specific Learning Objectives

		Self-Test Reference
1.	Define "inflation"	# 1
2.	Explain the common method used to measure inflation	# 2, 3
3.	Recognize that inflation poses problems for the economy	# 4, 5
4.	Explain basic causes of inflation which are demand-based	# 6-10
5.	Explain basic causes of inflation which are supply-based	# 11-15
6.	Recognize the significance of inflation psychology	# 16-18
7.	Define the relationship between inflation and the money supply	# 19-21
8.	Recognize factors which contributed to Canada's inflation in the 1970's	# 22-34

Self-Test

1. "Inflation" is defined as ____

____.

2. The statistic most commonly used to measure inflation is ___________________________

____.

3. If the Consumer Price Index rises over a 12-month period from 150 to 168, the rate of inflation for that year is _______%. If prices continued to increase at this annual rate, they will double in approximately _______ years.

4. State whether each of the following is **TRUE** or **FALSE**.

____ (a) Inflation tends to hurt groups that lack economic power.

____ (b) Inflation can impair a nation's exports.

____ (c) Inflation, if allowed to become very rapid, can cause slower economic growth.

____ (d) Inflation reduces the standard of living for all members of society.

____ (e) Inflation makes long-term financial planning (such as life insurance) easier.

____ (f) Inflation has no effect on interest rates.

____ (g) Inflation tends to benefit long-term borrowers.

____ (h) Inflation redistributes income from economically weak groups to economically powerful groups.

5. Which one of the following would be most severely affected by inflation?

   (a) a professional hockey player

   (b) an electrician

   (c) a retired steelworker living on a pension

   (d) an office clerk

   (e) a college student

6. "Demand-pull inflation" is caused by ______________________________

____

____.

7. Economists agree that the most basic cause of inflation is ______________________

____.

8. When a country is at war, demand-pull inflation can occur because ______________

____

____.

9. When trying to combat inflation, federal governments often are confronted with a trade-off between ______________ and ______________.

10. Governments may contribute to demand-pull inflation by ______________________________

____

____.

Using aggregate demand and supply schedules, illustrate the occurrence of government-induced demand-pull inflation.

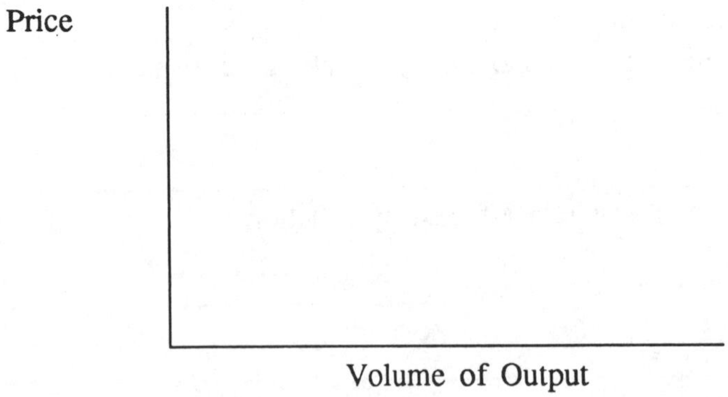

11. "Cost-push" inflation refers to

(a) inflationary pressures generated by the upward pressure of strong labor unions on wages.

(b) inflationary pressures generated by the pricing practices of some industries which are dominated by a few large firms.

(c) the interaction between (a) and (b).

(d) inflationary pressures which arise when heavy demand for goods and services forces producers to pay more for labor and materials, pushing up their production costs.

(e) none of the above.

12. Which of the following is the most accurate description of the process known as the "wage-price (price-wage) spiral?"

(a) The large wage increases won by the strongest labor unions automatically spread to other groups of workers throughout the economy, forcing up all wages (and prices) proportionately.

(b) Large corporations conspire among themselves to raise prices and profits, which in turn forces labor unions to bargain for higher wages, due to the rising cost of living.

(c) Excessive total demand for goods, services, and labor causes prices and wages to rise.

(d) In those industries in which there are a few large corporations and strong labor unions, there is a tendency for unions and employers to agree to unusually large wage increases. These are passed on to the consumer via price increases, which become the basis for further demands for increased wages, and so on.

(e) Labor unions force employers to pay higher wages, which in turn forces them to raise the prices of products in order to stay in business.

13. During economic booms, the wage-price spiral tends to become ____________________ severe, because ____

____.

14. During recessions, the wage-price spiral tends to become ____________________ severe, because ____

____.

15. If wage rates increase by 8% and labor productivity (output per worker/ hour) increases by 4%, labor costs per unit of output will ____________by ________ %. Illustrate the net result of these increases on the graph in Question 10 with the aid of an aggregate supply curve.

16. "Inflation psychology" refers to

(a) the tendency of people to seek larger income increases during periods of severe inflation.

(b) the tendency of people to spend a higher proportion of their disposable income during periods of severe inflation, and save less.

(c) (a) and (b) together.

(d) the tendency of people to save more money during periods of severe inflation, in order to cope with rising prices.

(e) none of the above.

17. The behavior(s) arising from "inflation psychology" tends to ____________________ ______________ the rate of inflation.

18. During a period of inflation which is expected to continue, interest rates will ____________

because lenders will ____

____

____.

19. If the money supply is increased rapidly,

(a) the economy will go into a recession.

(b) inflation will become worse immediately.

(c) prices will decline.

(d) interest rates will rise immediately.

(e) inflation will become more severe after a time lag of about a year or so.

20. Cost-push pressures on wages and prices can put pressure on the government to increase the money supply more rapidly, because ____

____.

21. Monetary and fiscal policies aimed at generating "full employment" will ____________ the rate of inflation, because ____

____

____.

22. The fundamental cause of Canada's rapid inflation of the 1970's was ________________

____.

23. Underlying the cause in the previous question is the fact that

(a) there were oil and food shortages in the 1970's.

(b) government spending and the money supply increased rapidly during the first half of the 1970's.

(c) unions constantly demand (and get) big wage increases.

(d) the profit margins of big businesses are constantly rising.

(e) people have become increasingly concerned with their own self-interest in recent years.

24. When the USA increased its money supply rapidly in the late 1960's to finance the Vietnam War, the international value of the Canadian dollar (in terms of the US dollar) tended to ____

____.

25. As a result of the situation described in the previous questions, unemployment in Canada tended to ____ because

____

____.

26. In response to this situation, the Canadian government increased Canada's money supply ____

____________________rapidly in order to ______________________

____.

27. As a result of the policy described in the previous question

(a) employment in Canada was protected against declines in the short run.

(b) inflation in Canada slowed down.

(c) Canada imported more foreign goods.

(d) inflation in Canada would become more severe in the next few years.

(e) (a) and (d) together.

28. In the late 1960's and early 1970's, Canada's umemployment rate rose, due to:

(a) ____;

(b) ____;

(c) ____.

29. As a result of the situation described in the previous question, the Canadian government _____

____

____.

30. Which of the following best describes Canada's inflation of the 1970's?

(a) It originated with cost-push pressures from rapid wage increases in the early 1970's, and was made worse by rapid increases in the money supply later.

(b) It was purely a cost-push inflation; the result of rapid increases in the prices of oil, energy and food, and rapid increases in wages.

(c) It originated with rapid increases in the government spending and the money supply in the early 1970's, but had by 1974 been made worse by heavy cost-push pressures, especially from wages.

(d) There were no significant cost-push pressures involved in the process; it was simply the result of excessive aggregate demand.

31. The situation described in the previous question

(a) made it likely that inflation would slow down automatically after the 1970's.

(b) made inflation more persistent and more difficult to combat during the second half of the 1970's.

(c) made it likely that if curbs were placed on government spending and the money supply, inflation could be combatted effectively.

(d) led the government to reduce government spending and the money supply during the second half of the 1970's.

(e) (c) and (d) together.

32. Given the strong cost-push pressures in the economy by the mid-1970s, a government policy of reducing the rate of growth of the money supply considerably would have caused ________

____.

33. Explain what economists generally believe to be the basic cause of inflation. Explain what the general public tends to believe the cause(s) of inflation to be, and what accounts for this difference between the views of the public and economists.

____

34. "The Federal Government's proposed Goods and Services Tax (GST) is likely to to be inflationary." Comment.

Chapter 13

GOVERNMENT POLICIES TO COMBAT INFLATION

This chapter deals with anti-inflation policies, emphasizing the fundamentals of inflation established in Chapter 12. Any anti-inflation program which fails to attack the basic cause of inflation by restricting aggregate demand cannot possibly succeed over any significant period of time. The apparently simple solution of legislated wage and price controls is in reality far from simple. Unless aggregate demand is curbed, controls face the problem of regulating the behavior of millions of buyers and sellers (both of whom are prepared to violate the controls). It is somewhat like the task of policing a law against "scalping" Grey Cup tickets, but on a nationwide scale. Also, the fact that any determined attempt to control prices and wages will inevitably lead to controls over a myriad of matters, from product design and quality to personnel practices of employers, makes the enforcement of a long-term comprehensive controls program not only objectionable to many people, but also administratively impossible. Another problem which should be stressed is the basic dilemma of price controls. Unless the government is prepared to impose simple and arbitrary limits on prices and thus risk production cutbacks, business closings and unemployment, it must allow price increases to cover production-cost increases. However, once this is allowed, the government must monitor cost increases — a horrendously complex task. Another problem is that in an open economy such as Canada's, import prices must of necessity be exempted from the controls, so that over a quarter of the CPI is beyond the controls. At best, controls are a temporary supplement to a real anti-inflation program which restrains aggregate demand, as illustrated by the "wet towel" analogy in the text.

Combatting inflation remains a very difficult policy problem. While it would be economically disastrous in the long term to allow inflation to continue unchecked, the short-term economic and political costs of a determined policy of curbing inflation are intimidating to governments (which perhaps explains why inflation remains a serious problem). In Chapter 12 we saw that, on the most basic level, inflation is generated by the unrealistic expectations of people generally. This suggests that the fundamental solution to inflation must involve more realistic expectations and more discipline, on the part of consumers, business, labor and governments. However, it is far from easy to achieve this in a society such as ours.

General Learning Objective

Describe methods to combat inflation and the implications of using these methods.

Specific Learning Objectives

		Self-Test Reference
1.	Match inflation types with possible remedies	# 1-11
2.	Describe impacts of wage and price controls	# 12-19
3.	Explain the government's approach to fighting inflation in Canada during the 1970's	# 20-31

Self-Test

1. Economists maintain that the basic cause of inflation is ______________________ ______________. This basic factor causes ______________________ ______________________.

2. The ability of some large corporations and some powerful labor unions to push up prices and wages refers to ______________________. This factor is regarded generally as a ______________________ ______________________.

3. Inflation psychology refers to ______________________. This factor can generate ______________________ ______________________.

4. Which of the following would be the most effective policy for dealing with the basic causes of inflation?

   (a) sales of bonds by the Bank of Canada.

   (b) legal restrictions on wage and price increases.

   (c) legal restrictions on the activities of labor unions.

   (d) "indexing" of all incomes to the rate of inflation.

   (e) reductions in interest rates.

5. In order to attack the basic cause of inflation, government policies must ________________.

____.

6. State which of the following policies would be appropriate if the government were attempting to restrain inflation.

______ (a) sales of government bonds by the Bank of Canada to the chartered banks.

______ (b) a reduction of interest rates.

______ (c) a federal policy of not hiring additional civil servants for one year.

______ (d) a temporary increase in personal income tax.

______ (e) a reduction in the rate of growth of the money supply.

7. Specific government policies to attack the basic cause of inflation would include __________ ____ growth of the money supply, ______________________________ interest rates, ________________ government spending and ________________________ taxes.

8. The policies referred to in the previous question will cause unemployment to __________ ______, because ____

____.

9. If prices are rising due to shortages of goods (i.e., supply is less than demand), it is likely that government controls which hold prices **down** would ______________________________

____.

10. A policy of indexing all incomes so that they would rise at least as rapidly as the Consumer Price Index would

(a) protect everyone against the effects of inflation.

(b) effectively curb inflation.

(c) make inflation more severe.

(d) fail to attack the real causes of inflation.

(e) (c) and (d) together.

11. If productivity (output per worker per hour) were rising slowly, there would be a tendency for inflation to be ______________________________ rapidly, because ______________________________

____

______________________________.

12. State whether it is **TRUE** or **FALSE** that each of the following statements represents the views of most economists concerning wage-price "guidelines."

____ (a) They are based on a reasonable theory, but have proven generally ineffective in practice, mainly because they are voluntary.

____ (b) They are a very effective way to combat demand-pull inflation, but are not effective against cost-push inflation.

____ (c) They are undesirable because they prevent wages from rising, but not prices.

____ (d) They are undesirable because they keep prices artificially low and hold business profits at unreasonably low levels.

____ (e) They are the most effective way to prevent inflation because they prevent wages from rising faster than productivity.

13. The difference between "selective" and "general" wage and price controls is that ____________

____

____

______________________________.

14. The historical record of wage and price controls shows that they have been

(a) ineffective in curbing inflation.

(b) very effective in curbing inflation only if the controls are kept in effect for long periods of time (i.e., several years).

(c) the source of negative side-effects on the operation of the economy.

(d) very effective in curbing inflation.

(e) both (a) and (c) above.

15. The reason why the historical record of controls has been as described in the previous question is that

(a) controls attack only the symptoms of inflation, not the causes.

(b) controls stop the wage and price increases which are the real cause of inflation.

(c) the penalties for violations have not generally been severe enough to make controls effective.

(d) like other economic policies, controls are really effective only after a substantial time lag.

16. State whether each of the following statements concerning wage and price controls is **TRUE** or **FALSE**.

____ (a) They are generally regarded by economists as the only really effective anti-inflation policy.

____ (b) They attack the symptoms of inflation rather than its causes.

____ (c) They are of possible short-term value at the beginning of an anti-inflation program.

____ (d) They are the most desirable anti-inflation policy due to the fact that they do not have any negative side-effects on the economy (such as increased unemployment).

____ (e) They are supported more by the general public than by economists, largely due to the public's misunderstanding of the causes of inflation.

____ (f) They are a relatively simple anti-inflation policy, which is easy to administer and enforce.

____ (g) If controls hold down prices, shortages of products tend to result.

____ (h) Controls can be evaded in many ways, making them difficult to enforce.

____ (i) The enforcement of controls can lead to government regulation of a wide range of business decisions regarding production and personnel.

____ (j) Controls must allow businesses to raise prices sufficiently to recover increases in their production costs.

____ (k) Controls will be effective if the penalties for violation of the controls are severe enough.

____ (l) Controls have a tendency to undermine business confidence and depress capital investment.

17. A basic dilemma of price controls is that if the controls impose simple, arbitrary limits on prices, there is the risk that ____

____,

whereas if they allow businesses to raise prices in order to recover production costs, they ____

____.

18. Most economists would agree that controls on wages and prices are most likely to be useful if

(a) a complete freeze is placed on wages and prices.

(b) the controls apply to all prices and incomes.

(c) the controls are backed up by sufficiently severe penalties to deter people from violating them.

(d) the controls are temporary only, and a supplement to a program which curbs aggregate demand.

(e) (a) and (c) together.

19. Explain the circumstances under which most economists consider wage-price controls to be useful as an anti-inflation measure and why most economists would limit their use.

____

____

____

____

____

____

____

____

____

____.

20. Which of the following best describes Canada's inflation during the 1970's?

(a) It was simply a cost-push inflation; the result of rapid increases in the prices of oil, energy and food, leading to rapid increases in wages.

(b) It originated with rapid increases in government spending and the money supply in the early 1970's, but by 1974 had been made worse by strong cost-push pressures, especially from wages.

(c) It originated with cost-push pressures from rapid wage increases in the early 1970's, and was made worse by rapid increases in the money supply later in the decade.

(d) There were no significant cost-push pressures involved in the process; it was simply the result of excessive aggregate demand.

(e) None of the above is an accurate description of inflation in the 1970's.

21. Which of the following best describes Canada's anti-inflation program that was implemented late in 1975?

(a) The basic element of the program was wage and price controls.

(b) The program represented an all-out attempt to curb inflation as quickly as possible, regardless of the economic costs involved.

(c) The program was a novel policy designed to slow inflation without increasing unemployment.

(d) The program aimed at a gradual reduction in the rate of inflation over a period of several years.

(e) None of the above.

22. Comment critically on the following statements, giving reasons for your position.

(a) "The answer to curbing inflation is to reduce interest rates. Higher interest rates only make inflation worse by adding to the costs of businesses."

____

____

____

____

(b) "The answer to curbing inflation is to reduce the size of Canada's annual deficit and its National Debt."

____

____

____

____

____

23. The key element in determining the long-term success of Canada's anti-inflation program was ____.

24. Canada's wage-price controls of 1975-78 were

(a) the keystone of Canada's anti-inflation program.

(b) only a supplement to, and not the most important element of Canada's anti-inflation program.

(c) a temporary program only.

(d) (b) and (c) above.

(e) to become a permanent feature of Canada's economic policy.

25. Canada's wage and price controls of 1975-78 applied on a mandatory basis to

(a) all prices and incomes.

(b) all prices but only the incomes of unionized employees.

(c) all incomes and all prices except the prices of imports.

(d) only those groups (businesses and labor) which possessed the power to raise their incomes and prices.

(e) wages only, but not prices.

26. Regarding price increases, Canada's controls of 1975-78 permitted ____.

27. The reason for the rules described in the previous question was that

(a) the intention of the controls program was to stop inflation as quickly as possible.

(b) there was concern that, unless business firms could recover cost increases, shortages of some products would occur.

(c) the government intended to restrict wage increases with the controls, but not price increases.

(d) the political influence of big business forced the government to allow prices to increase as rapidly as wages.

(e) none of the above.

28. As a result of the regulations described in the previous question,

    (a) the price controls were very effective in curbing inflation.

    (b) the price controls were very simple to administer.

    (c) the price controls required business firms to fill out many complex forms involving many complicated calculations regarding production costs.

    (d) the price controls had virtually no effect on the rate of inflation.

    (e) none of the above.

29. The exemption from Canada's controls system of energy prices, farm prices, interest rates and the prices of imports reflects

    (a) the fact that the government was really seeking to restrain wages but not prices.

    (b) the fact that controls on the prices of these items would cause political problems for the governments.

    (c) concern that controls on the prices of these items would cause political problems for the government.

    (d) the fact that certain groups (e.g., oil companies, farmers, banks) possess enough political power to gain such exemptions.

    (e) (a) and (d) together.

30. In summary, Canada's wage and price controls of 1975-78

    (a) restrained prices more effectively than they restrained wages.

    (b) were more effective regarding both wages and prices in the last year of the program than during the first two years.

    (c) restrained both wages and prices with approximately equal effectiveness.

(d) failed to restrain either wages or prices significantly.

(e) restrained wages more effectively than they restrained prices.

31. Besides wage and price controls, what else might be done to curb inflation?

Chapter 14

THE NATURE OF UNEMPLOYMENT

This chapter deals with the critical economic problem of unemployment. We conclude that the level of unemployment is a function of both inadequate aggregate demand and excess supply of labor. The higher participation rates and the increasing numbers of young people and women in the work force are supply-side factors. On the demand side, the severe recession of 1981-82 was a primary factor and provided the major shock concerning the number of unemployed in Canada. Although production and output recovered from this recession, relatively high levels of unemployment have persisted.

Although we define terms to characterize the type of unemployment and use numbers to quantify the problem, we must be cognizant of the immeasurable social costs incurred when someone cannot find lasting work. Unemployment means lost output but it also contributes to higher crime rates, broken families and alcohol and drug abuse.

General Learning Objective

Examine briefly the nature and causes of unemployment in Canada.

Specific Learning Objectives

	Self-Test Reference
1. Identify the main determinants of unemployment	# 1-3, 5 # 14-17
2. Recognize the types of unemployment	# 4, 7-9
3. Define the unemployment rate	# 6
4. Consider the accuracy of official unemployment statistics	# 10-12
5. Calculate several labor force statistics	# 13

Self-Test

1. Find the demand for labor, in terms of the number of jobs available, for a community with a working age population of 1 000 000, a participation rate of 65% and an unemployment rate of 10%.

____

____

____

____.

2. Which of the following is the most basic factor influencing the level of unemployment in Canada?

   (a) The level of aggregate demand.

   (b) Factors generating voluntary unemployment.

   (c) Seasonal factors.

   (d) Factors generating structural unemployment.

   (e) None of the above factors.

3. "Higher productivity (output per worker) can increase unemployment." Comment:

____

____

____

____.

4. State whether each of the following is an example of frictional, structural or seasonal unemployment.

   ____ (a) A miner replaced by new machinery.

   ____ (b) A former employee of a textile mill closed due to competition from imports.

   ____ (c) A computer programmer taking two weeks to travel to British Columbia to start a new job there.

   ____ (d) A worker laid off from a fish processing plant during the winter.

5. Your age and the area of Canada in which you live are two major factors affecting your chances of being unemployed, in that ____

____

____

____

____.

6. The unemployment rate as defined in Canada

(a) is the number of unemployed expressed as a percentage of the total population.

(b) is calculated from a sample of 56 000 households.

(c) is the number of unemployed expressed as a percentage of the labor force.

(d) all of the above.

(e) (b) and (c) above.

7. To the extent that "hidden unemployment" exists to a significant degree in some parts of Canada

(a) the official unemployment rate statistics understate the true extent of unemployment.

(b) the official unemployment rate statistics are of little value in assessing Canada's economic performance.

(c) the true extent of unemployment is much less than what is officially recorded.

(d) the number of "discouraged workers" represents a major part of the official unemployment rate statistics.

8. "Voluntary unemployment"

(a) exists when people volunteer for work but no employer can be found who is willing to hire them.

(b) indicates a situation where people choose not to take jobs which are available.

(c) is reduced through the combination of unemployment insurance and the existing tax system.

(d) has added at least five percentage points to the unemployment rate, according to most economists.

9. Which of the following is NOT considered to have been a factor generating "voluntary unemployment"?

   (a) Increased selectivity of job-seekers.

   (b) The more accessible and more attractive unemployment insurance benefits available after 1971.

   (c) Increased laziness on the part of Canadian workers.

   (d) An increase in the number of secondary income-earners (such as young people and married women) in the labor force.

   (e) An increased tendency of people to remain unemployed longer than really necessary before finding jobs.

10. Since over half of the unemployed in Canada are not breadwinners, but rather second or third incomes in a family (according to studies done in the 1970's), the unemployment rate (is/is no longer) viewed as an accurate indicator of hardship.

11. The reason there has been less concern about a 10% unemployment rate in the 1980's than there was about a 7% unemployment rate during the 1950's is that ____.

12. Full employment is defined as ____.

13. The following table represents hypothetical employment data for two separate years.

Year	Population Of Working Age (Millions)	Participation Rate (%)	Labor Force (Millions)	Employed (Millions)	Unemployed (Millions)	Unemployment Rate (%)
I	20.0	60.0	12.0	10.8	1.2	10.0
II	30.0	64.0	—	—	1.8	—

In year I, the working-age population is 20.0 million, of whom 60% participate in the labor force. From this labor force, 10.8 million are employed and 1.2 million are unemployed.

Considering the increase in the working population for year II, determine the size of the labor force, the level of employment and the rate of unemployment for this year.

14. What measures might be taken to combat unemployment?

____

____

____

____

____.

15. Explain why supply-side policies are preferred to demand-side policies when it comes to fighting unemployment.

____

____

____

____

____.

16. Which of the following changes in the supply side of the labor market have been factors in the higher unemployment rates in Canada during the 1970's and into the 1980's:

(a) the entry into the labor market of the "baby boomers" born in the decade after World War II.

(b) an increase in the number of women seeking work.

(c) an increase in the proportion of married women in the labor force.

(d) Unemployment Insurance payments

(e) all of the above.

17. The main causes of unemployment in the late 1980's and into the 1990's are:

____

____

____

____

____.

Chapter 15

ECONOMIC POLICY IN PERSPECTIVE

This chapter summarizes much of what has been said regarding macroeconomic policy in previous chapters and places the issue of government macroeconomic policy into broader perspective. The most basic concept in Chapter 15 is that macroeconomic policy pursues goals which conflict with each other, and can therefore never achieve everything that we would like; we must accept trade-offs between policy goals such as reducing unemployment and curbing inflation. In addition to this trade-off problem, several other factors (some economic, some political) are examined which place limits upon the effective use of monetary and fiscal policies.

The concept of a trade-off between unemployment and inflation is complicated by the fact that both problems can exist simultaneously. Severe inflation coupled with economic stagnation, or "stagflation," has plagued our economy in recent years. On the surface, the appearance together of inflation and stagnation seems to contradict the idea of a trade-off. However, to understand stagflation, it is important to remember that:

(a) it is the result of **excessive** aggregate demand and severe inflation, and

(b) the negative effects of these are felt on the **supply side** of the economy, due to their effect on the sources of funds for capital investment.

The negative effects of severe inflation on the supply side of the economy can be confusing unless an overview of the problem is maintained. In broad terms, severe inflation erodes the ability of business to raise funds to finance capital investment, thus eventually depressing productivity and living standards, and stagnating the economy. The details of this process involve the effects of inflation on the reported and after-tax profits of business, on interest rates (and thus on the cost of borrowing funds for capital investment), and on stock prices (and thus on the ability of business to raise funds through share issues).

The irony of this situation is that excessive attempts by government to generate prosperity by stimulating the demand side of the economy during the late 1960's and early 1970's contributed (through severe inflation) to the undermining of the supply side of the economy and thus to economic stagnation after the mid-1970's. The result of these problems has been increased attention to the supply side of the economy, and to policies to stimulate investment, although these have been pursued more in the USA and the UK than in Canada. Should these problems persist, and/or the US and UK policies succeed, Canadian policy will likely shift in this direction. The economic policy trade-off here is the one discussed in Chapter 5: less consumption now in exchange for more prosperity in the future.

Chapter 15 concludes by placing the entire issue of government "demand management" policies (monetary and fiscal policy) in perspective, tracing them from the Great Depression of the 1930's (when the need for such policies became apparent) through the 1960's (when they were used most successfully) and the 1970's (when government mismanagement of aggregate demand created more economic problems than it solved). The policy errors in "demand management" in the recent past have led to several developments, including:

(a) the suggestion by some that governments cannot be trusted to use monetary and fiscal policies freely, and should therefore be required by law to follow fixed rules instead;

(b) new emphasis on the money supply as a "policy variable" and on the importance of restraint on money-supply growth in order to curb inflation ("monetarism"); and

(c) new concern for the supply side of the economy (as described in Chapter 5), particularly the saving/investment process which has been eroded by recent emphasis on the basics of economics — factors which influence a society's productivity and thus its potential prosperity. Some observers hoped that the 1980's would be a period of renewed capital investment, partly to offset the decade of the 1970's in which severe inflation caused low levels of capital investment. They didn't have to wait too long, after 1985 capital investment grew significantly in Canada.

General Learning Objective

Discuss the practical problems and limitations faced by government in applying the theory of monetary and fiscal policy.

Specific Learning Objectives

	Self-Test Reference
1. Define three major goals associated with the use of monetary and fiscal policy . . .	# 1
2. Consider the conflicts between economic goals when aggregate demand is increasing and the economy is operating at (a) high unemployment (b) near full employment (c) full employment	# 2-6
3. Resolve a problem of conflicting objectives by applying economic policy trade-offs.	# 7-9
4. Recognize the limitations of monetary and fiscal policy with respect to (a) time lags (b) political considerations (c) reduced federal government fiscal and monetary powers (d) international realities (e) inflation psychology	# 10-18

Self-Test Reference

5. Define "stagflation" and relate it to the excessive use of expansionary fiscal and monetary policy . . . . # 19-21

6. Develop the relationship between the rate of inflation and the level of funding sources for capital investment from bond or stock issues and retained earnings . . . . # 22-31

7. Demonstrate the effect of rapid inflation on society's allocation of resources . . . . . # 32-33

8. Review the current debate over the proper role of monetary and fiscal policy in promoting economic prosperity . . . . # 34-36

Self-Test

1. State the three major goals of government monetary and fiscal policy as described in Chapter 15.

   (a) ______________________________

   (b) ______________________________

   (c) ______________________________

2. State which one of the three goals in the previous question conflicts with the other two goals.

   ______________________________.

3. The conflict referred to in the previous question exists because ______________________________

   ____

   ______________________________.

4. If there is very high unemployment in the economy and aggregate demand increases,

   (a) real output, employment, and prices will all rise rapidly.

   (b) real output and employment will rise rapidly, and there will be little or no increase in prices.

   (c) real output and employment will rise, and prices will fall.

   (d) real output, employment, and prices will all fall.

   (e) none of the above.

5. If the economy is near, but not yet at, full employment (or capacity production) and aggregate demand increases, real output and employment will rise (more/less) rapidly, and prices will rise (more/less) rapidly than in the previous question.

6. If the economy is at full employment (or capacity production) and aggregate demand increases,

   (a) real output and employment will rise less rapidly than before capacity production was reached, and prices will stabilize.

   (b) real output, employment and prices will all stabilize.

   (c) real output and employment will fall, but prices will rise rapidly.

   (d) real output and employment will not increase further, but prices will rise rapidly.

   (e) none of the above.

7. An economic trade-off is involved whenever government decides to ____________________

____

____.

8. During the 1980's, any attempt to reduce the inflation rate to a level much lower than 5% involved a trade-off with unemployment that is generally considered to be

   (a) desirable, due to the dangers of even low levels of inflation.

   (b) undesirable, due to the already high levels of unemployment.

   (c) of no real consequence to the unemployment level.

   (d) impossible to achieve.

9. An acceptable economic policy trade-off occurs when there is a balance between __________

____.

10. Monetary and fiscal policies do not affect the economy as quickly as we would like. Name and explain briefly each of the three "time lags" which slow the response of the economy to these policies.

   (a) ____

   ____

   ____

(b) ____

____

____

(c) ____

____

____

11. State whether each of the following statements regarding monetary and fiscal policies is **TRUE** or **FALSE**.

____ (a) They often responded more to short-term political considerations than long-term economic considerations.

____ (b) They stabilized the economy, helping it to avoid the extremes of the business cycle.

____ (c) They contributed to economic instability, or repeated cycles of inflation and slowdowns.

____ (d) They were used increasingly wisely and effectively by governments in the 1970's, as they learned from their errors of the 1960's.

____ (e) They frequently changed direction, from stimulation to anti-inflation policies and back again.

12. State whether each of the following is a likely result of government overstimulation of aggregate demand.

____ (a) Increased economic prosperity in the short run.

____ (b) A higher rate of inflation immediately.

____ (c) A higher rate of inflation after a time lag of about one year.

____ (d) An economic downturn will become more likely in a few years.

____ (e) The resultant severe inflation will depress capital investment, and thus contribute to economic stagnation.

13. State whether each of the following is in fact a difficulty regarding the effective use of monetary and fiscal policy in Canada.

____ (a) Much of the nation's tax revenues and government spending are matters of provincial jurisdiction.

____ (b) The Canadian multiplier is relatively small.

____ (c) If aggregate demand is increased by fiscal policy, much of the increased spending will be on goods and services produced in other countries.

____ (d) There are difficulties in actually defining and measuring the nation's money supply for purposes of controlling it.

____ (e) There are quite long time lags in the impact of monetary and fiscal policy on the economy.

____ (f) Before changing its monetary policy, the Bank of Canada (i.e., the federal government) must consult with the ten provincial governments.

____ (g) Generally, Canadian interest rates must be kept sufficiently higher than US rates to attract an overflow of foreign capital.

14. The fact that Canada's imports are roughly 30% of GNP tends to (increase/decrease/not affect) the size of the multiplier effect in Canada.

15. Traditionally, the Bank of Canada has

(a) determined Canadian interest rates solely on the basis of economic conditions within Canada.

(b) sought to attract capital from foreign nations, especially the USA.

(c) kept Canadian interest rates slightly higher than US rates.

(d) (b) and (c) together.

(e) all of the above.

16. State whether each of the following would be a likely result if Canadian interest rates were not kept higher than US interest rates.

____ (a) Canadians' living standards would be reduced.

____ (b) There would be no significant effect on Canada economically, because Canadian interest rates are not related to US rates.

____ (c) Capital flows from the USA to Canada would be reduced.

____ (d) Capital investment in Canada would tend to be depressed by a lack of funds.

____ (e) The international value of the Canadian dollar (compared to the US dollar) would fall.

17. If Canada's rate of inflation significantly exceeded the USA's rate of inflation for long, which of the following would be likely to happen?

____ (a) Canada's exports to the USA would decrease.

____ (b) Canadians would travel less to the USA.

____ (c) Canada's imports from the USA would increase.

____ (d) Unemployment in Canada would increase.

____ (e) Eventually, a decline in the international value of the Canadian dollar relative to the US dollar would occur.

18. If people expect that a new round of inflation will be the consequence of government action to reduce unemployment then

(a) demand management policies will become more effective.

(b) higher levels of real output would result from government expansionary policies.

(c) price and income increases would be the likely result of government expansionary policies.

(d) incomes would rise, but prices would remain stable as government attempted to stimulate aggregate demand.

19. "Stagflation" refers to a situation where the economy is experiencing ____________________

____

____.

20. In a stagflation, the trade-off of more jobs for higher inflation

(a) is always possible.

(b) may no longer apply.

(c) can be achieved, but only if capital spending is depressed.

(d) is a valid course of action that will lead to economic recovery.

21. By accepting **some** additional inflation as a trade-off, the government can speed up economic growth and reduce unemployment. Which of the following is the most likely result if the government tolerates **very rapid** inflation for **several years?**

(a) more rapid economic growth and lower unemployment rates.

(b) more rapid increases in living standards.

(c) both (a) and (b) above.

(d) sluggish economic growth together with rapid inflation.

(e) more rapid economic growth but higher unemployment rates.

22. Suppose you invest $100 at an interest rate of 10% over a one-year period in which the rate of inflation is 8%. Express the rate of return on your investment:

(a) in terms of real before-tax rate of return: ____ %.

(b) in terms of real after-tax rate of return (assuming a tax rate of 40% on your interest income): ____ %.

23. From the viewpoint of many corporations, how does rapid inflation affect the attractiveness of long-term borrowing (through bond issues) as a means of raising funds for capital investment, and why?

____

____

24. The effect of the unusually rapid inflation of the early 1980's was generally to __________ the prices of corporate shares (stocks).

25. The effect described in the previous question is in turn the result of:

(a) ____

____;

(b) ____

____.

26. Suppose the Swell Sweets Company buys sugar for $10 000 and processes it into candies (processing costs — $3000) for sale at a price of $15 000, thus earning a profit of $2000. If the value (price) of sugar rises to $11 000 while it is in the company's inventory, and Swell Sweets raises its selling price by $1000 to reflect this:

(a) Swell Sweets' reported profit will become $ ___________.

(b) This amount:

(i) is an accurate measurement of the company's real profits.

(ii) (overstates/understates) the company's real profits by $___________________.

(c) The reason for the answer to (b) is that ______________________________________
____
____.

27. Suppose the Perfect Paperclip Company buys a machine which lasts 12 years and costs $180 000 but which will cost $240 000 to replace at the end of 12 years. If the company charges straight line depreciation of $15 000 per year, economists would argue the Perfect Paperclip Company is:

(a) accurately stating its depreciation expense.

(b) (overstating/understating) its depreciation expense by $____________ per year, and thus (understating/overstating) its profits by $__________ per year.

28. As a result of the factors described in the previous two questions, many businesses pay ______ ______ taxes than their real profits situation warrants.

29. In summary, the effect of inflation on business profits is to

(a) reduce both reported and actual after-tax profits.

(b) reduce reported profits but increase actual after-tax profits due to the lower taxes on the reduced reported profits.

(c) increase both reported profits and actual after-tax profits proportionately.

(d) increase reported profits and thus tax liabilities, leaving actual after-tax profits depressed.

(e) none of the above.

30. As a result of the situation described in the previous question, while many businesses reported apparently high profits, capital investment was in the 1970's generally ________________.

31. State whether each of the following policies would likely be helpful for dealing with the problem of "stagflation."

____ (a) Allowing businesses tax deductions for "inventory profits."

____ (b) Increasing the amount of government transfer payments to lower-income families.

____ (c) Allowing higher tax exemptions for incomes from investments (interest, dividends and capital gains).

____ (d) Allowing businesses to charge depreciation based on replacement costs rather than historical costs.

____ (e) Increasing taxes on corporate profits and using the funds thus obtained for direct "job creation" programs through which governments would hire unemployed people.

____ (f) Increasing the rate of taxation on capital gains (e.g., sale of corporate shares at a profit).

____ (g) Increasing government regulation of businesses generally.

____ (h) More strict restrictions on capital investment in Canada by foreign companies.

32. In summary, the combined effect of **inflation** and **taxation** in recent years has been to shift economic resources

(a) toward private investment, and away from consumption and government spending.

(b) toward private investment and government spending, and away from consumption.

(c) toward consumption and away from private investment and government spending.

(d) toward private consumption and investment, and away from government spending.

(e) toward consumption and government spending, and away from private investment.

33. How would the trend described in the previous question affect:

(a) the rate of economic growth over the longer term? ________________________________

____

(b) the rate of inflation? ____

(c) the rate of growth of living standards? ______________________________________

34. In contrast to the early 1960's, the application of Keynesian economics in the late 1960's appeared to

   (a) provide much needed stability to the economy.

   (b) have no effect on unemployment or inflation.

   (c) cause more instability, as the economy moved between rapid inflation and recession.

   (d) demonstrate the long term advantages of government intervention in the economy.

35. A reasonable goal for government economic policy in the early 1980's would have been to

   (a) increase the level of capital investment.

   (b) increase production for present consumption, at the expense of capital investment.

   (c) continue the trend established during the 1970's concerning output of consumption and investment goods.

   (d) encourage more investment spending by increasing interest rates.

36. A reasonable goal for government economic policy for the 1990's would be ____________

____

____

____

____.

Chapter 16

INTERNATIONAL TRADE

The matters covered in this chapter are of particular importance to Canada, which exports (and imports) roughly 30% of its GDP. The theory of international trade is quite simple: free trade promotes specialization, efficiency and therefore prosperity. In practice, however, nations tend to place barriers in the way of free trade for various reasons. For over a century, Canada has used tariffs to protect and stimulate the development of the nation's manufacturing sector. The positive results of this policy are that Canada now has a larger manufacturing sector and more diversified economy than would have existed otherwise. On the other hand, this manufacturing sector consists largely of small-scale "branch plants" of foreign firms which are not very efficient and are therefore vulnerable to foreign competition and must be subsidized by continuing protection against imports.

A major policy problem facing Canada is how to increase the international competitiveness of Canadian industry in the future. This goal has become more attainable now in light of the free trade agreement with the United States. Canadian manufacturers will be under increasing competitive pressure to use the most cost-efficient methods of production.

The conclusion of this chapter is that the long-run benefits of freer trade outweigh the costs. It is an important conclusion and one too easily forgotten by politicians and policy makers in the past.

General Learning Objective

Establish the economic costs and benefits of international free trade.

Specific Learning Objectives

		Self-Test Reference
1.	Examine the facts regarding Canada's trade with other nations	# 1-3
2.	Consider the benefits of specializing productive activities	# 4-7
3.	Demonstrate the possible gains in productivity in light of high wages	# 8
4.	Examine the arguments for protection	# 9-11
5.	Assess the economic effects of the import tariff	# 12-16

Self-Test
Reference

6. Identify the non-tariff barriers to trade . . . . # 17

7. Consider policies to alleviate the costs of freer trade . . . . # 18

8. Establish the intent and achievements of GATT . . . . # 19, 20

9. Review the concepts and definitions . . . . # 21, 22

Self-Test

1. Canada's exports are approximately __C__% of GDP:

   (a) 10
   (b) 20
   (c) 30
   (d) 40

2. As of 1988, which country or countries account(s) for over 70% of Canada's merchandise exports and almost 70% of our imports?

   (a) Japan
   (b) The United States
   (c) The European Common Market
   (d) Great Britain
   (e) The Soviet Union

3. The Canadian share of total world trade has __decreased__ (increased, decreased) from 1963 to 1987 from __40__ (22%, 40%) to __22__ (40%, 22%). This change appears to be a result of __weaker__ (weaker, stronger) natural resource markets and a __less__ (more, less) competitive manufacturing sector in Canada.

4. If Moravia is 30% more efficient than Grand Fenwick in producing kadiddles and 15% more efficient than Grand Fenwick in producing fradistats, Moravia can benefit economically by

   (a) producing both kadiddles and fradistats itself, and importing neither from Grand Fenwick.

   (b) concentrating on producing kadiddles, and importing fradistats from Grand Fenwick.

   (c) restricting the importation of Grand Fenwickian products into Moravia.

   (d) subsidizing exports of fradistats.

   (e) (a) and (c) together.

5. The basic economic benefit which nations and people obtain from international trade is __A better standard of living__.

6. A trend toward freer international trade would represent

(a) a threat to all sectors of the Canadian economy.

(b) a threat to some sectors of the Canadian economy.

(c) an opportunity for some sectors of the Canadian economy.

(d) an opportunity for all sectors of the Canadian economy.

(e) (b) and (c) together.

7. To demonstrate the advantages of international trade, number the following in the order that they are expected to occur.

C (a) The nation realizes increased efficiencies of production reflected in lower per unit costs.

B (b) Specialization occurs.

A (c) The nation considers what they do best.

D (d) The nation realizes an improved standard of living.

8. A western Canadian company using local poplar wood produces disposable unfinished chopsticks using the most advanced equipment. A major portion of the output is exported to Asian countries. The average hourly output is 3000 chopsticks and the hourly costs are $90.

A Chinese company using less capital but more labor produces an equivalent product. In China, hourly production is 200 chopsticks and hourly costs are $10.

(a) Complete the following chart.

	Canadian Firm	Chinese Firm
Hourly costs	90	10
Hourly output	3000	200
Cost per chopstick	.3	.5

(b) How do we measure productive efficiency in this example? $ per unit

(c) What factor of production might account for the difference in efficiency?

Advanced technology equipment

(d) Determine the total cost in each country for an order for 2 million chopsticks.
$100 000 china $60 000 in canada

9. "The products of North American manufacturers cannot compete in price with the products of low-wage nations such as Taiwan and Hong Kong".

State whether the above statement is **TRUE** or **FALSE**, and explain the reason for your answer. False because better technology overides high wages

10. "As a generality, it is true that Canadian producers favor protective tariffs."

Is this statement **TRUE** or **FALSE**? Why? False, efficent competitive producers favour freer trade, which would allow access to foreign markets

11. In the "infant industry" argument for protective tariffs, it usually happens that

(a) the protected industry matures and becomes sufficiently competitive so that it no longer requires tariff protection.

(b) the protected industries develop slowly, requiring tariff protection for much longer than was intended, perhaps indefinitely.

(c) the tax revenues from tariffs make it possible for the government to reduce the overall tax burden on the Canadian public.

(d) the protected industries often develop into leading exporters.

(e) (a) and (d) together.

12. The demand and supply schedules below represent the Canadian market for video game cartridges. The supply schedule is that of Canadian producers and the demand schedule indicates the desires of Canadian consumers.

Before international trade, the Canadian price is $50, with production and consumption at 100 000 units.

Now, assume an international price of $35 with no trade restrictions preventing Canadians from purchasing the identical international product.

Draw in a price of $35 on the graph.

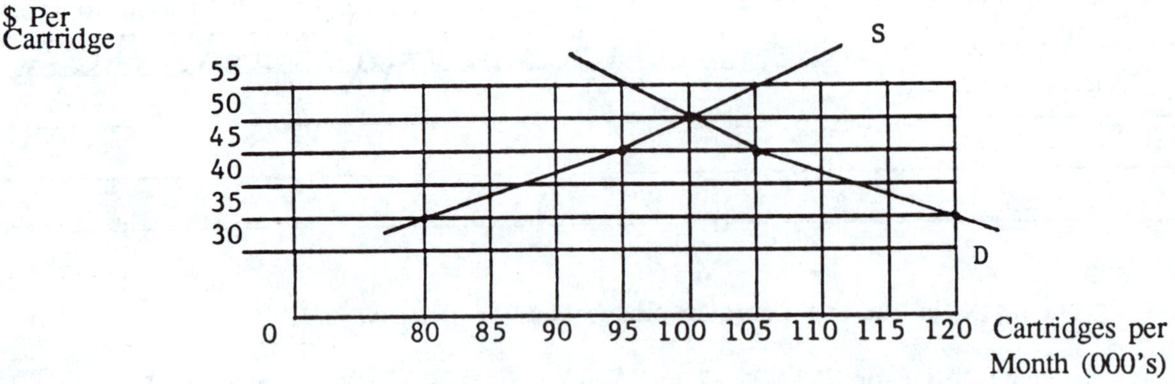

As a result of the lower priced imports, determine:

(a) Canadians' planned purchases 120 000

(b) production by Canadian firms 80 000

(c) imports 40 000

(d) tariff revenues resulting from imports zero

As a result of lobbying by Canadian producers of this product, the Canadian government levies a tariff of $10 per cartridge. The importers pass the tariff onto the consumer and the new market price is $45 per unit.

Draw the $45 price on the graph. Determine:

(e) Canadian purchases 105 000

(f) production by Canadian firms 95 000

(g) imports 10 000

(h) tariff revenues resulting from imports 100 000 p/month

(i) From the following groups, determine who gains and who loses as a result of the imposition of the Canadian tariff. Why do they gain or lose?

Consumers lose because they have to pay higher prices which reduces their

Foreign Suppliers loose have less to sell to canadians

Canadian Importers suffer the same as the foreign suppliers

Government gains as higher revenue is generated from higher taxes

Canadian Firms gain as a result of higher sales.

(j) If Canadian producers are new in the business of video cartridge production, is there a better way of providing some financial help?

13. If Canada has an unemployment problem which it tries to solve by increasing tariffs on foreign imports so as to encourage Canadians to buy goods produced by Canadian workers instead, the most likely effect that this will have on employment in Canada is that ________.

14. Which one of the following statements is **NOT** true?

A tariff on German widgets imported into Canada

(a) will reduce the economic prosperity of the Canadian public.

(b) will benefit the Canadian public in general.

(c) will result in higher widget prices in Canada.

(d) could result in fewer exports of Canadian products to Germany.

(e) will benefit Canadian widget producers and their workers.

15. From the viewpoint of the economist, state whether each of the following is a reasonable argument in favor of placing tariffs on foreign goods imported into Canada.

No (a) Tariffs protect the jobs of Canadians, and reduce unemployment.

No (b) Tariffs protect Canada against foreign competition.

Yes (c) Tariffs can assist in industrial development by getting "infant industries" established, whereas without tariffs they might not have survived.

Yes (d) Tariffs can encourage foreign manufacturers to establish branch plants in Canada, thus generating industrial development.

No (e) Several Canadian industries are experiencing strong competition from foreign producers, and are requesting that the government provide them with tariff protection.

Yes (f) Tariffs can help to diversify the economy, so that it is not dependent upon a few resource industries alone, but rather has manufacturing industries as well.

No (g) Tariffs (on foreign goods) will reduce the tax burden on the Canadian public.

No (h) Tariffs prevent other nations from taking money out of Canada.

16. State whether each of the following statements concerning Canada's manufacturing sector is **TRUE** or **FALSE**.

As a result of Canada's tariff policy over the past century,

F (a) the Canadian manufacturing sector is now able to provide the government with tax revenues which can be used to subsidize the rest of the economy.

T (b) the overall size of the Canadian manufacturing sector is larger than it otherwise would have been.

T (c) the Canadian manufacturing sector is characterized by relatively small-scale firms.

F (d) the Canadian manufacturing sector is generally not very competitive internationally.

T (e) the prices of manufactured goods in Canada are lower than they otherwise would have been.

T (f) Canada's manufacturing sector consists largely of "branch plants" owned by foreign firms.

17. Identify the non-tariff barriers to trade in the following list.

(a) A duty is levied on the value of potatoes imported from the USA.

(b) During the early 1980's, Canadian customs authorities delayed the processing of imported cars by a strict enforcement of paper work.

(c) A quota is imposed on imports of childrens' clothing.

(d) The provincial government provides subsidies for Canadian lumber exporters.

(e) Tax incentives are granted to selected Canadian exporters.

18. Name at least three ways in which governments could ease the negative effects of tariff reductions on protected Canadian industries.

(a) Provide Notice of Tariff reductions

(b) Provide financial/technical assistance

(c) Provide retraining for workers.

19. The purpose of the General Agreement on Tariffs and Trade (GATT) is to

(a) negotiate reductions in tariffs among major industrialized countries.

(b) prevent a return to protectionism experienced in the 1930's.

(c) increase world trade and prosperity for all nations.

(d) consider the reduction of non-tariff barriers to trade.

(e) all of the above.

20. Label the following **TRUE** or **FALSE**

T (a) The Uruguay Round of GATT talks started in 1986 and was scheduled to end in 1991.

F (b) There are now 50 countries involved in GATT.

T (c) Services account for 30% of the GATT trade.

F (d) GATT has had very little success in reducing world tariffs.

21. Answer the following questions on the basis of the diagram below. The diagram illustrates the supply of cars with free trade and with tariffs.

S(d) = total supply of domestically produced cars.
S(d+f) = total supply of domestic and imported cars with free trade.
S(d+t) = total supply of domestic and imported cars with tariffs.
D(d) = demand for cars in this particular country.

Assume this particular country is one of relatively small population.

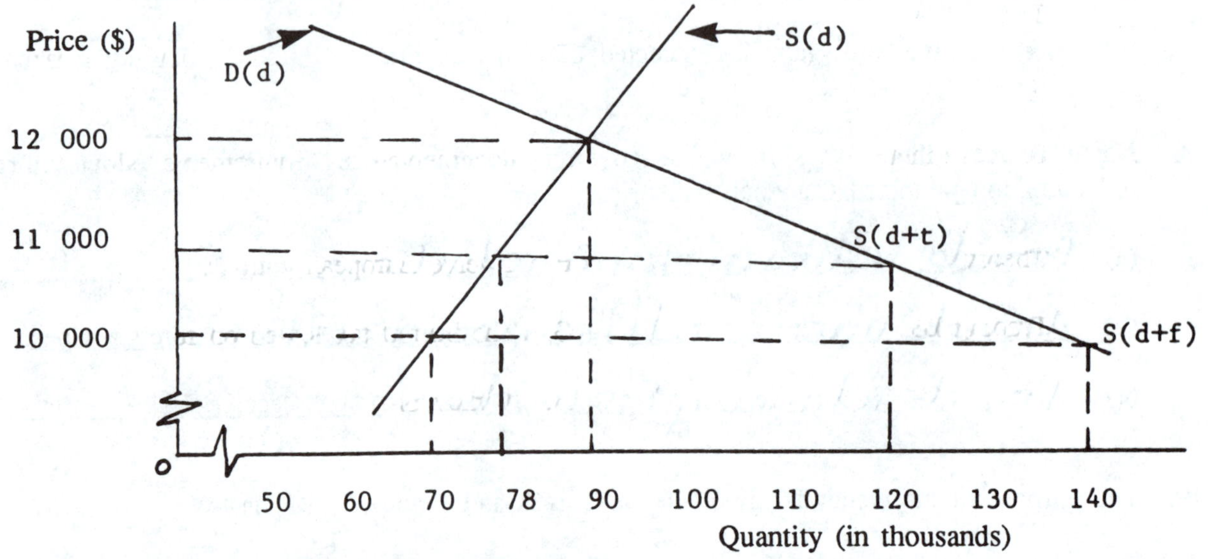

Insert your answers in the lettered spaces below.

If this economy was entirely closed to international trade, equilibrium price = (a) 12000; equilibrium quantity = (b) 90.

With free trade, equilibrium price = (c) 10 ; equilibrium quantity = (d) 140 ; domestic car sales = (e) 70; foreign car sales = (f) 70

With the tariff, equilibrium price = (g) 11 ; equilibrium quantity = (h) 120; domestic car sales = (i) 78; foreign car sales = (j) 42

Calculate the total revenue collected with the tariff: (k) 42m

22. Match the items of list B with the concepts of list A.

List A

- H Subsidy
- D GATT
- E Non-tariff barrier
- G Tariff
- A Import Quota
- B Branch Plant
- C Comparative Advantage Theory
- F Trading Bloc

List B

A. Canada limits imports of children's footwear.

B. Coca-Cola Canada Ltd.

C. Canada decides to produce and export steel in lieu of clothing production.

D. Negotiate multi-lateral reductions in tariffs.

E. Canadian customs officials enforce documentation requirements slowing down the importation of Japanese autos.

F. Twelve European nations.

G. The import tax levied on foreign wines.

H. Turkey producers receive 15 cents per pound to offset production costs.

Chapter 17

CANADIAN INTERNATIONAL TRADE AND INVESTMENT POLICY

This chapter expands on a problem discussed in an earlier chapter: the international competitiveness of the manufacturing sector of the Canadian economy. The tariff protection which fostered the development of Canada's manufacturing sector has had two side-effects: (1) much of Canada's manufacturing industry is foreign-owned, consisting of "branch-plant" operations, and (2) Canadian manufacturing operations tend to be relatively small-scale, inefficient and not competitive internationally.

While most of the public discussion of this matter tends to focus on the largely **emotional** issue of foreign **ownership**, the more serious concern is the **economic** issue of the **performance** of Canadian manufacturing, particularly its long-term future in the face of foreign competition.

The basic policy issue in Chapter 16 is what to **do** about this problem. The nationalistic approach does not appear particularly realistic without large-scale energy developments to use as the trade-off in bargaining with other nations; furthermore, Canada is not the only source of such resource products. Although the internationalist approach appeared threatening to many Canadian workers, especially in Ontario and Quebec's secondary manufacturing sectors, the Canadian government ratified a Free Trade Agreement with the United States on January 1, 1989.

The politics of international trade caught up with the reality of economics. To compete, Canada was forced to turn its attention from the national perspective to the global market. The signing of the trade deal was the first step in our quest to compete in that global market.

General Learning Objective

Examine the economic effects of Canadian international trade and investment policy, from the British policy of preferential tariffs in the 1800's to the current free trade agreement with the United States.

Specific Learning Objectives

	Self-Test Reference
1. Consider the National Policy of 1879 and the resulting effects of tariff protection on Canadian industry	#1-6
2. Compare the general level of Canadian interest rates to American rates	#7
3. Outline the Canadian government policy regarding foreign investment along with the response of Canadians	#8, 9, 15, 17-20
4. State five reasons why US investors have found Canada attractive for investment	#10
5. Compare the foreign-controlled share of total assets and sales in Canada for 1971 and 1985	#11-13
6. Consider the economic effects of foreign investment in Canada	#14, 16
7. Examine several reasons for the poor productivity performance in Canadian manufacturing	#21
8. Identify the forces of change in moving from a nationalist to a global perspective	#22, 23
9. Assess the basis of support for freer trade	#24
10. Consider the concerns of some sectors of the Canadian economy regarding a move to freer trade	#25
11. Recognize the factors inherent for competing in global markets	#26, 27
12. Define the terminology of the Free Trade Agreement	#28

Self-Test

1. The National Policy of 1879 was designed to protect which segment of the Canadian economy? Manufacturing Industry.

2. As a result of Canada's early high tariff policy, the Canadian manufacturing sector became larger (smaller, larger) in size, foreign ownership of Canadian manufacturing increased (increased, decreased) and the Canadian manufacturing sector became less (more, less) efficient.

3. Under the National Policy, foreign companies that desired to sell in Canada could avoid the higher Canadian tariffs by build a subsidiary Plant in canada.

4. As a result of the move towards smaller 'branch plant' firms and the reality of a smaller Canadian market for goods, determine if the following are true or false.

F (a) Manufacturing benefitted from 'economies of scale'.

T (b) Average costs per unit were relatively higher than in the United States.

T (c) Canadian consumers had to subsidize the manufacturing industry by paying relatively higher prices.

5. State whether each of the following statements regarding the form of foreign investment in Canada is **TRUE** or **FALSE**.

T (a) Mega projects, especially hydro-electric projects, have been financed by foreigners through loans.

F (b) Equity investment is preferred to debt investment because Canadian businesses have a greater chance of maintaining control.

T (c) Foreign investment has resulted in takeovers, plant expansion or closure, and the export of primary resources.

T (d) Of late, foreign firms in Canada appear to be content to use Canadian-earned profits to expand operations rather than import capital from abroad.

6. A basic purpose of Canadian tariff policy has been to promote the development of the manufacturing sector of the Canadian economy. Another effect of this tariff policy has been to

(a) benefit Canadian consumers.

(b) make manufacturing in Canada more efficient.

(c) reduce foreign ownership and control of Canadian manufacturing.

(d) increase foreign ownership and control of Canadian manufacturing.

(e) increase competition generally in the Canadian economy.

7. Historically, Canadian interest rates have been higher (higher, lower) than US rates. This has led to more (more, less) foreign investment in Canadian bonds and treasury bills.

8. Canada's policy toward foreign investment has been

(a) more restrictive than most nations' policies.

(b) about as restrictive as most nations' policies.

(c) less restrictive than most nations' policies.

9. The predominant attitude of the Canadian government over the years toward foreign investment has been

(a) neutral; the government has neither sought to encourage nor discourage it.

(b) favorable; the government has sought to encourage it.

(c) selective; the government has sought to encourage debt investment by foreigners but discourage equity investment.

(d) unfavorable; the government has sought to discourage it.

(e) none of the above.

10. United States investors have found Canada to be a particularly attractive country to invest in because:

(a) close by.

(b) Skilled low paid labour force.

(c) language & culture.

(d) easy market for U.S. firms.

(e) Many resources (wealth).

11. As of 1985, foreign control of Canadian industry is most concentrated in the mining and manufacturing sectors.

12. From Figure 17-3 in the text, as of 1971, the foreign controlled share of total assets was approximately 36% but declining to under 23% by 1985. Similarly, the foreign controlled share of sales was 37% in 1971 declining to about 29% in 1985.

13. Thus, from 1971 to 1985 there was a decrease in the foreign control of Canadian companies. Less foreign control was accompanied by a (an) increased (increase, decrease) in the growth of Canadian controlled corporations and increased. (decreased, increased) acquisitions of foreign firms by Canadians.

14. State whether each of the following statements regarding the effects of foreign investment in Canada is **TRUE** or **FALSE**.

F (a) Without foreign investment Canada's manufacturing sector would have grown much faster.

T (b) Foreign investors brought their savings, know-how and technology to Canada.

T (c) Foreign investment increases the value of the Canadian dollar and supplies Canadians with US dollars to purchase US imports.

T (d) Foreign investment has substantially added to Canada's standard of living.

T (e) Foreign investment in Canada has been accompanied by an increased outflow of interest and dividends from Canadians to foreigners.

15. List four criticisms which are made of foreign investment by Canadians.

(a) i) benefits them not canadians
ii) Profits leave canada
iii) foreign laws.
iv) non canadian leaders.

(b) State which of these criticisms you believe to be the most valid and serious, and explain the reason(s) for your selection.

i) investors only look for their benefits

(c) State which of these criticisms you believe to be the least valid, and explain the reasons(s) for your selection.

16. Are the following statements, regarding foreign investment in Canada, **TRUE** or **FALSE?**

T a) Economic growth in Canada is accelerated.

T b) The foreign investment is a source of American dollars allowing Canadians to purchase American products.

T c) Americans have been the largest source of foreign investment in Canada.

F d) Profits made by foreign corporations operating in Canada are seldom re-invested in Canada.

T e) Much of the foreign investment is made in manufacturing and the natural resource industries.

T f) The extent of foreign control of Canadian corporations peaked in the early 1970's and has declined since that time.

17. The Foreign Investment Review Act (FIRA) acted to screen

a) all proposals for foreign investment in Canada.

b) any expansion within Canada by foreign firms already operating in Canada.

(c) proposals for foreign takeovers of Canadian firms over a given size and the expansion into new businesses by foreign corporations.

d) foreign investment in certain "key sectors" of the Canadian economy, such as banking, publishing and communications.

e) any investments by foreign firms leading to control of Canadian firms.

18. Opponents of foreign investment in Canada have criticized FIRA on the grounds that

a) Applies to similar investment

b) Applies only to Future investment

c) Approved most Applications from Foreign Firms

19. Supporters of foreign investment in Canada have criticized the Foreign Investment Review Agency on the grounds that ____.

20. With the creation of Investment Canada in 1985, FIRA ceased to exist, and foreign investment became easier. The watchdog role of FIRA gave way to Investment Canada's role of investment in Canadian industry with the exception of the foreign oil and gas industries.

21. Indicate whether or not the following have contributed to Canada's inefficient and uncompetitive manufacturing sector. If it is not a reason, change the wording to make it one.

F a) relatively high Canadian productivity

F b) generally low levels of tariffs

F c) large Canadian market

T d) restricted use of modern mass-production technology.

F e) specialization in one or few products.

22. Canada was forced to change its thinking in the 1980's from a nationalist perspective to a global perspective. How did each of the following factors influence the Canadian decision?

a) World resource markets

Declining worldexports for canadian products

b) Competition

Increase in foreign competition

c) The U.S. market for Canadian goods

canadians had increasing access to u.s. markets

23. As a 'rule of thumb', what size of market is required to realize efficient production in manufacturing? 100 million people

24. The Canadian Manufacturers Association supported the move to freer trade on the grounds that

a) Canadians would move from manufacturing to the production of services.

b) the free trade agreement would encourage Canadians to do more processing of raw materials as opposed to exporting raw materials.

c) the experience prepares Canada for the inevitability of global competition.

d) both b) and c) are correct.

25. What were two concerns of Canadian food processors regarding implementation of the free trade agreement with the United States?

1) Canadians purchase Primary Food Products, prices high

2) strong competition from large US firms.

26. The concept of a company acquiring a mandate to design, manufacture and market a particular product for the world market on behalf of the parent company is known as world product Mandating.

27. Which of the following are applicable to the economic philosophy of gearing production to a global market as opposed to focusing on the Canadian market?

a a) find 'niche' markets

____ b) increase our sense of nationalism

c c) specialize

____ d) protect threatened industries

e e) develop new products

f f) corporate re-structuring

28. Place the letter of the description in List B that best fits the concept of List A.

List A

I Dumping

J Globalization

A Subsidies

G Disputes panel

F Duty remission

D Countervailing duty

E Direct acquisition

H Indirect acquisition

C Auto pact

B Marketing Board

List B

A. financial assistance from government to private firms

B. controls production and distribution of eggs

C. allows for product mandating

D. the U.S. retaliates against the EEC for unfair subsidies in the German steel industry

E. Thompson Newspapers buys controlling interest in the shares of a Canadian regional newspaper

F. Canada refunds import duties on foreign parts purchased by the Honda Canada Company

G. a neutral panel to arbitrate American-Canadian trade disputes

H. the Bank of Hong Kong, a Canadian subsidiary bank, buys the Canadian assets of another foreign owned bank

I. a South Korean steel producer sells steel in North America below the market price in Korea

J. a movement away from national markets

Chapter 18

THE CANADIAN DOLLAR IN FOREIGN EXCHANGE MARKETS

There are two basic concepts in Chapter 18:

(a) foreign exchange markets, and

(b) the international Balance of Payments of a nation.

Regarding (a), nations' currencies are bought and sold in markets, in which demand and supply cause their prices in terms of each other (their exchange rates) to fluctuate. Regarding (b), a nation's international financial transactions can be summarized into its Balance of Payments, which shows all of that nation's receipts from and payments to other nations.

The interactions between the exchange rate and the Balance of Payment can be quite complex, but are essentially two-way:

(a) the Balance of Payments influences the exchange rate: Balance of Payments deficits cause the exchange rate to fall, while surpluses cause the exchange rate to rise.

(b) the exchange rate influences the Balance of Payments: a decline in the exchange rate increases a nation's receipts and reduces its payments, while a rise in the exchange rate increases a nation's payments and reduces its receipts.

When these international economic forces are allowed to work themselves out freely in markets, a "floating" exchange rate system is said to be in effect. Under a floating exchange rate system, the international price of a nation's currency will rise and fall in response to changes in the demand for and supply of it, in exports and imports, and in the flows of capital into and out of that nation. However, governments often do not allow their exchange rates to float freely; rather, many governments (including Canada's) practise what is called a "dirty float," in which they influence their exchange rates. This is done mainly through purchases or sales of Canadian dollars in foreign exchange markets by the Bank of Canada. If the Bank of Canada buys Canadian dollars, the exchange rate tends to rise: such a policy would depress import prices and restrain inflation, but also would depress exports and thus add to unemployment. If the Bank of Canada sells Canadian dollars, the exchange rate tends to decline: this would increase exports and reduce unemployment, but at the expense of higher import prices and more inflation.

Thus, exchange rate policy, like monetary and fiscal policy, involves trade-offs between the goals of full employment and stable prices, with lower exchange rates contributing to one and higher exchange rates contributing to the other. As with monetary and fiscal policy, the government tries to achieve a balance between these conflicting policy goals.

In the mid-seventies, the Canadian dollar traded at par with the American dollar. Since that time, depreciating forces have forced a decline in Canada's exchange rate, which has reduced Canadians' living standards but increased employment by making Canadian industry more internationally competitive. For several years during the mid-1970's, Canadians' incomes rose too fast for productivity, forcing production costs out of line with our competitors. The decline in Canada's exchange rate was therefore quite similar to the nation's work force taking an international pay cut in exchange for improved job security, somewhat like auto workers did in the early 1980's, but on a grand scale.

The Canadian dollar has come under attack by foreign holders several times during the 1980's. The most serious selling of our dollar occurred in early 1986 as the price fell below the benchmark $.70 American. This prompted the Bank of Canada to embark on a massive buying of Canadian dollars and selling of foreign currencies. It also necessitated a substantial rise in our short-term interest rates at a time when lower rates were warranted to sustain the economic expansion and enhance employment. This latter crisis is an excellent example of the necessary trade-offs involved in public policy — especially the trade-off of higher interest rates to gain an appreciated currency.

The Canadian dollar gained strength as of 1988, reflecting the large inflows of foreign capital in our debt and equity markets. This was more than enough to offset our declining merchandise balance and Canada's increasing deficit on tourism and investment income flows. The result was a Canadian dollar in the range of $.85 Am. over 1989 and 1990.

General Learning Objective

Explain the operation of foreign exchange markets and interpret a nation's International Balance of Payments statement.

Specific Learning Objectives

	Objective	Self-Test Reference
1.	Define the "exchange rate"	# 1-3
2.	Determine the factors that affect the foreign exchange value of the Canadian dollar	# 4
3.	Explain the concept of a "floating" exchange rate	# 5, 6
4.	Analyze a Balance of Payments statement	# 7-10c
5.	Define "dirty float"	# 10d-11
6.	Identify the costs and benefits of a depreciating or appreciating Canadian dollar	# 12-20
7.	Consider the activity of foreign exchange speculators	# 21
8.	Analyze long-run changes in Balance of Payments statements since 1970	# 22-30

Self-Test

1. The foreign exchange rate is defined as ______________________________

2. If $1 Canadian = $.8585 American; then $1 American = ______ Canadian.

3. If 1 pound Sterling = $1.9121 Canadian; then $1 Canadian = ________ pounds Sterling.

4. (a) If foreign businesses increase the flow of investment capital into Canada over last year's levels with other factors constant, this will tend to cause the international value of the Canadian dollar to ______________________________.

   (b) If Canadian imports of foreign automobiles increase over the level of the previous year with other factors constant, this will tend to cause the international value of the Canadian dollar to ______________________________.

   (c) If the Canadian subsidiaries of American corporations increase the amount of dividends which they pay to their US-based parent companies with other factors constant, the international value of the Canadian dollar would tend to ____________________.

   (d) An increase in the number of immigrants coming to Canada (and bringing funds with them) would tend to cause the international value of the Canadian dollar to ________.

   (e) If many Canadians travel abroad to the World Bejuniaberry Festival in the Duchy of Grand Fenwick, this would tend to cause the international value of the Canadian dollar to ______________________________.

   (f) An increase in Canadian short-term interest rates relative to equivalent American interest rates tends to cause the international value of the Canadian dollar to __________.

   (g) For the above answers (a through f), distinguish between a depreciation (D) of the Canadian dollar and an appreciation (A).

5. If Canada is operating on a floating exchange rate system, the international value of the Canadian dollar will

   (a) remain stable (at one fixed level as decided by international agreement).

   (b) float steadily upwards in relation to other currencies.

   (c) gradually decline in relation to other currencies.

   (d) rise and fall as the supply of and demand for Canadian dollars in international money markets change.

   (e) none of the above.

6. Suppose that Canada is operating on a floating exchange rate system and that Canada has a Balance of Payments **surplus**. In these circumstances, the international value of the Canadian dollar would tend to ______________________________.

7. Classify each of the following transactions as a Canadian "receipt" or "payment."

   (a) Foreign tourists spend money in Canada.

   (b) Canada imports Japanese automobiles.

   (c) Canadian companies build plants in the USA

   (d) Canadian subsidiaries of foreign companies pay dividends to their parent companies in Europe.

   (e) Foreign firms buy controlling interest in Canadian companies.

   (f) Ontario Hydro pays interest to US bondholders.

   (g) Canadians visit Disney World in Florida.

   (h) B.C. Hydro borrows $500 million in New York.

8. (a) If Canada's receipts exceed payments, Canada has a Balance of Payments ____________.

   (b) If Canada's payments exceed receipts, Canada has a Balance of Payments ____________.

   (c) Balance of Payments deficits tend to (depreciate/appreciate) the Canadian dollar, whereas a balance of payments surplus tends to ________________ the dollar. The latter results from the increased (demand/supply) for our currency.

9. A SUMMARY OF CANADA'S BALANCE OF PAYMENTS, 19-5
(Millions Of Dollars)

CURRENT ACCOUNT	RECEIPTS	PAYMENTS	BALANCE
Merchandise	$900	$1200	— $300
Travel	150	50	+ 100
Interest and Dividends	150	350	— 200
Government Contributions	—	100	— 100
BALANCE ON CURRENT ACCOUNT	$1200	$1700	— $500
CAPITAL ACCOUNT			
Capital Movements	$600	$ 200	+ $400
BALANCE ON CAPITAL ACCOUNT	$600	$ 200	+ $400
OVERALL BALANCE (Current and Capital Accounts)			— $100

(a) State whether each of the following statements is **TRUE** or **FALSE**.
In 19-5:

____ (i) Canada sold more merchandise internationally than it bought.

____ (ii) Foreign tourists spent more money in Canada than Canadian tourists spent in foreign countries.

____ (iii) Canada received more in interest and dividends than were paid out of Canada.

____ (iv) Canada gave foreign aid to other nations.

____ (v) Canadian investment in foreign countries exceeded foreign investment in Canada.

(b) In 19-5, Canada had a Balance of Payments ______________________________.

(c) If the price of the Canadian dollar were allowed to "float" freely, in 19-5 it would tend to ____.

(d) One group within Canada which would **benefit** economically from the change in the price of the Canadian dollar in (c) above would be ______________________,

because, ____

____.

(e) The group(s) within Canada that would be hurt economically by this change in the price of the Canadian dollar would be ____________________, because ______________

____.

10. There are two important facts about the current account of the Canadian Balance of Payments. Because of our long Canadian winters, increasing numbers of Canadians take winter holidays in foreign countries. Secondly, Canadians pay increasing amounts of interest and dividends to foreigners who have both invested in Canada and loaned funds to Canadians.

How does the above affect:

(a) The current account of Canada's Balance of Payments______________________

____

____.

(b) The foreign exchange price of the Canadian dollar assuming a purely floating exchange rate ____

____.

(c) The prices of Canadian imports, as a result of (b), ______________________.

(d) If the Bank of Canada desires an appreciation of the Canadian dollar, it could:

(i) ____;

(ii) ____.

(e) Assuming floating exchange rates, the activity of the Bank of Canada in (d) is referred to as a ____

____.

11. Under a dirty float, the government

(a) allows the international value of its currency to fluctuate freely with supply and demand.

(b) manipulates the international value of its currency contrary to the wishes of its trading partners.

(c) prevents any fluctuations in the international value of its currency.

(d) intervenes in foreign exchange markets to moderate fluctuations in the international value of its currency.

(e) permits the international value of its currency to float, but prevents speculative purchases and sales of the currency which could cause its value to fluctuate.

12. If the international value of the Canadian dollar were to decline unusually rapidly, there would be a risk of

(a) more severe inflation in Canada.

(b) more severe competition from foreign manufacturers.

(c) less severe competition from foreign manufacturers.

(d) (a) and (b) above.

(e) (a) and (c) above.

13. If the international value of the Canadian dollar were to rise unusually rapidly, there would be a risk of

(a) more severe inflation in Canada.

(b) more severe competition from foreign manufacturers.

(c) an increase in unemployment in Canada.

(d) (b) and (c) above.

(e) none of the above.

14. If the international value of the Canadian dollar were under downward pressure which the Canadian government wished to resist, the Bank of Canada could ______________________ interest rates in Canada.

15. If the Bank of Canada takes steps to increase the international value of the Canadian dollar, unemployment will _______________ since export sales decrease, and inflation is likely to decrease since imported goods cost ___________.

16. If the Canadian government attempted to maintain the international value of the Canadian dollar far above its equilibrium level,

(a) Canada would deplete its foreign exchange reserves.

(b) over the longer run, the international value of the Canadian dollar would eventually fall to a more realistic level.

(c) (a) and (b) above.

(d) the result would be large increases in Canada's foreign exchange reserves.

(e) there would be downward pressure on Canadian interest rates.

17. If the Canadian government attempted to maintain the international value of the Canadian dollar far below its equilibrium level,

(a) the government would have to either "print" or borrow Canadian dollars on a large scale.

(b) the Bank of Canada buys Canadian dollars.

(c) (a) and (b) above.

(d) the Bank of Canada would have to hold Canadian interest rates at high levels relative to rates in other nations.

(e) Canada's holdings of foreign exchange reserves would decline.

18. "Under a system of floating exchange rates, monetary policy might be more effective than fiscal policy." Explain.

19. Suppose that the Canadian dollar falls in price against the American dollar and the Bank of Canada takes action to increase the value of our currency.

(a) Canadian pulp and paper executives are against the Bank of Canada intervention because __________.

(b) Canadian importers support the action of the Bank because __________.

(c) What is the Bank trying to accomplish? __________.

20. (a) Dawna Rose is a Canadian automobile dealer who sells imported cars from Japan. In one year she imported 1000 new cars at an average price of 2.2 million yen per car. The exchange rate was 200 yen = $1 Canadian. The total Canadian dollar cost of cars for that year was $ ______________________.

(b) The next year, the Canadian dollar depreciated against the yen to 140 yen = $1 Canadian. The total Canadian dollar cost to Dawna who again imports 1000 cars at an average price of 2.2 million yen per car, was $ ______________________.

(c) Based on the relative change in prices caused by the dollar depreciation, Canadians reduce their purchases of Japanese goods and services whereas our exports to Japan increase.

Thus, Canadian exports (increase/decrease) and our Japanese imports ______________. This adjustment to our Balance of Payments resulting from floating exchange rates is referred to as the ______________________.

21. State whether each of the following statements is **TRUE** or **FALSE**. If there were widespread rumours of a decline in the international value of the Canadian dollar, the actions of foreign exchange speculators would tend to

____ (a) put an additional downward pressure on the international value of the Canadian dollar.

____ (b) contribute to lower interest rates in Canada.

____ (c) cause the Bank of Canada to buy Canadian dollars in foreign exchange markets.

____ (d) make it more difficult for the Bank of Canada to stabilize the international value of the Canadian dollar.

____ (e) contribute to lower prices of goods imported into Canada.

22. State whether each of the following statements concerning Canada's international economic position in the 1950's and 1960's is **TRUE** or **FALSE**.

____ (a) Surpluses on merchandise trade provided the funds for a net outflow of capital to other nations.

____ (b) Deficits on current account, mainly due to travel and interest and dividends, were offset by inflows of foreign capital, particularly foreign direct investment.

____ (c) Both the current and capital accounts showed deficits, mainly due to travel and interest and dividends, together with a net outflow of direct investment.

____ (d) Deficits on current account, mainly due to travel and interest and dividends, were financed for the most part by heavy borrowing abroad, especially through bond issues.

____ (e) None of the above is an accurate representation of Canada's international economic position in the 1950's and 1960's.

23. State whether each of the following statements is **TRUE** or **FALSE**. By the early 1970's,

____ (a) the inflow of foreign direct investment into Canada increased considerably, as Canada's energy resources were developed.

____ (b) Canada's current account deficits increased, but were financed increasingly by heavy borrowing abroad, mainly through bond issues.

____ (c) Canada's reliance on foreign capital decreased, as the current account deficit shrank, reducing Canada's need for foreign capital.

____ (d) Canada was widely believed to be maturing economically to the point where the nation's capital requirements could be financed within Canada.

24. State whether each of the following would help to reduce Canada's need for foreign borrowing.

____ (a) Reductions in Canada's personal income tax.

____ (b) Reductions in the federal government's budget deficit.

____ (c) Increased exports of Canadian resources and other products.

____ (d) Reduced consumption by Canadians of foreign goods and services.

____ (e) Increased saving (and reduced consumption) by Canadians.

____ (f) Increases in federal government spending.

25. The Canadian dollar appreciation of 1988 resulted from

a) a higher merchandise trade surplus

b) a smaller deficit on the services sector of the Current Account

c) both a) and b)

d) rising capital inflows

26. It appears that the Bank of Canada intervened in foreign exchange markets in 1987-88 to prevent the Canadian dollar from appreciating too much against foreign currencies.

The Bank accomplished this objective by ______________________ (buying, selling) ______________________ (Canadian dollars, foreign exchange) and ______________________ (buying, selling) ______________________ (Canadian dollars, foreign exchange).

27. What was the cost in Canadian dollars of the Bank of Canada intervention of Question 26?

______________________.

28. Why is the flow of investment income classified as a service in our Balance of Payments statement?

______________________.

29. From Figure 18-14 of the text, we discover that the interest portion of the services deficit has grown substantially during the 1980's. The two possible reasons for this change are:

1) ______________________.

2) ______________________.

30. The trend of Canadians increasing their requirements of borrowing foreign capital is worrisome since

a) debt servicing costs as a percentage of exports are increasing.

b) we are increasing our indebtedness to foreigners.

c) our increasing indebtedness to foreigners means that future current account deficits will be increasing.

d) a debt that doesn't increase productive assets but instead finances current operating budgets of governments, leaves future generations with increased costs but little benefits.

e) all of the above are true.

Chapter 19

THE INTERNATIONAL MONETARY SYSTEM

The basic concepts of international trade and finance have been established in Chapters 16 and 18. Chapter 19 uses these concepts to trace the evolution of the international monetary system over more than 50 years, from the extreme instability of the 1930's to the rigidity of the pegged system from 1945 to 1973, to the development of the dirty float after that. When the present situation is seen in historical perspective, it is apparent that nations are continuing the long search for an international monetary system that is neither too unstable nor too rigid to be workable and sustainable.

Chapter 19 also touches on a number of matters of international interest and importance such as the shift of world industrial power in favor of Japan and West Germany, currency devaluations, the role of gold in the international monetary system, gold speculation, the trials and tribulations of the US dollar and, finally, its devaluation.

We also consider the economic impact of the evolution of petro-dollars and how the growth of euro-dollar deposits and loans precipitated a commercial banking crisis in the early eighties. We look at the reasons for the strength of the American dollar during the first half of the 1980's and the causes of the American dollar depreciation during the latter half of the decade. Inevitably, the persistent federal government deficits and the Balance of Payments deficits played a role in the American dollar depreciation.

General Learning Objective

Explore the historical events from the 1930's to the present that had an impact on the evolution of the international monetary system.

Specific Learning Objectives

	Self-Test Reference
1. Distinguish between a "floating rate" system and a system of "pegged" currency prices	# 1-3
2. Examine the effect of the Great Depression of the 1930's on foreign exchange rates	# 4-5
3. Identify the main features of the pegged exchange rate system established after World War II	# 6-12

Self-Test Reference

4. Relate the effect of Balance of Payments problems to the exchange rate . . . . # 13-15

5. Assess the role of the international monetary fund in foreign exchange crises . . . . # 16-19

6. Review the concept of devaluation . . . . # 20-22

7. Recognize the role of the US dollar as a key world currency from 1945-59 . . . . . . # 23-24

8. Examine the causes of the breakdown of the pegged system of exchange rates . . . . # 25-29

9. Identify possible solutions to restore the pegged rate system during the late sixties . . . . # 30-34

10. Consider the 1973 devaluation of the American dollar . . . . # 35-37

11. Define "euro-dollars" . . . . # 38-39

12. Recognize the causes of the world banking crisis of the early eighties . . . . # 40

13. Describe the measures designed to alleviate the banking crisis . . . . # 41

14. Establish the reasons for the strong American dollar from 1980 to 1985 . . . . # 42-43

15. Summarize the events that led to the G-5 Agreement of 1987 . . . . # 44

16. Review the record of co-operation among major industrialized countries regarding the international monetary system . . . . # 45, 46

17. Assess the present role of gold in the international monetary system . . . . # 47

18. Describe the present system of International Exchange Rates . . . . # 48

Self-Test

1. The difference between "floating" and "pegged" currency prices (exchange rates) is that:

   (a) floating currency prices are free to move both up and down, while pegged currency prices are only permitted to move upwards.

   (b) with pegged currency prices, governments act so as to prevent the prices of currencies from moving significantly upwards or downwards.

   (c) only nations with Balance of Payments surpluses have floating exchange rates.

(d) floating currency prices are usually higher than pegged currency prices.

(e) pegged currency prices are considered to be appropriate for nations with Balance of Payments deficits.

2. Under a pegged system, a country's level of foreign exchange reserves is (more/less) important relative to the reserve holdings under a floating rate system.

3. Question 2 is true since under a pegged system the government (buys/ sells) foreign exchange reserves and (buys/sells) its own currency if market forces push the value of the domestic currency below the pegged rate.

4. During the Great Depression of the 1930's

   (a) nations agreed to peg exchange rates at agreed levels so as to encourage international trade.

   (b) many nations sought to increase the value of their currency in order to increase the purchasing power of their consumers in international markets.

   (c) exchange rates became very unstable as nations repeatedly devalued their currencies in attempts to gain competitive advantages over each other.

   (d) the floating system of exchange rates worked quite successfully as currency values were able to respond quickly to the economic pressures of the Depression.

   (e) none of the above.

5. The situation referred to in the previous question caused international trade to (flourish/stagnate) making for an (increase/decrease) in unemployment.

6. Immediately after World War II

   (a) the international monetary system fell into confusion due to the lack of a generally acceptable currency for use in international trade.

   (b) nations were unable to agree on which type of monetary system to use, so each nation acted according to its own preferences.

   (c) the nations of the world agreed to establish a single world currency to simplify international trade and finance.

   (d) the major trading nations of the world agreed to use a system of floating exchange rates.

   (e) the major trading nations agreed to set up a system of pegged exchange rates.

7. Which of the following are true regarding the international monetary system after World War II?

____ (a) The system was designed to prevent exchange rate fluctuations.

____ (b) There had to be an agreement to eliminate protectionist policies that destabilized international trade and investment.

____ (c) Governments would not intervene in foreign exchange markets to restore the 'pegged' exchange rates.

____ (d) Unlike the concept of the 'dirty float', the objective under a fixed exchange rate system is to prevent exchange rate fluctuations as opposed to moderating fluctuations.

8. For example, if Canada were operating on a pegged exchange rate system and had a Balance of Payments surplus, the international value of the Canadian dollar would tend to (rise/fall) and the Canadian government would have to (buy/sell) Canadian dollars and (buy/sell) foreign currencies and gold in order to maintain it at its pegged level.

9. Using the same choices as Question 8, if Canada were operating on a pegged exchange-rate system and had a Balance of Payments deficit, the international value of the Canadian dollar would tend to ________________, and the Canadian government would have to ________ Canadian dollars and ________________ foreign currencies and gold in order to maintain it at its pegged level.

10. Which of the following best describes the position of the US dollar internationally during most of the post war period (until about 1968)?

(a) Considered to be a valuable asset for speculators to hold, not only because of its gold backing, but also because it was generally considered to be undervalued, and therefore likely to increase in value.

(b) Not considered by most nations to be an acceptable medium of exchange in international trade because of its record of instability.

(c) Less acceptable than gold to most nations for purposes of international trade, due to the fact that it could not actually be converted to gold.

(d) The most commonly used currency in international trade and finance; the centre of the world's system of pegged exchange rates--largely due to the fact that it was backed by gold.

(e) Widely used in international trade; the centre of the world's monetary system despite the fact that it had undergone two devaluations over the period.

11. Experience with the international monetary system established after World War II indicates that

(a) exchange rates can be held at pegged levels for as long as governments possess the determination to do so.

(b) the only really workable international monetary system is one that requires nations to peg their exchange rates rigidly and indefinitely.

(c) exchange rates cannot be pegged at fixed levels for indefinite periods of time--sooner or later, some rates will change despite the pegged system.

(d) the floating system established after World War Two works extremely well in most circumstances.

(e) (a) and (b) above.

12. Why is it not possible to peg the international values of all currencies indefinitely?

____

____

____.

13. Nations can experience Balance of Payments deficits for a variety of reasons. State whether each of the following would or would not tend to cause Britain to have a Balance of Payments deficit.

____ (a) The British pound is pegged at an unrealistically high level.

____ (b) Foreign corporations invest more in Britain than the British invest in foreign nations.

____ (c) Britain experiences a more rapid rate of inflation than other nations.

____ (d) British industry is not increasing its efficiency as rapidly as other nations.

____ (e) Imports of Japanese cars into Britain increase significantly.

14. If Britain has a Balance of Payments deficit and is operating on a pegged exchange rate, the international price of the British pound will tend to ____________________, and the Bank of England will have to ______________ British pounds and ______________ foreign currencies.

15. If the Balance of Payments deficits referred to in the previous question continued over a considerable period of time, Britain's holdings of foreign currencies and gold would ________________, and the international price of the British pound would ______________ relative to other currencies. If this situation persisted ____________________(devaluation, revaluation) is inevitable.

16. State whether each of the following is a way in which the International Monetary Fund would **assist** nations experiencing problems due to Balance of Payments deficits.

____ (a) Asking other nations to reduce tariffs on that nation's goods.

____ (b) Allowing that nation to increase its tariffs on foreign goods.

____ (c) Lending that nation foreign currencies and gold.

____ (d) Purchasing goods from that nation.

____ (e) Purchasing that nation's currency.

17. The condition which the IMF would usually attach to the assistance referred to in the previous question would be that the nation receiving the assistance ____________________

____.

18. An austerity program tends to relieve Balance of Payments deficits by ______________

____

____

____

____.

19. The major difficulty encountered with the use of an austerity program is that such programs

____.

20. Assuming a pegged exchange rate system, if Italy experienced persistent Balance of Payment deficits and central bank interventions to stabilize the currency did not help, then the lira would be (revalued, devalued, depreciated, appreciated) ____________________

21. Assuming pegged exchange rates, which of the following would be true regarding a devaluation of the Italian lira?

____ (a) More Canadian dollars would be required to purchase the lira.

____ (b) More Italian lira would be required to purchase foreign currencies.

____ (c) Holding the lira exchange rate at the pre-devalued price would tend to postpone rather than prevent exchange rate fluctuations.

22. Indicate whether each of the following is an expected result after the change in value of the

lira of Question 20.

____ (a) If there is continued downward pressure on the price of the lira, the Italian central bank is no longer obligated to intervene in the market.

____ (b) Italian export sales should improve.

____ (c) Italian imported goods are less expensive.

____ (d) The purpose of the devaluation is to eliminate the Italian Balance of Payments deficit.

____ (e) Italy might now experience more severe inflation.

23. What was the major feature of the U.S. dollar that made it the most commonly used currency in international trade during the post war era?

____

____

____

____

24. During the 1950's, the USA had large Balance of Payments (deficits, surpluses) and a(n) (decreasing, increasing) level of gold reserves.

25. (Use the choices of Question 24.) In the 1960's, the USA had Balance of Payments ________ ______ and a(n) ________________ level of gold reserves.

26. State whether each of the following was or was not a reason for the US Balance of Payments situation described in the previous question.

____ (a) US manufacturers were experiencing strong competition from Western European and Japanese manufacturers.

____ (b) The US military was spending large amounts of money in foreign countries.

____ (c) The US dollar was pegged at an unrealistically high level.

____ (d) Subsidiaries of US corporations in foreign countries were paying dividends to their US-based parent companies.

____ (e) American corporations were investing large amounts of funds in foreign nations.

27. Which of the factors in the previous question was the **most fundamental** source of the USA's problem? ____

____

28. As a result of the US Balance of Payments situation described in the previous two questions, the volume of U.S. dollars held by foreigners

____

____.

29. Which of the following best describes the attitude of most other nations to the situation described in the previous question?

   (a) They were pleased, because there had not been a sufficient volume of US dollars held by foreigners to finance world trade.

   (b) They were concerned that the volume of US dollars in the hands of foreigners would fall, possibly causing a world depression.

   (c) They viewed it as the USA's problem and as not having any particular significance for other nations.

   (d) They were concerned that holders of US dollars might panic and convert them to gold, causing the USA's gold stock to run out and the US dollar to lose its acceptability.

   (e) They were hopeful that the U.S. dollar would be revalued upwards, which would cause the value of their holdings of U.S. dollars to rise greatly.

30. One solution to the problems described in the previous questions would have been for the USA to ________________ its currency. However, the USA preferred instead that certain other nations particularly Japan and Germany (devalue, revalue) their currencies.

31. These nations (supported or opposed) the US proposal referred to in the previous question, because ____

____

____.

32. To encourage Japan and West Germany to agree to their proposals for revaluation, the USA imposed ____,
____
____.

33. The intention of these steps was to ______________________ US receipts (e.g., exports) and ______________________ US payments (e.g., imports), thus ______________________ the US Balance of Payments deficits.

34. The actual result of these steps was that the US Balance of Payments

(a) improved (i.e., the annual deficits decreased), but remained in a deficit position.

(b) moved from a deficit position to an equilibrium position.

(c) moved from a deficit position to a surplus position.

(d) deteriorated (i.e., the annual deficits became more severe).

(e) did not change.

35. In response to the situation described in the previous question, in February of 1973, the USA
____
____.

36. The action referred to in Question 35 was expected to help because it would (increase/decrease) US receipts (e.g., exports) and (increase/ decrease) US payments (e.g., imports).

37. However, the US Balance of Payments deficits did not dwindle, but instead increased after 1973, because ____
____
____.

38. Eurodollars are best defined as ____
____.

39. Besides the Vietnam War, Eurodollar deposits increased mainly as a result of ____________

____.

40. The banking crisis of the early eighties was precipitated as a result of the following.

The OPEC nations were able to (increase/decrease) oil production causing (surpluses/shortages) and forcing the price of oil to (fall/rise). Since the Americans were large importers of OPEC oil, this meant (increasing/decreasing) payments by the United States for foreign oil.

The OPEC nations deposited their American dollar oil receipts in European banks. These deposits are (regulated/unregulated) by American authorities. Large loans were made from these Eurodollar deposits to (rich/poor) countries who were willing to pay (low/high) interest rates. The ability of these nations to pay the interest on the loans and to repay the principal was based on their future sales of higher priced ______________________________.

The 1981-82 recession caused (higher/lower) world commodity prices. Growth of Eurodollar deposits declined and tight monetary policy led to (lower/higher) interest rates. As a result, the debtor countries such as Mexico, Brazil and Poland were unable to meet the interest payments on their loans. Now it was clear that the banks of the industrialized nations were left with some very (good/poor) loan assets on their balance sheets.

41. To ease the bad loan problems of the commercial banks, the major central banks undertook the following steps

(a) reduced United States interest rates.

(b) converted the bank loans of poor nations from US dollars into other currencies.

(c) implemented policies to keep the US dollar from rising further.

(d) initiated IMF action to enforce strict regulations on borrowing nations.

(e) all of the above.

42. State whether each of the following statements regarding the price of the American dollar on foreign exchange markets from 1980 to 1985 is **TRUE** or **FALSE**.

____ (a) The American dollar remained strong (i.e., high priced) on foreign exchange markets.

____ (b) Large US government deficits were financed by foreign capital. As foreign capital inflows were converted to American dollars, the extra demand forced an appreciation of the US dollar.

____ (c) American interest rates were relatively low causing an outflow of American dollars seeking higher rates elsewhere.

____ (d) Low American interest rates were caused in part by the low savings rates of Americans that reduced the supply of loanable funds.

____ (e) The US-led recovery from the Great Recession of 1980-81 proved beneficial to the rest of the world.

43. During the 1980s, when American interest rates were high, Canadian interest rates were higher. This policy was designed to (decrease/ increase) the flow of foreign capital into Canada and to (decrease/ increase) the outflow of Canadian dollars seeking higher rates of interest in foreign countries (especially the United States). With this policy, the Bank of Canada attempts to prevent a(n) (appreciation/depreciation) of the Canadian dollar since the latter causes price inflation in Canada to (increase/decrease).

44. Number the following from (1) to (7) to illustrate the correct sequence of events during the years 1983 through 1987.

____ American imports increased more rapidly than exports.

____ American 'trade protection' measures were considered.

____ The American dollar appreciated.

____ The American federal government was incurring a large budget deficit.

____ Foreigners were investing large amounts in American Government securities.

____ The American rate of savings was too low to cover the financing needs of the federal government in the United States.

____ The G-5 Agreement and the Louvre Accord were both designed to solve American Balance of Payments problems.

45. Which of the following statements are true regarding the G-5 Agreement?

____ (a) Concerted action among nations seemed necessary to appreciate the U.S. dollar.

____ (b) The 5 in G-5 referred to the five point plan.

____ (c) It appeared that the high value of the U.S. dollar was more a symptom of the problem than a cause.

____ (d) The U.S. dollar was strong because of the massive inflow of foreign capital to cover the large U.S. government deficit.

____ (e) In the eighteen months following the agreement, the U.S. dollar declined by about 30 percent against the yen and the Deutsche Mark.

46. The Louvre Accord of __________ and the G-5 Agreement were designed to solve (the same, a different) problem.
At the time of the Louvre Accord, the U.S. dollar was (declining in value, accelerating in value) too rapidly. In this case, the (five, seven) industrialized countries would spend over $100 billion of foreign currencies (buying, selling) U.S. dollars.

47. State whether each of the following is an accurate description of the present role of gold in the international monetary system.

____ (a) The US dollar is still backed by gold, which makes the US dollar acceptable internationally.

____ (b) The US dollar has not really been backed by gold since the late 1960's, and gold is presently being phased out of the international monetary system.

____ (c) The exchange rate system is pegged with the values of all currencies tied rigidly to the US dollar.

____ (d) Speculators have been selling gold because they fear that a devaluation of the US dollar would sharply reduce gold prices.

____ (e) While the US dollar is not backed by gold at present, it is generally believed that the USA will return to gold backing in the near future.

48. Which of the following best describes the present situation concerning the international monetary system?

(a) The system is basically one of floating exchange rates but with governments sometimes intervening in foreign exchange markets to prevent the prices of their currencies from floating too far away from their previous levels (called a dirty float).

(b) The exchange rate system is pegged and based on gold, with all major currencies convertible into gold at fixed rates.

(c) The exchange rate system is pegged with the values of all currencies tied rigidly to the US dollar.

(d) The system is one of floating exchange rates, with currency prices totally free to rise and fall as economic forces dictate.

(e) Only the US dollar is backed by gold.

Chapter 20

THE CANADIAN ECONOMY: A TIME FOR RENEWAL

Chapter 20 pulls together several of the major issues of the past decade. More importantly it challenges us to examine how the nation's economic resources are allocated between current consumption and investment for the future, and the effects of government policies on the allocation of resources.

The 1980's were characterized by high unemployment, low investment in capital goods, high real interest rates and rising federal government deficits. The growing concern regarding government deficits prevented the government from embarking on expansionary monetary policy both through a fear of renewed inflation and a desire to stabilize the value of the Canadian dollar.

The difficulty of applying traditional fiscal and monetary policies suggested that fresh policies were needed to revitalize the Canadian economy; for example — freer trade to offset growing protectionism and declining markets.

In this light, the following priorities regarding future policies are recommended: contain inflation; encourage capital investment; reduce government deficits; negotiate for freer trade; and create wealth through the creation of small business.

General Learning Objective

Review the Canadian economy of the 1980's and consider appropriate economic policies for Canada's future.

Specific Learning Objectives

	Self-Test Reference
1. Examine the difficulty of applying traditional fiscal and monetary policies to enhance Canadian economic growth and employment	#1-8
2. Review the relationship between price stability and productivity	# 9,10
3. Consider the new policy directions for Canada emphasizing the creation of wealth and the globalization of markets	#11-13

Self-Test

1. Which of the following are likely reasons for the low level of investment spending in Canada during the first half of the 1980's?

____ (a) Canadian businesses preferred to invest abroad.

____ (b) substantial unused plant capacity.

____ (c) balance sheets of private companies reflecting more equity than debt.

____ (d) a growing concern about U.S. protectionism.

____ (e) government policies aimed at promoting economic nationalism.

____ (f) strong business confidence.

____ (g) concern over the size of government deficits.

____ (h) a large inflow of foreign capital.

____ (i) high real rates of interest.

2. List four major benefits of investment spending.

(a) ____;

(b) ____;

(c) ____;

(d) ____.

3. (Lenders/borrowers) benefit from unanticipated inflation because the future dollars paid back as interest and principle have (less/more) purchasing power than the dollars originally (borrowed/lent).

On the other hand, (lenders/borrowers) lose as a result of unanticipated future inflation since present dollars have (more/less) purchasing power than future dollars.

4. A reason for the high real rates of interest in Canada during the mid-1980's is

____

____

5. Offer two reasons to explain why the Government of Canada was reluctant to deal with the growing deficit:

____

____.

6. In the mid-1980's, the Government of Canada was not in the position to use expansionary fiscal policy to alleviate high unemployment in Canada because ______________________

____

____.

7. Similarly, the Bank of Canada did not wish to embark on an expansionary monetary course because of the fear of ____

____.

In addition, the Canadian dollar was supported to prevent a(n) (depreciation/ appreciation) which was meant to curtail a(n) (decrease/increase) in import prices. (Higher/lower) import prices could lead to a new round of (demand-pull/cost-push) inflation in Canada.

8. Which of the following encourage entrepreneurship and enterprise?

____ (a) tax incentives for saving and investing;

____ (b) more government regulations to encourage the formation of business;

____ (c) freer trade with the United States.

9. From 1987 through 1990, the Bank of Canada maintained relatively high interest rates in Canada in an attempt to stabilize prices.

In light of the financing needs of the Government of Canada by 1990, what is one other reason for the high rates?

____

____

____

10. Choose the best description of the relationship between price stability and improvements in productivity:

(a) Price stability leads to lower rates of interest. This means higher consumer spending and less saving. Higher levels of production mean improved productivity.

(b) Lower interest rates result from price stability. This improves business confidence and investment spending increases. The new investment means up-dated plant and equipment — a most important contributor to higher productivity.

(c) Price stability means higher export sales for Canadian companies. This leads to increased foreign capital inflows to Canada resulting in improvements in productivity.

(d) Economists have concluded that there is no relationship between price stability and productivity.

11. It appears that the Government of Canada has made a subtle but fundamental shift in policy away from redistribution of wealth and economic nationalism and toward the creation of wealth and economic internationalism.

Here is a list of possible policies of the Government of Canada:

1) An increase in child allowances.

2) A movement to join the Mexico/United States Free Trade Agreement.

3) Replacement of the Manufacturer's Sales Tax with the General Sales Tax on consumer purchases.

4) Elimination of investment tax credits from the determination of tax payable.

5) An increase in corporate tax rates.

6) Removal of provincial restrictions on the production and sale of brewery products.

7) Assistance in the formation of Canadian high-tech knowledge based industries.

8) Stricter enforcement of legislation on Canadian Competition policy.

Place the numbers from 1) through 8) of each of the above policies in either the category of List A or List B below:

List A	**List B**
Redistribution of Wealth and Economic Nationalism	**Creation of Wealth and Economic Internationalism**
____________________	____________________

12. Describe the economic relationship that exists among the following factors:

- A government policy of encouraging freer trade
- Increased competition
- Economic internationalism
- The creation of wealth

13. a) Why was the imposition of the General Sales Tax favored by the Canadian Manufacturers Association?

13. b) How does the option of the General Sales Tax as opposed to the Manufacturer's Sales Tax relate to the policy move away from the re-distribution of income towards the creation of wealth?

MICROECONOMICS

Chapters 1 through 3 of the microeconomics text are identical to Chapters 1 through 3 of the macroeconomics text. As a result, the study guide materials relating to these chapters may be found in the macroeconomics section of the Study Guide.

Chapter 4

INTRODUCTION TO MICROECONOMICS

This chapter deals in general terms with the factors that determine the prices of particular goods and services, thus laying the groundwork for subsequent chapters on demand, supply and prices. To place the question of price determination in better perspective, Chapter 4 reviews briefly the role played by prices in our economy, and the role of markets in determining answers to the three basic questions of what to produce, how to produce it and for whom it will be produced. This concept of markets and their role in the economy runs through much of the remainder of the book.

General Learning Objective

Describe the role that prices and markets play in allocating resources.

Specific Learning Objectives

	Self-Test Reference
1. Define "microeconomics"	# 1-2
2. Identify the major determinants of the price of a good or service	# 3-5
3. Explain the role played by prices in allocating resources within a market-type economy	# 6-8
4. Describe important characteristics of competition in the marketplace	# 9-10

Self-Test

1. Microeconomics is ____

____

____.

2. The utility theory of value proposes that the price of an individual product should be determined by ______________________________.

3. The paradox of value refers to:

(a) the fact that an increase in the supply of a product will cause its price to fall.

(b) the fact that an increase in the demand for a product will cause its price to rise.

(c) both (a) and (b) together.

(d) the fact that the prices of products are often unrelated to the usefulness of those products.

(e) the fact that supply and demand often fail to explain prices or changes in prices.

4. The answer to the paradox of value lies in the fact that prices are

____

____

______________________________.

5. In a market system type of economy, prices play an important role in determining

(a) ______________________________;

(b) ______________________________;

(c) ______________________________.

6. Which of the following best describes how the question of what to produce is decided in a market system type of economy?

(a) The most important factor is the government, which, through its own purchases and the regulations it places on business activity, has the dominant influence concerning what is produced.

(b) The most important factor is consumer demand, which influences prices and profits and thus incentives for businesses to increase or reduce production of particular goods and services.

(c) Privately owned businesses (producers) decide what to produce in the final analysis.

(d) The most important factor is the public which, through the election of governments, exerts the strongest influence on what to produce.

(e) Both (a) and (d) together.

7. In a market system type of economy, which of the following best describes how the question of how to produce goods and services is decided?

   (a) The consumer decides this question, through the demand for goods and services.

   (b) The major factor influencing this decision is the government.

   (c) Those productive inputs which are more scarce will be more costly, so that production methods will be used which economize more on them.

   (d) The actual decisions regarding production methods are made by businesses or producers.

   (e) Both (c) and (d) are correct.

8. In a market system type of economy, the division of the economy's output among groups and individuals is basically determined by:

   (a) the social status of groups and individuals.

   (b) the marketing departments of businesses.

   (c) markets, in which the incomes of individuals and groups are decided mainly by the supply of and demand for various occupational skills.

   (d) governmental taxation and welfare programs that redistribute income.

   (e) none of the above.

9. For a market system to operate effectively, there must be ______________________________

   and ____.

10. Two important aspects of competition in the marketplace are that:

   (a) ____

   ____

   (b) ____

   ____

   ____

Chapter 5

BUSINESS ORGANIZATION IN CANADA

This chapter provides descriptive background material for subsequent chapters on how prices are determined in various types of industries, such as industries characterized by many small firms and those dominated by a few large firms. The major new concept comes at the end of the chapter, when the material on small business and big business is related to the concept of "market structures," ranging from highly competitive to monopolistic, and the relevance of these to the analysis of price determination to follow in subsequent chapters.

General Learning Objective

Describe the nature of the business sector of the Canadian economy.

Specific Learning Objectives

	Self-Test Reference
1. Compile a list of the relative advantages and disadvantages of three legal forms of business ownership	# 1-6
2. Identify the challenges and opportunities facing small business owners in Canada	# 7-14
3. Explain the challenges and opportunities confronting some of Canada's largest corporations	# 15-26
4. Assess pros and cons of government-owned enterprises	# 27-28

Self-Test

1. State whether or not the story of Dan's Doughnut Dens illustrates each of the following.

    ____ (a) Sole proprietorship often involves a great deal of strain on the owner-manager.

    ____ (b) Partnerships are often subject to severe strains owing to differences among the partners.

    ____ (c) The corporate form of business enterprise can involve the risk of the original founder/owner/manager losing control of the business.

____ (d) Life insurance on the partners' lives is a common way to ensure the continuity of the business in the event of the death of one of the partners.

2. Name at least two advantages of the sole proprietorship as a form of business organization.

(a) ______________________________

(b) ______________________________

3. List at least four disadvantages of the sole proprietorship as a form of business organization.

(a) ______________________________

____

(b) ______________________________

____

(c) ______________________________

____

(d) ______________________________

____

4. In addition to the problems listed in the previous question, the partnership as a form of business organization faces the possible problem of ______________________________

____

5. List four advantages of the corporation as a form of business organization.

(a) ______________________________

____

(b) ______________________________

____

(c) ____

____

(d) ____

____

6. The most common form of business ownership in Canada today is ____________________

____.

7. State whether each of the following statements would be **ACCEPTABLE** or **UNACCEPTABLE** as a definition of a small business.

____ (a) A business qualifying for a lower tax rate of 25% on the first $150 000 of active income per year.

____ (b) Any business employing less than 100 employees.

____ (c) A business with sales of less than $2 million annually.

____ (d) Any business that qualifies for a government-guaranteed loan.

____ (e) Any business independently owned and operated and not dominant in its field of endeavour.

8. Small business in Canada takes the form of:

(a) sole proprietorships, partnerships and corporations.

(b) sole proprietorships and partnerships only.

(c) sole proprietorships only.

(d) corporations only.

(e) none of the above.

9. Small businesses employ about ______ % of Canada's labor force.

10. Which of the following is not likely to be a small business?

(a) a dental clinic with annual fees totaling $500 000.

(b) a seafood restaurant.

(c) a student enterprise.

(d) a chain of nationally operated retail shoe outlets.

(e) a turkey hatchery.

(f) a carbide-tip saw blade manufacturer.

11. Small businesses serve the economy by helping to keep economic power and concentration in check. They also

____

____

____

____

____

____

____

12. List at least four problems commonly faced by small businesses.

(a) ____________________________________

(b) ____________________________________

(c) ____________________________________

(d) ____________________________________

13. Government assistance to small business comes in a bewildering array of programs which essentially come down to

(a) ____________________________________;

(b) ____________________________________;

(c) ____________________________________;

(d) ____________________________________;

(e) ____________________________________;

14. The Canadian Federation of Independent Businesses (CFIB) is ______________________

____,

the purpose of which is to ____

____

____.

15. Large businesses in Canada generally take the form of ______________________,
because this form of business organization is most suited to the task of ______________

____

____

16. The largest industrial enterprise in Canada is ______________________________

____

which is _____ % ____________ owned. The second-largest business is ____________

____

and it is _____ % ________________ owned.

17. Industrial corporate concentration is a concern to Canadians because ______________

____

____.

18. A "conglomerate" is

(a) a group of companies in the same industry which are controlled by a central management group, through holding companies.

(b) any company exercising a significant degree of monopoly power in a market.

(c) a corporation producing a wide variety of goods and services.

(d) a group of companies in various industries which are controlled by a central management group, through holding companies.

(e) none of the above.

19. Two examples of Canadian conglomerates are ______________________________
and ______________________.

20. Normally, the ultimate control of a corporation lies in the hands of ____________________.

____

However, when the shareholders are numerous and dispersed, control of large corporations is often exercised by ____

or by ____.
It should be noted that control is often separated from ownership. While 50% ownership in a corporation buys control in theory, often (more, less) is required in practice. Corporate executives or money managers can claim control and influence decisions based on their ______ ____rather than on ownership.

21. A Crown corporation is ____

____

____

____

22. State whether each of the following statements concerning Crown corporations in Canada is **TRUE** or **FALSE.**

____ (a) They are few in number and therefore not a major part of the Canadian economy.

____ (b) Only the federal government has the power to create Crown corporations.

____ (c) They are an important part of the Canadian economy, comprising about 10% of Canada's very large corporations.

____ (d) Their objective is not merely to make a profit, but also in some cases to provide certain services for the public.

23. List four types of industries in which Crown corporations play a significant role.

(a) ____

(b) ____

(c) ____

(d) ____

24. The three largest Crown corporations in Canada are probably ____________________________

____________________, ____,

____.

25. What is meant by "privatization"?

26. Write a brief description of the role of Crown corporations in Canada, including references to fields of enterprise in which Crown corporations are most commonly involved.

27. In support of government enterprises, such as Canadian National Railways and Via Rail, it may be argued that

28. In opposition to the above argument, critics point out that

Chapter 6

THE NATURE OF DEMAND

This chapter examines the area of consumer demand, focusing on major factors that affect demand. Demand is one of the most basic concepts in economics, and will be referred to frequently in subsequent chapters.

Chapter 6 also introduces the concept of "price elasticity of demand", which is a measure of the sensitivity of quantity change to price change.

General Learning Objective

Examine the concept of consumer demand and describe the factors which influence demand.

Specific Learning Objectives

	Self-Test Reference
1. Explain the terms "demand" and "quantity demanded"	# 1-6
2. Describe factors which influence consumer demand	# 7-12
3. Recognize factors affecting the elasticity of demand	# 13-17
4. Indicate the relationship between elasticity and total revenue	# 18-25

Self-Test

1. Which one of the following portrays a typical demand curve?

(a) 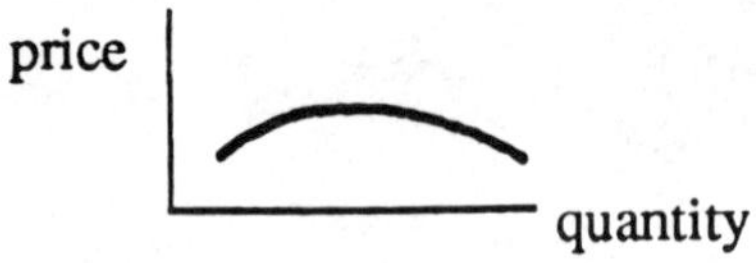

(b) 

(c) 

(d) 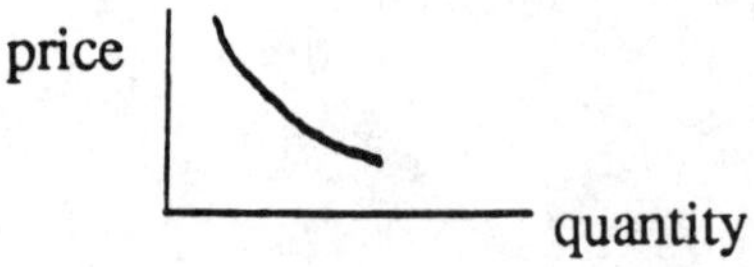

(e) 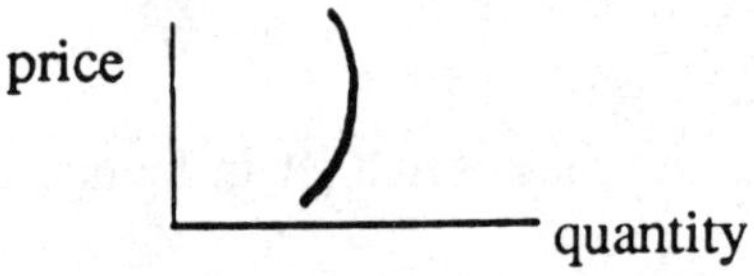

2. The demand curve in the previous question shows that, as the price of a product rises,

____.

3. The change referred to in the above question is graphically illustrated by ____________

____

____.

4. The term "quantity demanded" refers to ____________________

____

____.

5. Given the following data, plot the points and draw and label the curve and the axes.

Price	**Quantity Demanded**
$ 2	50
4	40
6	30
8	20
10	10

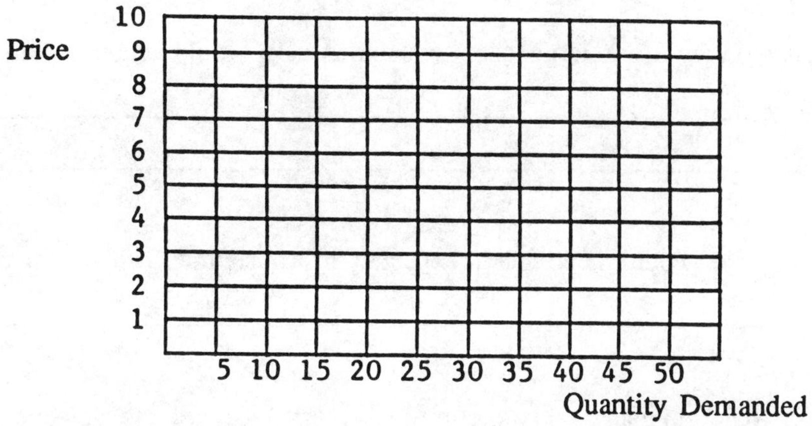

6. As the price rises from $4 to $6 in the above question, the demand ______________________________
____.

7. State three factors that could cause the demand curve for a product to shift, and indicate how those factors would have to change in order for the demand to increase.

(a) ____
____
____

(b) ____
____
____

(c) ____
____
____

8. As consumer incomes rise, the demand curve for beef steak would tend to
____.

9. If the price of imported wine falls, the demand curve for Canadian-produced wine would tend to ______________________________.

10. If consumers in general began to prefer margarine to butter, the demand curve for butter would tend to ______________________________.

11. A switch on the part of the public from large cars to smaller cars would tend to cause the demand curve for gasoline to ______________________________

______________________________.

12. The invention of the automobile would have been expected to cause the demand curve for horse-drawn carriages to ______________________________

13. List three criteria which aid sales managers in determining whether or not the demand for a product is inelastic.

(a) ______________________________

(b) ______________________________

(c) ______________________________

14. When the demand for a good or service is elastic, it means that the product is ____________

______________________________.

____

15. For which one of the following pairs of products would the demand be more **elastic**? Explain the reason(s) for your choices

(a) automobiles/Ford Mustangs

____

____

(b) soft drinks/Pepsi Cola

____

____

(c) toothpaste/Crest

___

___

16. State whether each of the following events would tend to make the demand for the product involved more **elastic** or **inelastic**, and explain the reason(s) for your answers.

(a) In the summer, the demand for steak would likely become more ________, because ________

___

(b) The development of a good-quality Canadian-produced white wine would tend to make the demand for imported white wine more ________, because ________

___

17. Arrange the following products in order of the elasticity of demand for them, with the most elastic listed first.

(a) beef
(b) steak
(c) porterhouse steak
(d) meat

18.

Price	Quantity Demanded	Total Revenue
$ 5	100	$
6	90	
7	80	
8	70	
9	60	

State whether the demand represented in the above schedule is elastic, inelastic or of unitary elasticity for price changes:

(a) from $5 to $6: ________

(b) from $6 to $7: ________

(c) from $7 to $8: ________

(d) from $8 to $9: ________

19. Based on the above question, if the firm lowered the price from \$9 to \$8, would the firm be better off or not? Explain your answer.

____

____

____

____

20. Elasticity may be defined as the percentage change in quantity divided by the percentage change in price:

$$\text{coefficient of elasticity} = \frac{\text{percentage change in quantity}}{\text{percentage change in price}}$$

$$\text{or } e = \frac{\% \ \Delta \ Q}{\% \ \Delta \ P}$$

You have just been appointed General Manager of a chain store outlet with sales of \$40 000 per week. Head Office has instructed you to increase sales volume (quantity) by 10%.

You are considering a sales promotion, a better location or a price change. You conclude that the promotional budget is insufficient and a new location raises lease problems so you decide a price change is in order.

Past experience shows that a 10% change in price will generate a 20% change in quantity of goods sold.

The elasticity coefficient is ______________________________
and demand is (elastic/inelastic/unitary).

To generate a 10% increase in sales (quantity), price should be ______________

__________ by ______%. If the average price of the products for sale is \$20, the new price will be \$ ____________.

21. If the coefficient of price elasticity of demand for a product is 10, it means that

(a) a 10% change in price results in a 1% change in quantity demanded.

(b) the product is insensitive to price changes.

(c) a 1% change in price results in a 10% change in quantity demanded.

(d) a change in price changes demand by an equal amount.

22. Calculate the various elasticity coefficients for the demand curves below using the following formula:

$$e = \frac{Q_2 - Q_1}{Q_2 + Q_1} \div \frac{P_2 - P_1}{P_2 + P_1}$$

Where Q_1 is the original quantity, P_1 is the original price. Q_2 and P_2 are the new quantity and price.

e is used as the symbol for elasticity coefficient.

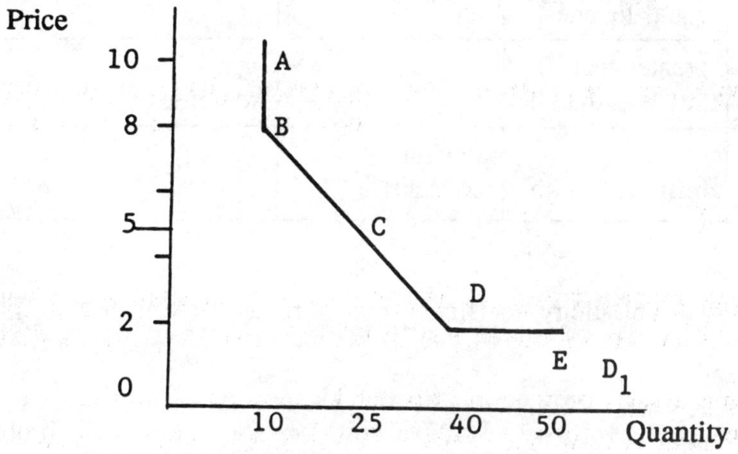

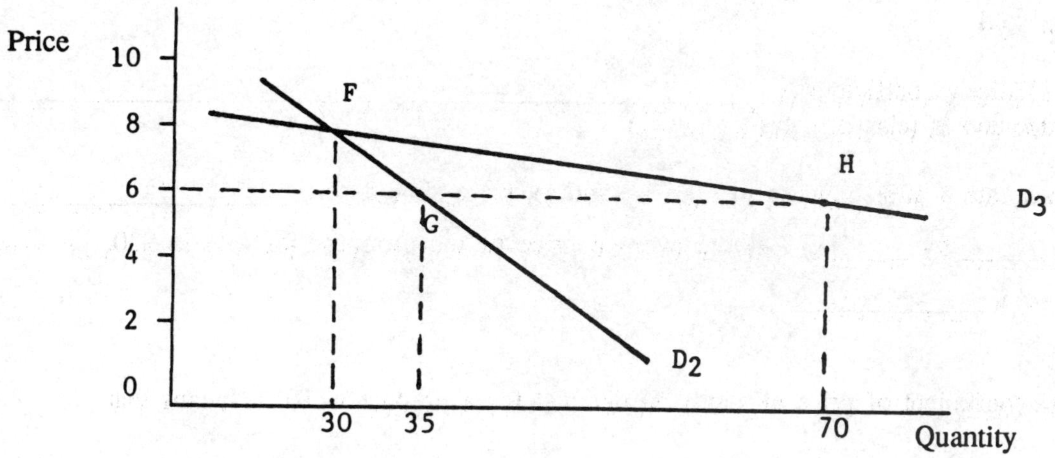

For A-B, e = __________________.　　D-E, e = __________________.

B-C, e = __________________.　　F-G, e = __________________.

C-D, e = __________________.　　F-H, e = __________________.

23. If the minimum wage were to increase above the market-clearing wage, then the total wages for industrial workers would fall if the demand for labor is (elastic/inelastic).

24. Complete the following table.

If Demand is	Then e is	If Price	Then Total Revenue Will
perfectly inelastic		decreases	
elastic		decreases	
	equal to one	increases	
inelastic	greater than 0 but less than 1		increase
	infinitely large	remains constant	

25. The (larger/smaller) the elasticity coefficient the more sensitive a product is to a price change.

Chapter 7

THE NATURE OF SUPPLY

This chapter presents the concept of "supply" and how supply and demand interact in competitive markets to determine prices. One possible source of confusion is the terminology used to describe industries: the terms "competitive" and "non-competitive" are intended to focus on industries' behavior **regarding prices**, and to convey the idea that, in competitive industries, competition can be counted upon to hold down prices and profits, while in non-competitive industries it cannot. This does not mean that there is **no** competition between firms in non-competitive industries; for instance, they often compete extensively through advertising. However, there is a tendency for firms in such industries to seek to avoid competing on prices.

It is very important to remember that this chapter's analysis of supply deals only with competitive industries. In an equally important part of the economy, prices are determined differently, as will be seen later. Finally, static equilibrium analysis such as the supply/demand analysis of Chapter 7 can be misleading. The equilibrium price is **not** "the" price; it is merely the result of the interaction between buyers and sellers in a market at a particular time. The behavior of buyers and sellers (demand and supply) will constantly change, and so will the equilibrium price. It is helpful to think of the supply and demand curves as representing a **snapshot** of a changing situation at a particular point in time.

General Learning Objective

Examine the concept of producer supply and describe the factors that influence supply.

Specific Learning Objectives

		Self-Test Reference
1.	Describe conditions distinguishing competitive industries from non-competitive industries	# 1-6
2.	Explain the terms "supply" and "quantity supplied"	# 7-10
3.	Describe factors which influence producer supply	# 11-12
4.	Recognize factors affecting elasticity of supply	# 13-15
5.	Explain market equilibrium and its significance with respect to price	# 16-18

Self-Test

1. Competitive industries are different from non-competitive industries in that competitive industries

   (a) are those which compete for sales in international (export) markets.

   (b) are those in which there is any form of competition between firms (price, advertising, product differentiation, etc.).

   (c) are those in which there are many firms, which compete strongly on price.

   (d) include all industries in which there are more than one firm.

2. List the two basic characteristics of competitive industries.

   (a) ______________________________

   (b) ______________________________

3. As a result of the characteristics described in the previous question,

   (a) producers are unable to control either the supply of the product or its price, and profits tend to be low.

   (b) producers are able to control the supply of the product, forcing up its price and their profits.

   (c) producers can control the price of the product but not the supply of it.

(d) producers can control prices, but are unable to keep out new firms and thus control supply.

(e) product prices tend to be high because there are too many producers.

4. State two ways in which the basic characteristics of non-competitive industries differ from the basic characteristics of competitive industries as listed in (2) above.

(a) ______________________________

(b) ______________________________

5. Because of the characteristics in (4) above, the behavior of noncompetitive industries differs from the behaviour of competitive industries in that ______________________________

____

______________________________.

6. State whether an economist would classify each of the following industries as competitive or non-competitive.

(a) stereo shops ______________________________

(b) brewing ______________________________

(c) automobile manufacturing ______________________________

(d) restaurants ______________________________

(e) window washing ______________________________

(f) airlines ______________________________

(g) tourist agencies ______________________________

7. Which of the graphs below represents the typical supply curve of a competitive industry?

(a) 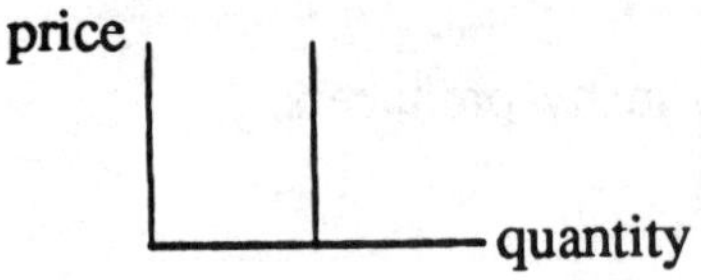

(c) 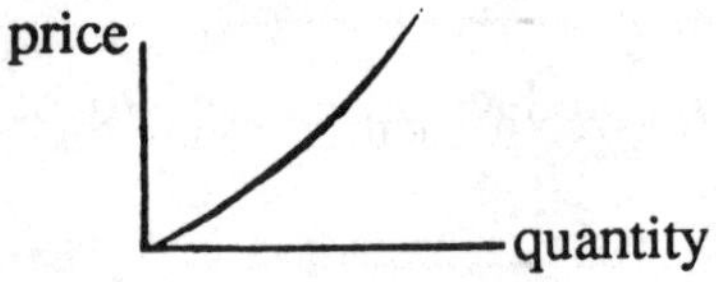

(b) 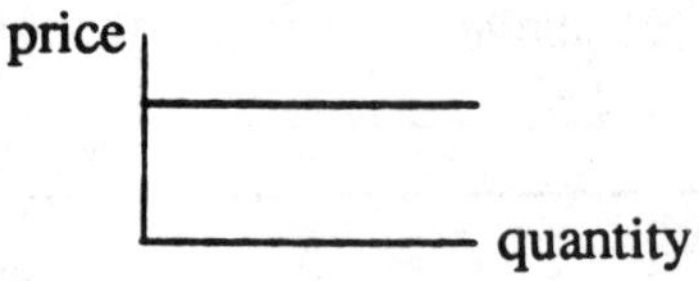

(d) 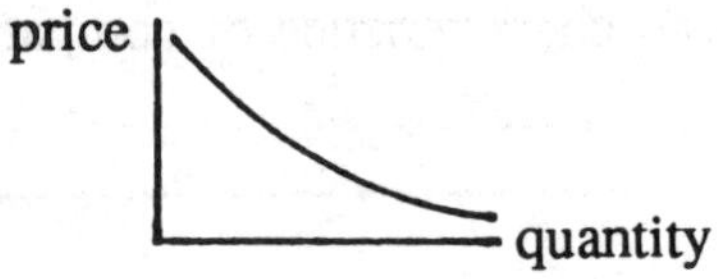

8. The supply curve reflects the fact that in competitive industries, as price increases, __________
____.

9. (a) If supply increases, the supply curve will ________________________________
____.

(b) Such an increase in supply could be caused by ____________________________
____
____.

10. (a) If supply decreases, the supply curve will ________________________________
____.

(b) Such a decrease in supply could be caused by ____________________________
____
____.

11. As the costs of production rise in a given industry, the supply in that industry will ________ ____________. This is illustrated graphically by a shift ________________ in the supply curve.

12. As the number of firms in a given industry increases, the supply in that industry will _______ ________. This is illustrated graphically by a shift ______________________________ in the supply curve.

13. (a) If the supply of a product is inelastic, an increase in its price will ______________

____.

(b) What factors could make the supply of a product inelastic?

____

____

____

14. (a) If the supply of a product is elastic, an increase in its price will ______________

____

(b) What could make the supply of a product elastic?

____

____

____

15. As time passes, does the supply of most products become more elastic or more inelastic? ___

Why? ____

____

16. 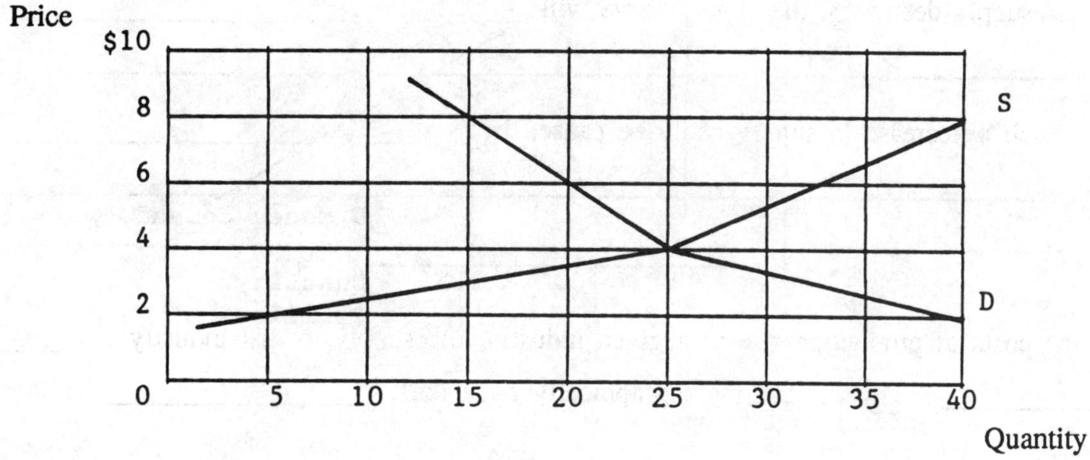

In the market represented by the above diagram,

(a) the equilibrium price will be $ ______________________.

(b) the equilibrium quantity will be ______________________.

(c) if the price were $6, the result would be ______________________

____.

(d) if the price were $2, the result would be ______________________________

____.

(e) between $2 and $6 the elasticity coefficient of supply is ____________________

____.

17. Based on the diagram in the preceding question, assume that there is an increase in population. Draw the impact of this on your diagram. As a result of the change, identify the impact on the following factors:

(a) demand ____

(b) supply ____

(c) price ____

(d) quantity demanded ____________________________________

(e) quantity supplied _____________________________________

18.

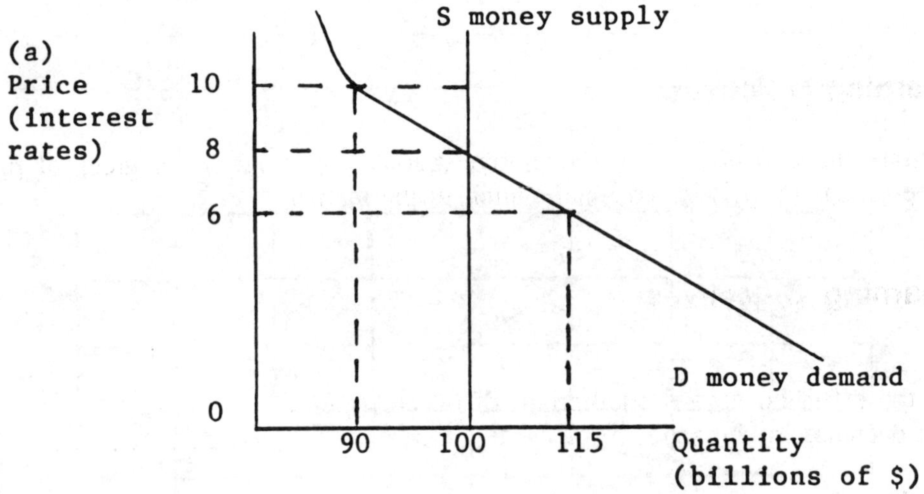

At a 10% rate of interest there is a (shortage/surplus) of dollars equal to $____________.

If interest rates decline from 8% to 6%, there is a (shortage/surplus) of $ equal to ________.

Chapter 8

THE DYNAMICS OF COMPETITION

This chapter uses the basic tools of supply and demand to show how competitive markets respond to changes in supply and demand. To illustrate the dynamics of competitive markets, various examples are used, including the markets for professional hockey players, capital, and gold. The only new concept in this chapter is that the more elastic demand and supply are, the more smoothly a market will adjust to changes in supply or demand. It is important to remember that this type of supply-and-demand analysis relates only to the types of markets that we have classified as "competitive," that is, markets characterized by large numbers of sellers.

General Learning Objective

Demonstrate the dynamics of a competitive market under varying degrees of price elasticity and analyze the effects of government intervention in the market.

Specific Learning Objectives

	Self-Test Reference
1. Illustrate the effect on market equilibrium of (a) an increase and (b) a decrease in demand	# 1-2
2. Illustrate the effect on market equilibrium of (a) an increase and (b) a decrease in supply	# 3-4
3. Establish the effect of demand elasticity on market equilibrium when supply shifts	# 5
4. Establish the effect of supply elasticity on market equilibrium when demand shifts	# 6
5. Compare the short run effect (supply inelastic) with the long run effect (supply more elastic) of a change in demand on market equilibrium	# 7

		Self-Test Reference
6.	Observe the operation of demand and supply forces in other markets	# 8-11
7.	Analyze the effect on the market of a government price support, backed up by an offer to purchase	# 12-13
8.	Analyze the effect on the market of a maximum, or ceiling price imposed by government	# 14-15

Self-Test

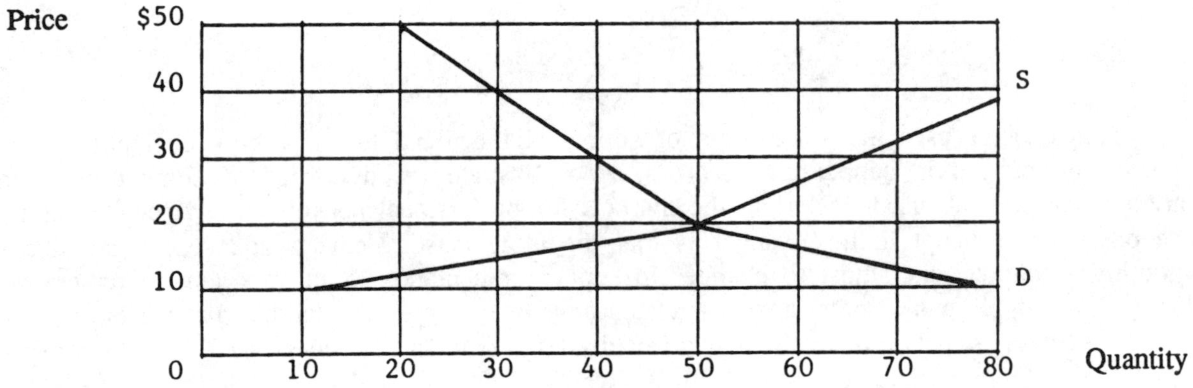

In answering Questions 1-4, you may find it helpful to refer to the above diagram.

1. If the demand for the product increased (and the supply remained unchanged), the equilibrium price would ________ and the equilibrium quantity would ______.

2. If the demand for the product decreased (and the supply remained unchanged), the equilibrium price would _______ and the equilibrium quantity would _______.

3. If the supply of the product increased (and the demand remained unchanged), the equilibrium price would ________________ and the equilibrium quantity would ____________________.

4. If the supply of the product decreased (and the demand remained unchanged), the equilibrium price would _______ and the equilibrium quantity would _______.

5. When the demand for a product changes, the resultant change in its price will be greater,

   (a) the more inelastic is the supply of the product.

   (b) the more elastic is the supply of the product.

   (c) the larger is the supply of the product.

   (d) the smaller is the supply of the product.

   (e) none of the above.

6. When the supply of a product changes, the resultant change in its price will be greater,

   (a) the more elastic is the demand for the product.

   (b) the more inelastic is the demand for the product.

   (c) the larger is the demand for the product.

   (d) the smaller is the demand for the product.

   (e) none of the above.

7. As time progresses, the supply of products tends to become

   (a) less elastic.

   (b) more elastic.

   (c) neither more nor less elastic.

8. With the expansion of the NHL in the late 1960's, players' salaries increased substantially, even though the quality of players diminished. This could be explained by

   (a) a decrease in supply of good players.

   (b) a decrease in demand for good players.

   (c) an increase in supply of good players.

   (d) an increase in demand for good players.

9. Which of the following is true with respect to the market for gold?

(a) An elastic supply, combined with a steady demand, causes prices to be stable.

(b) An inelastic supply, combined with a fluctuating demand, causes prices to be volatile.

(c) Both demand and supply are inelastic, resulting in an unchanging market.

(d) Both demand and supply are highly elastic, causing prices to fluctuate widely.

10. The following diagram refers to the market for cauliflower.

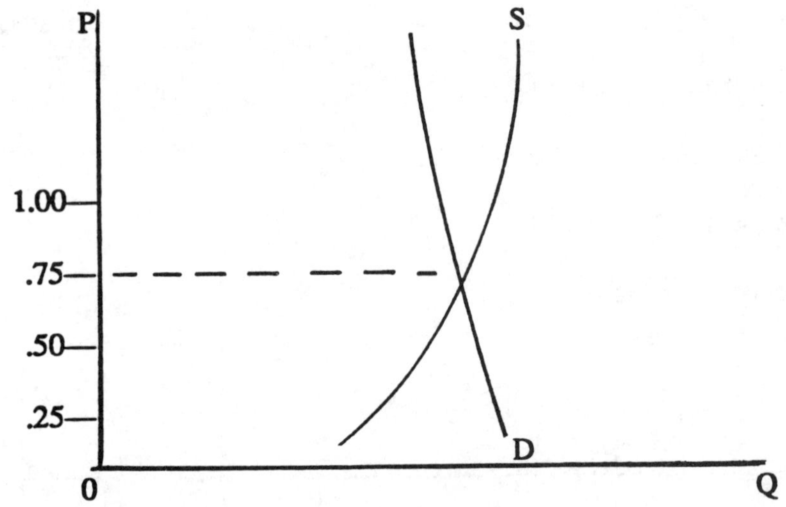

Producers currently are selling cauliflower at a price of $1.00 each. Can this price prevail in this market? Why or why not?

____

____

____

____

____

____

____

____

____

11. Improved technology generally is welcomed as a positive factor for the producer and the economy in general. In the case of grain farmers, there have been significant improvements in production methods over the past twenty years due to technological innovation. Has the position of the grain farmer, with respect to income, improved? Explain fully.

____

____

____

____

____

____

____

____

____

Answer Questions 12-14 on the basis of the following graph.

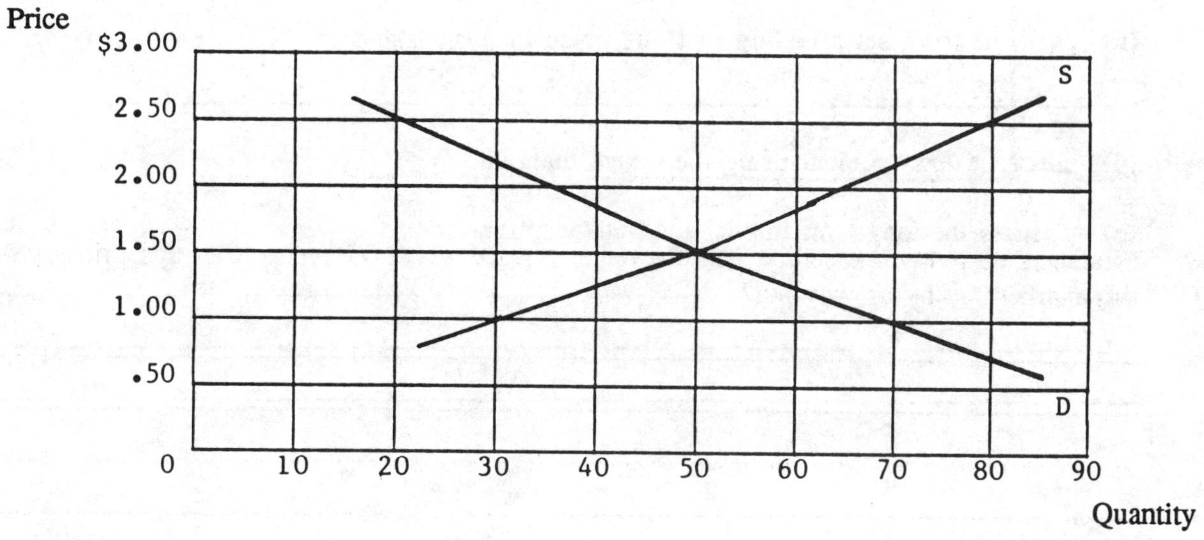

12. The equilibrium price of this product will be $ _______________ per unit.

13. If the government supported the price of this product above the equilibrium price, at a price of $2.50, the result would be _______________

____

14. If the government placed controls on the price of this product to hold it below the equilibrium price, at a price of $1, the result would be ____________________

____

15. The following diagram illustrates the market for rental accommodation in Red Lake for 2-bedroom walk-up apartments. Equilibrium price is P_1 and equilibrium quantity is Q_1 in the market.

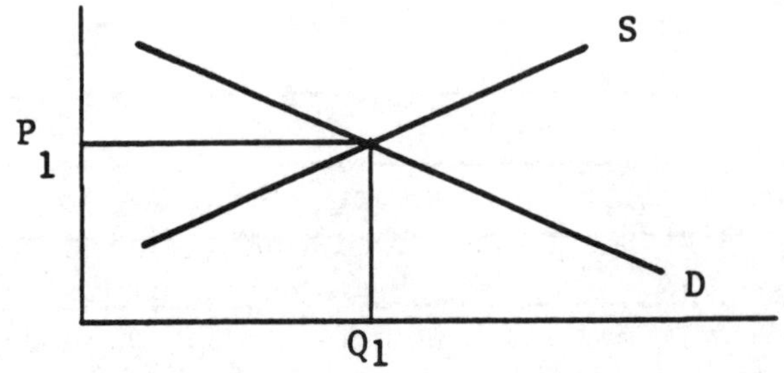

Now suppose that there is an enormous increase in the town's population due to a mining boom resulting from the opening of three new gold mines in the area. Assume that the Mayor wishes to maintain rent levels at P_1 and therefore initiates rent controls to do so.

(a) Will the town set a **ceiling** or **floor price** in this instance?

____

(b) Illustrate this problem using the above diagram.

(c) Discuss the long-term implications of these rent controls.

____

____

____

Chapter 9

COMPETITIVE INDUSTRIES

This chapter examines the operation of industries which we have described as competitive in the sense of being comprised of many small firms which compete vigorously on prices. These industries are divided into two types: "perfect competition" and "monopolistic competition." Perfect competition is a rather abstract and theoretical concept, but it does provide a useful starting point, or benchmark, for comparing the performance of other types of industries, since it represents the most extremely competitive situation possible — one in which each seller has absolutely no control over the price of its product.

Monopolistic competition represents a much more realistic and relevant type of industry. Unfortunately, monopolistic competition is a label which many students find confusing, as the term "monopolistic" leads them to think of Bell Canada rather than Harry's Hamburger Stand. It is essential to remember that monopolistically competitive industries are also highly competitive, and that the product differentiation which characterizes these industries only gives some sellers a **small** degree of control over the price of their products. Only when there are a few sellers (or one monopolist) are sellers in a position to exercise considerable control over prices, as Chapter 10 will discuss.

General Learning Objective

Recognize the nature of a competitive market and distinguish between perfect and monopolistic competition.

Specific Learning Objectives

	Self-Test Reference
1. Identify the conditions necessary for perfect competition	# 1
2. Diagram the theory of market prices determination under perfect competition	# 2-3(a)
3. Develop a profit maximizing strategy for a perfectly competitive firm	# 3(b)-(c)
4. Recognize perfect competition and analyze available options	# 4-5

Self-Test Reference

5. Identify the characteristics of monopolistic competition . . . . # 6-8

6. Compare the demand curve facing a monopolistically competitive firm with that of a perfect competitor . . . . # 9-11

7. Develop a profit maximizing strategy for a monopolistic competitor . . . . # 12

8. Recognize the extent of monopolistic competition and assess its significance in a self-regulating free enterprise economy . . . . # 13-14

9. Identify the reasons for the relatively low prices and profits of competitive industries . . . . # 15

Self-Test

1. Name the three characteristics of perfect competition.

   (a) ______________________________

   (b) ______________________________

   (c) ______________________________

2. As a result of the situation described in the previous question, if an individual seller raises the price of its product, its sales will ______________________________

   ____

3. (a) On the graph, draw the demand curve for the product of an individual firm in a perfectly competitive industry in which the market price is $4.

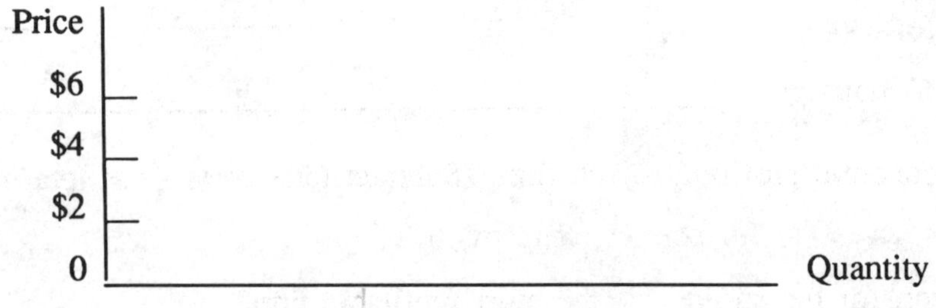

   (b) How does this firm react regarding:

   (i) its price? ______________________________

   ____

(ii) its output? ______________________________

____

(c) What can the firm do to increase its profits above minimal levels?

____

____

4. The following demand and supply schedules represent the interaction of 20 000 different firms and 20 million consumers. The current market price found at the intersection of D and S_1 is \$5 per unit with an equilibrium quantity of 15 million units.

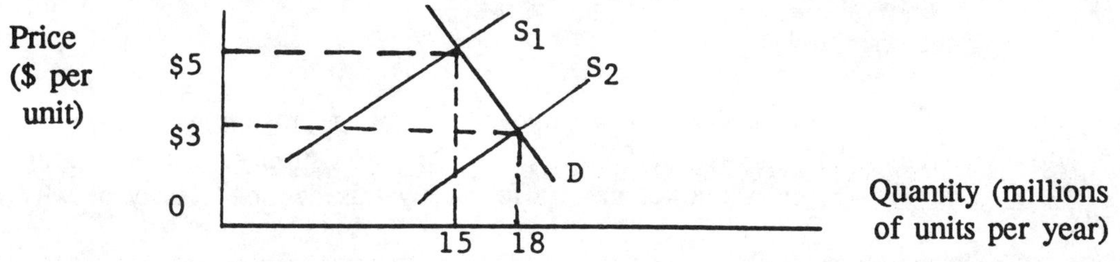

Consider three firms, A, B, and C competing in this industry. Each firm is faced with a perfectly elastic demand schedule at \$5 per unit. Assuming a normal profit of 10% is included in costs, the following table shows the output levels and per-unit costs of production of the three firms.

Firm	Costs of Production (per unit)	Yearly Quantity Produced (units)	Total Profits in Excess of a Normal Return (b)	(d)
A	\$5.00	1000	______	______
B	4.25	1500	______	______
C	3.00	3000	______	______

(a) Name the type of industry. ______________________________

(b) Determine the economic profits for each firm. (Subtract total costs from total revenues for each firm)

(c) What is the reason for the success of the most profitable firm?

____

____

(d) Suppose new firms enter the industry and supply shifts to S_2.

(i) The market price is now ____.

(ii) Re-determine economic profits for each firm under (d) in the table.

(iii) Determine which of the following options are possible for firms A and B.

____ Keep charging $5 and hope some buyers are ignorant of the new market price.

____ Increase price in the hope that industry demand is inelastic above $5.

____ Reduce costs of production.

____ Reduce costs and increase output.

____ Shut down.

(iv) Suppose firms A and B were unable to adapt to the new market conditions prompted by the supply shift to S_2. Market supply is then reduced by ______________. Is market price affected by this decline? Why or why not?

____

____

5. Frank Smith is one of thousands of grain farmers who produces only #1 Northern wheat. Last year he harvested and sold 320 000 bushels. The market price was $3.80 per bushel and the total Canadian production was 2 billion bushels. Assume no government intervention.

(a) Choose the best description of the industry.

(i) monopoly (iii) oligopoly

(ii) monopolistic competition (iv) perfect competition

(b) Why did you make the choice in part (a)?

____

(c) Draw the demand schedule facing Mr. Smith.

(d) What happens if Smith increases his price slightly above the market price? ____________

____

(e) Should Smith lower his price below $3.80 to capture more of the wheat market? Why or why not? ____

____

____

(f) Should Smith spend money on advertising?

____

6. State two characteristics of perfect competition and monopolistic competition which are similar.

(a) ____

(b) ____

7. Monopolistic competition is different from perfect competition in that, in monopolistic competition ____

____

____

8. State whether each of the following is an example of monopolistic competition. Give reasons.

____ (a) automobile manufacturing ________________________________

____ (b) stereo shops ________________________________

____ (c) Bell Canada ________________________________

____ (d) airlines ________________________________

____ (e) restaurants ________________________________

____ (f) Quebec Hydro ________________________________

____ (g) florist shops ________________________________

9. As a result of the situation described in Questions 6 and 7, in monopolistic competition:

   (a) each seller has a great deal of control over the price of its product.

   (b) producers usually make agreements not to compete on prices.

   (c) the demand for each seller's product is more elastic than in perfect competition.

   (d) while profits are still quite low, individual sellers have a small degree of control over the prices of their products.

   (e) the one seller has total control of the market.

10. In what two ways does the situation in the previous questions make the incentives for the firm in a monopolistically competitive industry **different** from the incentives for a firm in a perfectly competitive industry?

    (a) ____

    ____

    (b) ____

    ____

11. As product differentiation increases, demand tends to

    (a) rise.

    (b) fall.

    (c) become more elastic.

    (d) become neither more nor less elastic.

    (e) become more inelastic.

12. Bob Van Heyden owns a bakery in a city where there are over one-hundred other bakeries. Bob specializes in Belgian pastries and is known for his fine birthday cakes. Last year he lowered his prices for one month only to find that total sales revenues declined from $16 000 to $13 500.

    (a) Choose the best description of the industry.

    (i) monopoly　　　(iii) monopolistic competition

    (ii) oligopoly　　　(iv) perfect competition

(b) Demand for Bob's bakery products appears to be (inelastic/ elastic).

(c) What accounts for the nature of the elasticity of (b)? ______________________

____

____

(d) What is Bob's most important advantage in capturing and holding his market relative to his competitors? ______________________________________

____

____

13. According to the doctrine of laissez-faire

(a) the economy functions best if businesses are privately owned and operated, but are subject to extensive government regulation.

(b) the economy cannot function well unless the government takes over the ownership and operation of all business.

(c) the economy functions best when government regulation and intervention are kept to a minimum.

(d) all non-competitive industries should be controlled by the government.

(e) none of the above.

14. The doctrine of laissez-faire assumes that the economy is generally comprised of industries which are (competitive/non-competitive) in nature.

15. Competitive industries are characterized by low prices and low profits. The origin of this situation is best described by

(a) aggressive price cutting.

(b) extraordinary advertising expenditures.

(c) a large number of firms.

(d) easy entry into the industry.

(e) an inability of producers to control supply.

(f) choices (c), (d), and (e).

Chapter 10

NON-COMPETITIVE INDUSTRIES

Chapter 10 completes the section on market structure by examining monopoly and oligopoly — the market structures described as "non-competitive." The term non-competitive can be misleading, so it must be remembered that this term refers not to the absence of any kind of competition, but rather to the fact that these industries are not competitive in the sense described in Chapter 9, that is competitive forces cannot be counted upon to hold prices and profits down.

The section on monopoly is straightforward, readily understood and refers to a relatively small sector of the economy. Oligopoly, by contrast, is a very large and important sector of the Canadian economy, yet predicting the behavior of oligopolists regarding price and output decisions is not simple. When all is said and done (which takes a while), we can only say that the potential for increasing prices and profits above competitive levels exists, with the actual results depending on the circumstances in each particular case.

General Learning Objective

Examine the effects on market price and output of non-competitive industry.

Specific Learning Objectives

	Self-Test Reference
1. Define a monopoly industry and be able to distinguish a natural monopoly	# 1-4
2. Identify the key factors in the creation of a diamond monopoly	# 5
3. Consider a case where monopoly serves the "best interests" of society	# 6
4. Recognize an oligopoly market structure and assess the extent of oligopoly in the Canadian economy	# 7-10
5. Examine the barriers to entry that are typical of an oligopolistic industry	# 11-12
6. Analyze price determination in an oligopolistic structure	# 13-15
7. Inspect the forms of non-price rivalry that oligopolists may engage in	# 16-19
8. Recognize the necessary conditions for the continued existence of a cartel	# 20

Self-Test

1. The best definition of a monopoly industry is ______________________________

____.

2. A natural monopoly refers to a situation in which __________________________

____.

3. List two possibilities regarding the role of government concerning natural monopolies.

   (a) ____

   (b) ____

4. Consider the following information regarding a **capital intensive industry**. To achieve the desired levels of output there are two possibilities with respect to the structure of the industry. It is possible to have only one firm (a monopoly) or to have four firms (an oligopoly).

	Monopolist			Oligopolist		
Output Desired	(1) Output Of Mono-polist	(2) Total Costs ($)	(3) = (2) ÷ (1) Average Costs	(4) Total Costs Per Firm ($)	(5) Output Per Firm	(6) = (4) ÷ (5) Average Costs
100 000	100 000	$ 200 000	____	$ 75 000	25 000	____
600 000	600 000	1 000 000	____	450 000	150 000	____
1 800 000	1 800 000	2 000 000	____	1 000 000	450 000	____

   (a) Fill in the blanks in the table by determining average costs per unit for both the monopolist and the typical oligopolist. (NOTE: The average cost per unit is equal to total costs divided by the level of output.)

   (b) What is the most significant feature regarding average costs for the monopoly-oligopoly comparison? ______________________________

   ____

   ____

   ____

   (c) As a result of our analysis of average costs and the oligopoly-monopoly comparison, we label this industry as a typical ______________________________

(d) Check which of the following are possibilities for the type of industry.

____ telephone services ____ service station

____ breweries ____ hydroelectric

____ power generation ____ restaurant

5. The secret of the De Beers monopoly of the diamond market could be attributed to

(a) influencing demand through the advertising campaign of "A diamond is forever."

(b) limiting production and the number of dealers.

(c) forcing Russian diamonds off the market thorugh negative advertising.

(d) a policy of selling diamonds at the wholesale level.

(e) both choices (a) and (b).

6. The text material makes the point that where the depletion of natural resources is a concern a monopoly tends to serve the interests of society best. Take the example of timber.

(a) If a number of firms are involved in processing timber what is the tendency regarding production in the shortrun? Why?

____

(b) What happens to price and the supply of the resource?

____

(c) How does the monopoly option provide incentives for replenishing the resource?

____

7. Oligopoly refers to a situation in which

(a) an industry is dominated by a few large firms.

(b) prices and profits are above competitive levels.

(c) two or three firms do all of the business in a particular market.

(d) one very large corporation is the largest (but not the only) firm in a particular market.

(e) none of the above.

8. "Oligopoly" is defined as a situation in which ____________ or fewer producers account for _________ % or more of an industry's sales.

9. Classify each of the following industries as perfectly competitive, monopolistically competitive, oligopolistic or monopolistic.

(a) postal service for letters ______________________________

(b) steel mills ______________________________

(c) many small farmers selling vegetables ______________________________

(d) record stores ______________________________

(e) automobile manufacturing ______________________________

10. Regal Steel Ltd. is a privately owned steel manufacturer competing in an industry where three firms have a near equal share of the market. Each firm specializes in a unique steel product ranging from steel for automobiles to the rolled steel of pipelines. Regal sells its product for $1500 per ton and sold 2 million tons last year. The owners feel that a 10% price increase will cause a reduction in sales to 1.6 million tons. It also seems apparent that a 10% price reduction will increase sales to 2.1 million tons.

(a) This is an example of

(i) monopoly (iii) monopolistic competition

(ii) oligopoly (iv) perfect competition

(b) Three reasons for choosing the answer in (a) are ______________________________

____

____

______________________________.

(c) Should Regal increase the price of the product by 10%? Why or why not?

____

____

____

(d) Should Regal decrease its price by 10%? Why or why not? ______________________________

____

____

(e) Draw the demand schedule facing the Regal Steel Co. in the following space.

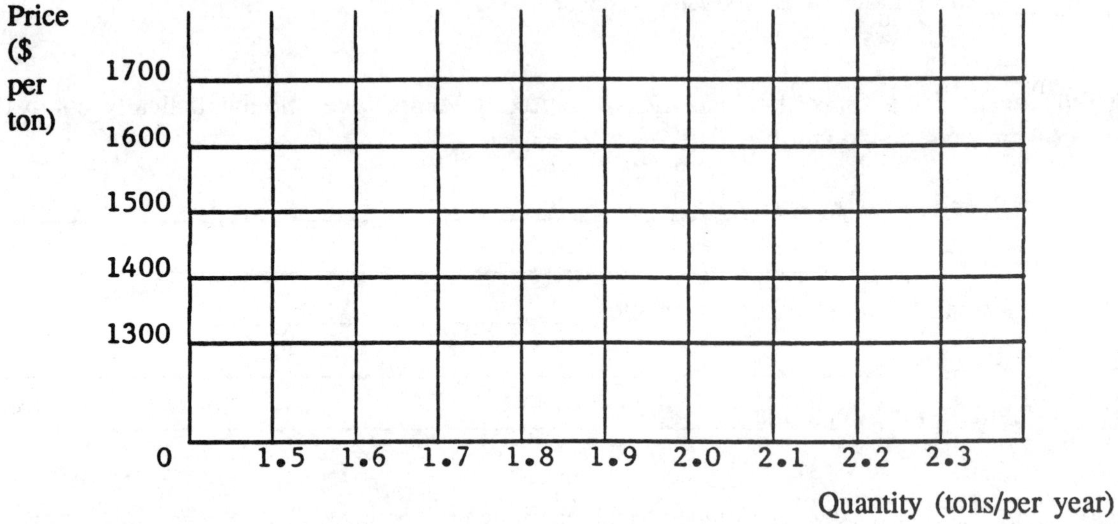

(f) Above $1500 demand is (inelastic/elastic) whereas below $1500 demand is (inelastic/elastic).

11. List six different type of barriers to entry which may make it difficult for new firms to enter an industry.

(a) ______________________________

(b) ______________________________

(c) ______________________________

(d) ______________________________

(e) ______________________________

(f) ______________________________

12. State whether it is **TRUE** or **FALSE** that barriers to entry to an industry tend to have each of the following effects

____ (a) To increase competition and reduce prices and profits.

____ (b) To restrict competition and increase prices and profits.

____ (c) To make existing producers more efficient, thus reducing product prices.

____ (d) To increase production by existing producers in the industry.

13. The demand curve faced by an oligopolist creates an incentive for the oligopolist to

(a) increase its price.

(b) leave its price at the present level.

(c) change its price only if the other firms in the industry do so.

(d) (b) and (c) are both correct.

(e) reduce its price.

14. Which of the following most accurately describes the position of oligopolists with respect to pricing of their products?

(a) They have total control over the price of their products, and can set whatever price they wish.

(b) Governments keep such close watch on and control over their prices that they can be said to have practically no real power over their prices.

(c) While they often have (and use) considerable power over prices, they are limited in the use of this power by various forces, including market forces as well as governmental forces.

(d) The fact that the demand for their products is usually elastic means that they have little power over prices.

(e) While they have considerable potential power over prices, they seldom charge prices higher than would exist under competitive conditions.

15. If oligopolists are to succeed in controlling the price of their product, they must succeed in controlling the ______________________ of it.

16. List four factors which may serve to limit the ability of oligopolists to increase their prices.

(a) ____

(b) ____

(c) ____

(d) ____

17. Which statement best describes the competitive behavior of most oligopolists?

(a) They engage in vigorous competition of all sorts: advertising, price cutting, etc.

(b) They focus mostly on price competition, using relatively little advertising and other non-price methods.

(c) They use extensive advertising to save money and increase profits.

(d) They generally avoid all forms of competition of any sort: advertising, price cutting, etc.

(e) They often seek to avoid price competition so as to protect prices, and use other forms of competition, such as advertising and product differentiation.

18. State whether each of the following types of competition would likely be used by oligopolists.

____ (a) advertising

____ (b) customer services

____ (c) product differentiation

____ (d) price reductions

____ (e) style changes

19. During a recession, competitive industries tend to adjust to reduced demand by ____________ ____________, whilc oligopolistic industries tend to adjust to reduced demand by ____________

20. For any cartel to survive certain conditions must be met. Place a check mark by the following factors that appeared to influence the breakdown of the OPEC cartel.

____ the trend to smaller cars reduced demand for oil.

____ because of higher prices, consumers were switching use, where possible, from natural gas to oil.

____ OPEC nations had not agreed on price increases.

____ although agreement between OPEC members had been made on price increases, there was no agreement on production quotas.

____ because of the self interest of members, each country was producing and selling too much oil between 1973 and 1979.

____ non-OPEC oil producers such as the United Kingdom, Mexico and Norway were reducing their supply between 1973 and 1979.

____ OPEC was able to maintain its market share of the world non-socialist oil market between 1979 and 1985.

Chapter 11

THE COSTS AND REVENUES OF THE FIRM

Chapters 9 and 10 have covered the four types of Market Structures (perfect competition, monopolistic competition, oligopoly and monopoly) and the behavior of these industries regarding **price** and **output** decisions. In explaining the incentives facing the individual firm regarding its price and output decisions, we have so far assumed that the firm's objective was to maximize its total revenue (sales revenue), rather than profits. This made the analysis simpler, as it enabled us to focus on the revenues of the business, whereas analyzing profits would have required consideration of **production costs** as well as sales revenues.

There are two exceptions to this format in Chapters 9 and 10. Per unit costs of production were provided in Question 4 of Chapter 9 in the illustration of a perfectly competitive industry. Then, in Chapter 10, the concept of average costs was considered in Question 4 to illustrate the existence of a natural monopoly. In both of these cases there was no explanation as to the derivation of production costs.

Chapter 11 adds to the analysis of Chapters 9 and 10 the topic of production costs to make that analysis more complete. This requires the introduction of some new concepts (in particular, the Law of Diminishing Returns and its effect on costs, and the concepts of marginal cost and marginal revenue and the analysis associated with them). These new concepts can only be learned effectively by working with them and by doing the problems in the discussion questions and the self-test questions.

When these new tools of analysis are used, our understanding of the behavior of the individual firm under various market structures is more thorough. However, the results of the analysis — our conclusions regarding the incentives facing the firm regarding its price and output decisions under various market structures — are the same as we reached in Chapters 9 and 10.

General Learning Objective

Using production cost data and sales revenue projections, determine the maximum profit output under conditions of both perfect and imperfect competition.

Specific Learning Objectives

		Self-Test Reference
1.	Distinguish between fixed and variable costs	# 1-2
2.	Relate average variable costs to average product per worker	# 3-5
3.	Schedule average costs of a typical firm	# 6
4.	Calculate marginal costs from marginal productivity data	# 7-9
5.	Consider average and marginal costs of a typical firm	# 10-11
6.	Relate productivity data to the firm's costs, revenues and profits	# 12
7.	Determine the maximum profit output for a perfectly competitive firm	# 13-14
8.	Illustrate a monopolist's maximum profit price and output position	# 15-16
9.	Analyze the break even position and the shut down point for a business firm	# 17-18
10.	Determine whether a firm should raise, lower or maintain its price and output levels to maximize profits	# 19

Note: When constructing graphs, plot the marginal cost and marginal revenue data at the midpoint of the appropriate range of output. For example, if marginal cost is $10 between 100 and 200 units, plot the $10 at 150 units.

Self-Test

1. State whether each of the following is a fixed or variable cost

____ (a) property taxes

____ (b) flat-rate telephone costs

____ (c) direct materials costs

____ (d) direct labor costs

____ (e) the salary of the president

____ (f) mortgage payments

____ (g) long-distance telephone services

2. As output increases, fixed costs per unit

(a) increase.

(b) remain constant.

(c) decrease.

3. As successive units of one production input (e.g., labor) are added to fixed amounts of other inputs (e.g., capital equipment), the average output of the variable input will

(a) increase at a constant rate.

(b) remain unchanged.

(c) increase at first, then decline.

(d) decrease gradually.

(e) none of the above.

4. The phenomenon described in Question 3 is known as the ______________________________
______________________________.

5. As output is increased, average variable cost per unit

(a) falls at first, then rises.

(b) rises at first, then falls.

(c) falls continually.

(d) rises continually.

(e) none of the above.

6. Average total cost per unit is a dish-shaped curve.

(a) It is high at low levels of output because ______________________________
______________________________.

(b) It is high at high levels of output because ______________________________
______________________________.

7. Marginal cost per unit is

   (a) the addition to total costs arising from the production of one more unit.

   (b) the total costs divided by the total number of units produced.

   (c) the total variable costs divided by the number of units produced.

   (d) the net effect of declining fixed costs per unit and rising variable costs per unit as output is increased.

   (e) none of the above.

8. If output is increased from 25 units to 26 units and total costs increase from $615 to $638, marginal cost per unit is

   (a) $24.60

   (b) $24.54

   (c) $23

   (d) $638

   (e) none of the above

9. Fill in the "marginal cost per unit" column

Output	Total Costs	Marginal Cost Per Unit
0	$200	—
5	300	$ _______ (a)
10	385	$ _______ (b)
15	460	$ _______ (c)

10. If average cost per unit is falling,

   (a) marginal cost per unit must be falling faster than average cost per unit.

   (b) marginal cost per unit must be rising.

   (c) marginal cost per unit must be less than average cost per unit.

   (d) marginal cost per unit must be falling, too.

   (e) none of the above.

11. The marginal cost per unit curve intersects the average cost per unit curve

(a) to the left of the lowest point on the average cost per unit curve.

(b) at the lowest point on the average cost per unit curve.

(c) to the right of the lowest point on the average cost per unit curve.

12. Joe Smith has a business manufacturing television tables. His building is 2000 square feet and his fixed costs are $600 per week.

Each employee hired costs the company $1500 per week.

The owner discovered the following changes to weekly output as more labor was hired. Determine average output for the various levels of employment.

Labor per week (employees)	Output per week	Average output (tables/employee)
1	20	______________
2	40	______________
3	90	______________
4	150	______________
5	160	______________

(a) Peak efficiency for this business seems to occur at ______________________ tables per week and ______________ employees.

(b) The law of diminishing returns is illustrated when the ______________________ employee is hired.

(c) The costs incurred when hiring extra employees is known as ______________________.

(d) Complete the following table by determining costs at each output level.

(1) Employees	(2) Tables	(3) Total Fixed Costs (TFC)	(4) Total Variable Costs (TVC)	(5) Total Costs	(6) ATC
0	0				
1	20				
2	40				
3	90				
4	150				
5	160				

(e) Suppose the selling price for each table is $55.00 and the firm can sell all that it produces. Complete the following.

Tables/week	Total Revenues	Total Costs	Profits
20	$________	________	____
40	$________	________	____
90	$________	________	____
150	$________	________	____
160	$________	________	____

(f) Thus, for this business, the best level of production is ______ tables per week. The firm hires ________ employees and total profits are $________ per week.

(g) Under what conditions would this firm decide to shut down rather than continuing to operate in the short-run period?

____

13. The Rory Street Bike Works is a small bicycle manufacturing company. Presently, there are two employees who are manufacturing 3 bicycles per day. The owners wish to know whether to expand their operation and if so by how much? After completing part (a), make their decision in (b) given the following data.

Each worker is paid $60 per day.

Total fixed costs are $50 per day.

There are $20 of materials in each bicycle.

Each bicycle sells for $75.

(a) Fill in the blanks on the following tables and complete the graphs. Plot total revenues and total costs on one graph and marginal cost and marginal revenue on the other.

Labor	Daily Output	Total Fixed Costs	Total Variable Costs	Total Cost	Average Total Cost	Mar-ginal Cost	Total Reve-nues	Profits	Marginal Revenues
0	0								
1	1								
2	3								
3	7								
4	9								
5	10								

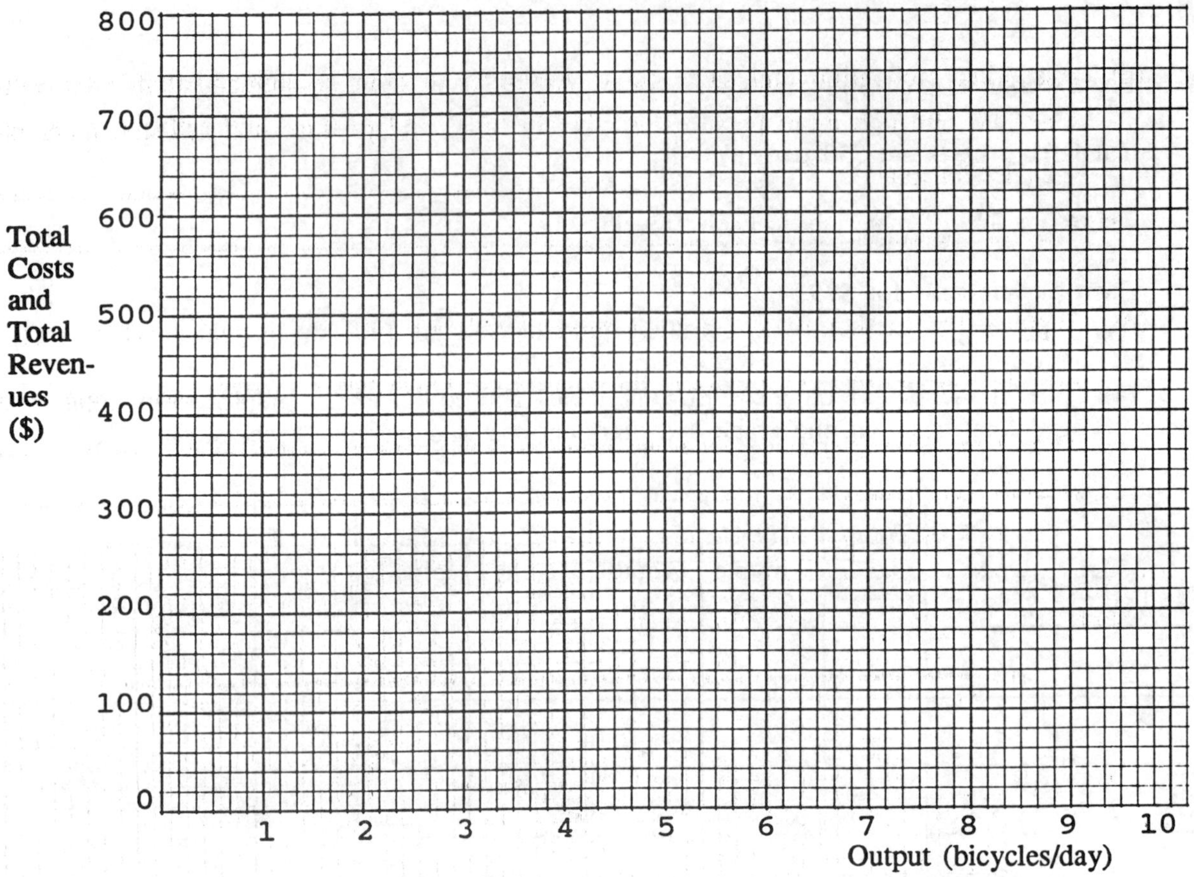

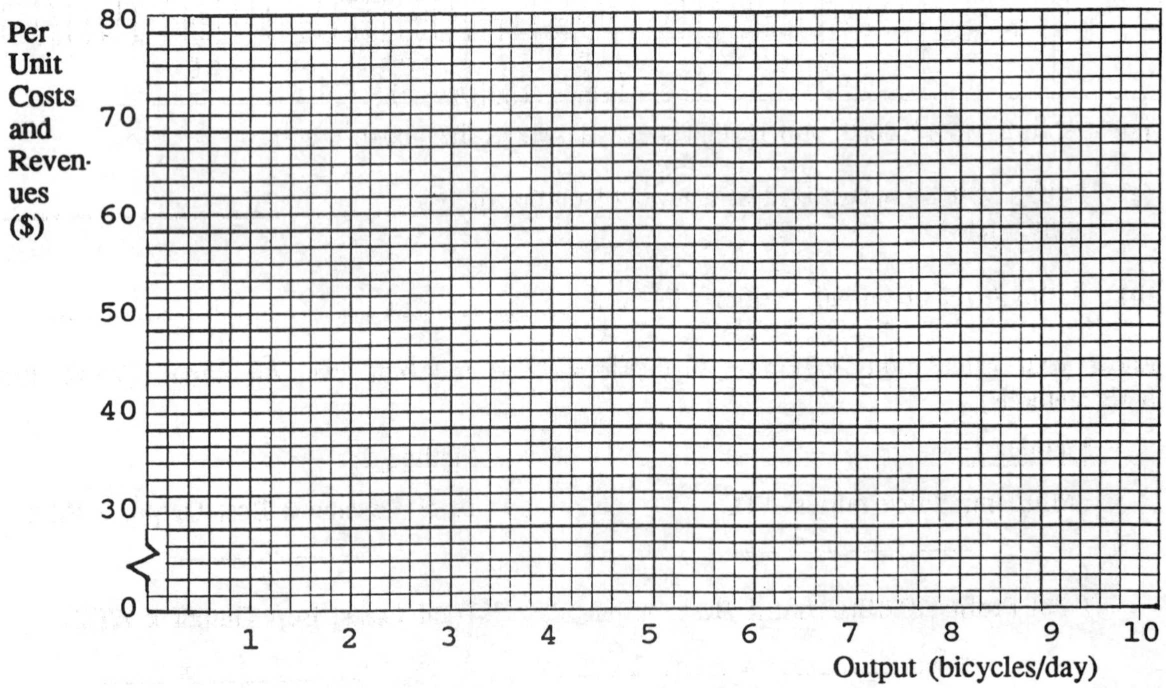

(b) Decision: Employees ______________________

Output ______________________

Profits ______________________

(c) Assuming production and sales occur according to your recommendation, why wouldn't this firm hire one more person (i.e., five in total) and produce and sell one more bicycle (i.e., ten in total)? ______________________________

____

(d) Suppose the market price for their product falls to $40 per bicycle. What is the best decision for the owners assuming these costs are unchanged? Why? __________

____

____

14. Price ($/unit)

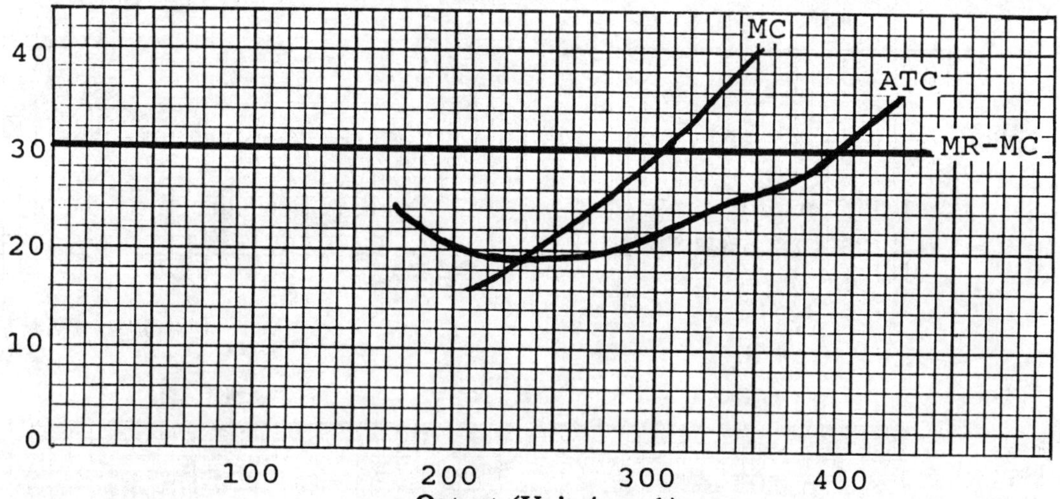

Output (Units/month)

For the firm whose costs and revenues are shown in the above graph,

(a) profits will be maximized at a level of output of ______________ units, and

(b) at this level of output, profits will be $ ______________

Show your calculations assuming that ATC=$22 at the best level of output. (Work through both methods).

Method 1:

Profit/Unit: Price minus ATC

____ - ____ = ____

Total Profits: Profits/Unit x Best Output

= $________ x ________

= $____________

Method 2:

Total Revenues: Best Output x Price

______ x ______

Total Costs: Best Output x ATC

________ x _____

= $____________

Total Profits: TR - TC

= ________

(c) Is this firm operating in a perfectly competitive market?

YES ____

NO ____

If this firm is in a perfectly competitive industry and is a typical firm which is making extra profits, what adjustment will occur in the price of the product and how will this affect the profits of this typical firm? What will be the final equilibrium level of the price?

____

____

____

____

15. Following are the cost and revenue data for the Ronson Reemistram Company.

If the company charges this price per reemistram:	It will sell this many reemistrams per week:
$ 5.00	0
4.50	300
4.00	600
3.50	900
3.00	1200
2.50	1500
2.00	1800

The company's total fixed costs (TFC) are $300 per week, and its total variable costs (TVC) are shown in the following table.

Daily Output	$ TFC	$ TVC	$ Total Costs	ATC	(AR) Average Revenue Or Price	(TR) Total Revenue	(MC) Marginal Cost	(MR) Marginal Revenue
0	300	0	_____	_____	_____	_____		
							_____	_____
300	_____	850	_____	_____	_____	_____		
							_____	_____
600	_____	1550	_____	_____	_____	_____		
							_____	_____
900	_____	2050	_____	_____	_____	_____		
							_____	_____
1200	_____	2500	_____	_____	_____	_____		
							_____	_____
1500	_____	3100	_____	_____	_____	_____		
							_____	_____
1800	_____	4300	_____	_____	_____	_____		
							_____	_____

(a) Determine the values for the blanks in the above table.

(b) Draw the ATC, MC, AR and MR schedules on the graph. (Remember to plot MC and MR at the midpoints of the range).

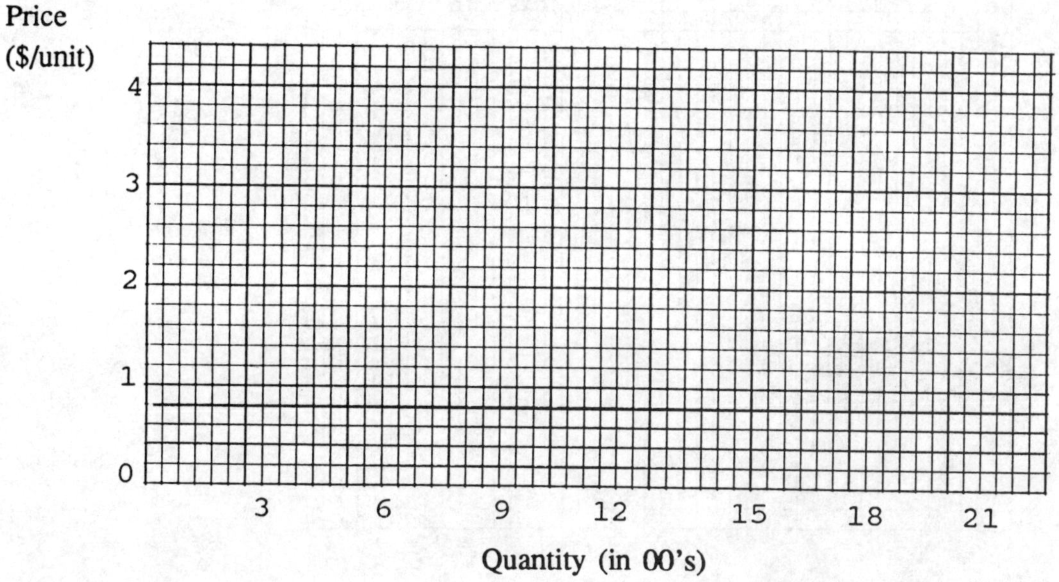

(c) According to the table, the best level of output for the maximum profits is in the range of __________ units.

(d) According to the graph, the best profit point occurs at _______ units.

(e) If ATC = $2.40 and price is $3.25 at the best output, total daily profits are $__________.

(f) Is the Ronson Company operating in a perfectly competitive market?

Yes _______ No _______

How do you know in this situation? ____

____

16. $ Per Unit

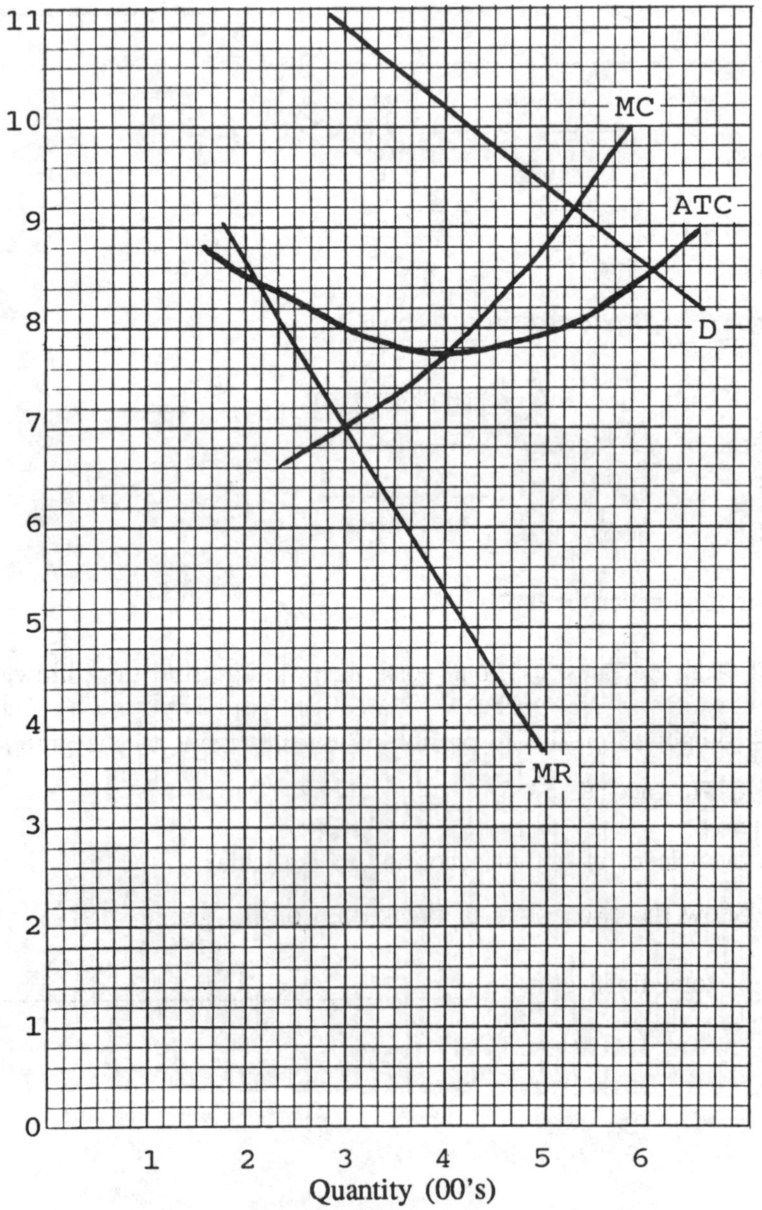

From the graph above determine:

(a) The best output for maximum profits ______________________

(b) Price at the best output ______________________

(c) Average cost at the maximum profit output ______________________

(d) The best profits are ______________________

(e) Is this firm in perfect competition? ______________________

Reason: ______________________

____

____

____

____

17. Given the following data:

Quantity	Price	Total Costs	Total Revenues
0	$ 50	100	________
10	$ 50	500	________
20	$ 50	950	________
30	$ 50	1400	________
40	$ 50	1600	________
50	$ 50	3000	________

(a) Fill in the table for total revenues.

(b) Draw the graph of total revenues and total costs using the grid on the following page.

(c) Determine the best output to maximize profits. Show this point on the graph by drawing a vertical line up to TC and TR. ______________________

(d) What is the break-even level of output according to the table?

________. Show the two points of break-even on the graph.

(e) What is the level of total fixed costs? ______________________

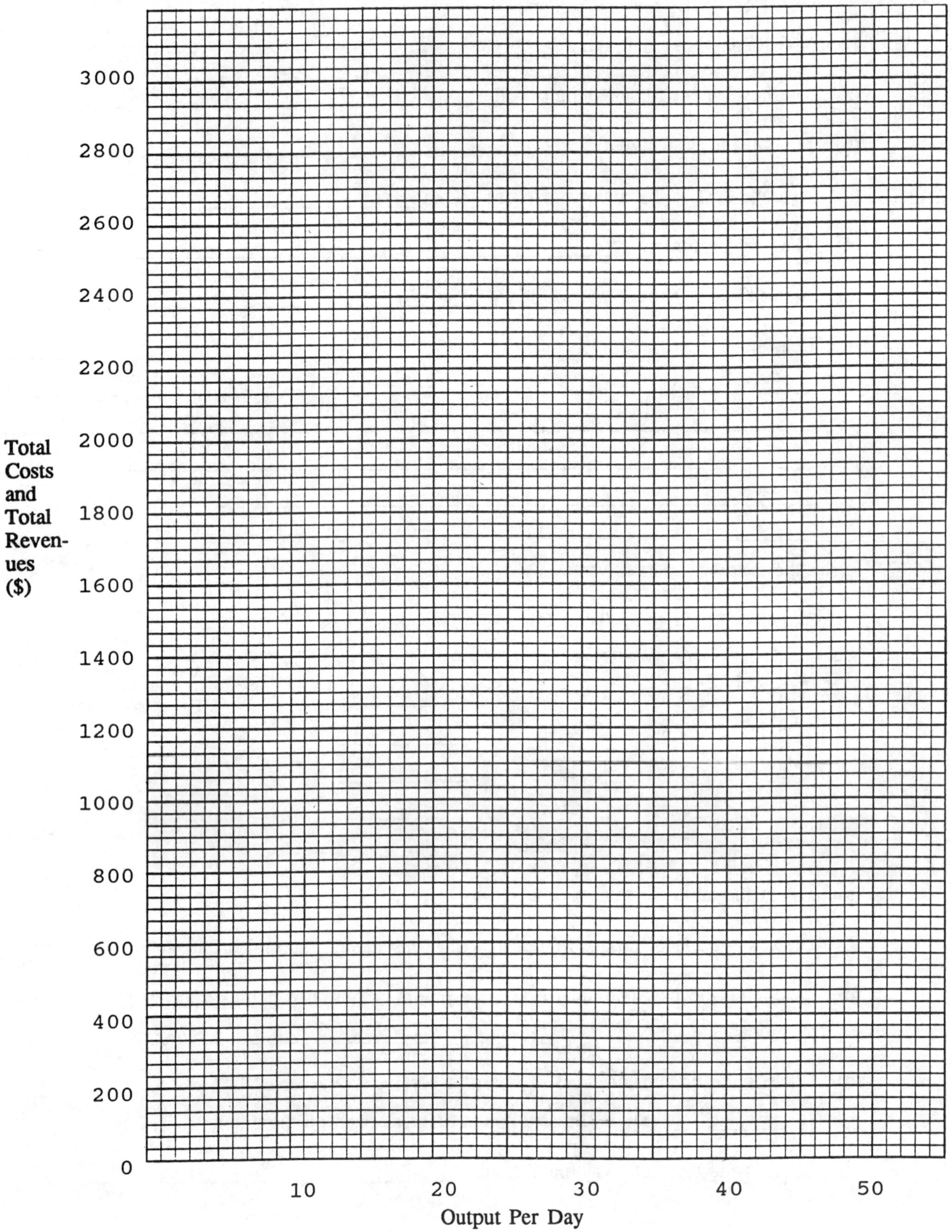
Total Costs and Total Revenues ($)
3000
2800
2600
2400
2200
2000
1800
1600
1400
1200
1000
800
600
400
200
0
10
20
30
40
50
Output Per Day

18. Francesca's Fradistats Ltd. sells fradistats at a price of $3.50 each. Francesca's fixed variable costs are shown in the following table.

Units of Output Per Day	Fixed Costs	Vari-able Costs	Total Costs	Total Revenue
0	$ 300	$ 0	____	____
200	300	900	____	____
400	300	1600	____	____
600	300	2100	____	____
800	300	2400	____	____
1000	300	3100	____	____
1200	300	4300	____	____

(a) Complete the remaining 2 columns in the table.

(b) On the graph below, draw the total revenue, total costs and variable costs curves.

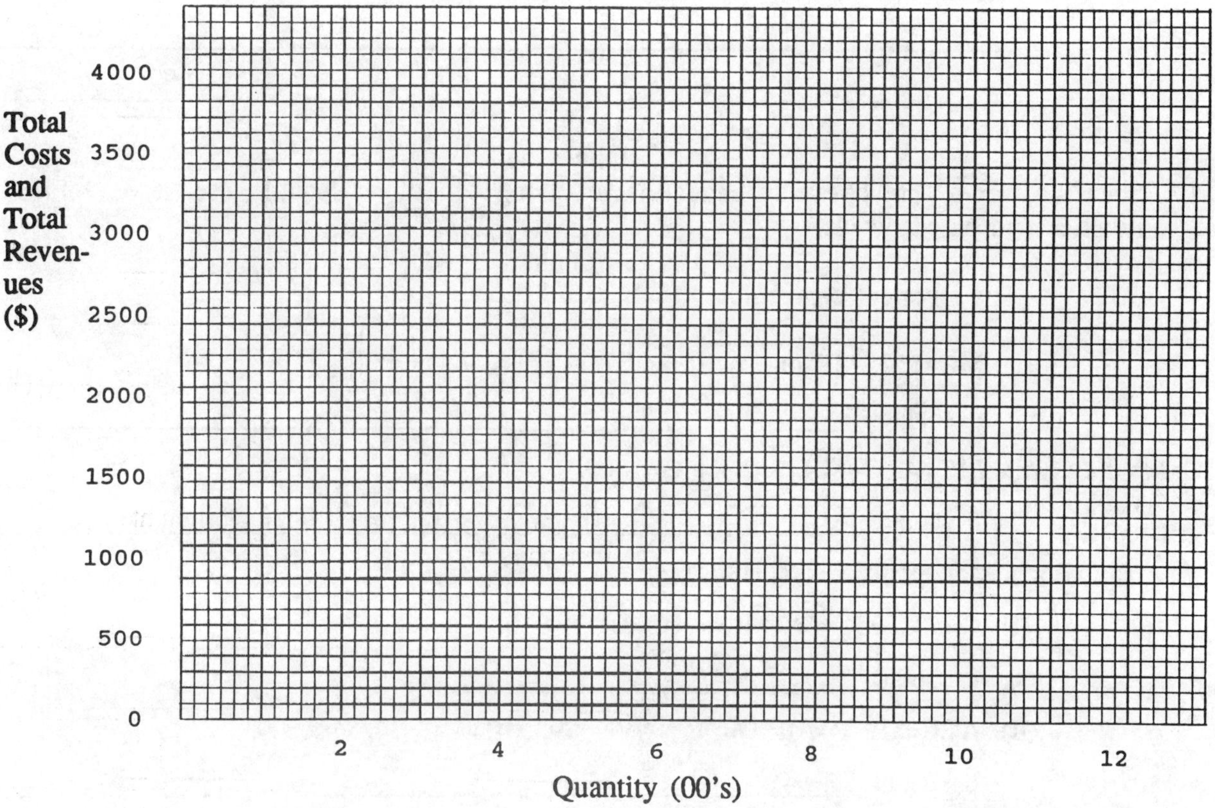

(c) The graph indicates that the minimum level of output and sales required for this firm to start up in business (its break-even point) is ____________ units per day.

(d) The graph indicates that, before this firm should go out of business its sales should fall below a level of _________ units per day.

Explain the reasons for your answers to (c) and (d).

____

____

____

____

____

____

____

____

____

____

____

____

____

19. State whether a firm operating under the following conditions should raise, lower or maintain its price and output levels.

(a) For a perfect competitor

(i) MC=$12, MR or P=$10, and ATC=$10 at Q=1000.

It should ____.

(ii) MC=ATC=MR=$12 for Q=1000.

It should ____.

(b) For a monopolistic competitor

(i) Q=500, MC=$4, MR=ATC=$8, P=$10.

It should ________________________.

(ii) ATC=$12 P=AR=D=$10, AVC=$9, MR=MC=$4, Q=1000.

It should ____.

(c) For an oligopolistic competitor

(i) Q=100,000, ATC=$5, MC=MR=$6, D=$8.

It should ______________________________.

(ii) Q=80,000, ATC=$5, MC=$3, MR=$7, P=$9.

It should ______________________________.

(d) For a monopoly

(i) MR=$2, Q=1000, ATC=$8, MC=P or D=$10.

It should ______________________________.

(ii) MR=MC=ATC=$10, Q=1000, D=$15.

It should ______________________________.

(e) For a natural monopoly

(i) MC=MR=$5, ATC=$7, D=$10.

It should ______________________________.

(ii) AC or ATC=$4, D=$4, MC=$2.

It should ______________________________.

Chapter 12

INDUSTRIAL CONCENTRATION: IS BIG BAD OR BETTER?

This chapter deals with issues of big business in Canada. This is an important policy issue due to the small size of much of the Canadian manufacturing sector's operations and its vulnerability to foreign competition.

Chapter 12 examines the traditional view that "big is bad." It is difficult to estimate the effect that oligopolistic practices have on prices, and the estimate that oligopoly results in prices being 25% higher than would exist under competitive conditions is based on a limited amount of research; however, it is the best estimate available.

Subsequently, it is argued that the traditional view is not correct, for various reasons. The key element in this argument is that the price comparisons presented may not always be appropriate because the lower production costs associated with the larger operations of big businesses make it possible for prices to be reasonable despite their higher profits. Thus, it is argued, big business actually contributes to our prosperity through its productivity by increasing capital investment.

The policy dilemma which flows from these differences of opinion is discussed, stressing its relevance to the importance of improving the international competitive position of the Canadian manufacturing sector. While Canadian industry is more concentrated than industry in other countries, Canadian firms are small by international standards and not particularly competitive internationally. So, if revisions to Canadian competition policy result in increasing the restrictions on the growth of big business in order to give consumers more protection, they risk preventing Canadian firms from becoming larger and more competitive internationally. Recent changes to Canadian competition policy appear to be geared to **legal** considerations, such as anti-competitive behavior, as opposed to **economic** considerations, such as the desirability of larger, more efficient Canadian manufacturing enterprises.

General Learning Objective

Discuss whether or not industrial concentration is in the best interests of the Canadian economy.

Specific Learning Objectives

		Self-Test Reference
1.	Give reasons for and examples of increased industrial concentration in Canada's manufacturing sector	# 1-6
2.	Describe the probable costs of increased industrial concentration to Canada	# 7-16
3.	Describe the probable benefits of increased industrial concentration to Canada	# 17-20
4.	Discuss the policy dilemma facing the Canadian government regarding industrial concentration	# 21-28
5.	Identify major changes in emphasis in the new competition policy in Canada	# 29-34

Self-Test

1. List four major corporate takeovers in Canada during the 1980's.

(a) ____

(b) ____

(c) ____

(d) ____

2. From the early 1980's to 1987, mergers in Canada increased from about __________ to __________.

3. Industrial concentration refers to

(a) situations in which one firm controls over half of the sales of an industry.

(b) the extent to which an industry is dominated by a few firms.

(c) only those industries in which profits are significantly above the average for the economy as a whole.

(d) industries in which the major firm(s) concentrate(s) on acquiring the shares of their competitors.

(e) none of the above.

4. Industrial concentration is generally measured by the concentration ratio, which is

____

____.

5. Industrial concentration is of interest and concern to economists because

(a) larger firms are sometimes more progressive technologically, and thus contribute to higher productivity and higher living standards.

(b) when a few firms dominate an industry, the potential exists for monopolistic practices such as price-fixing.

(c) it is generally agreed that big business and the domination of industries by a few firms are economically and socially undesirable.

(d) (b) and (c) together.

(e) (a) and (b) together.

6. In Canada, the overall degree of industrial concentration is higher than in the USA. **TRUE** or **FALSE?**

7. State whether each of the following is a reason why large corporations have come to play such a dominant role in much of the economy.

____ (a) Larger businesses often enjoy cost advantages, due to large-scale production, and are thus better able to compete.

____ (b) Modern manufacturing often requires such vast amounts of capital investment and large plants that large corporations are required.

____ (c) Government prefers large corporations to smaller businesses, and it is government policy to encourage the development of large corporations, through tax advantages and other measures.

____ (d) Businesses often merge with their competitors.

____ (e) The small size of the Canadian market allows for the development of relatively few firms in some industries.

8. The number of corporate mergers and takeovers has increased sharply over the past decade. Four plausible reasons are

(a) ____

(b) ____

(c) ____

(d) ____

9. The traditional view is that the existence of big business tends to result in ______________ prices and ______________ output and ________________ product quality than would be the case in competitive industries.

10. The after-tax rate of return on owner's investment in oligopolistic industries is approximately ____________________________ times as high as the average rate of return on investment for all industries.

11. The most basic reason for the higher-than-average **profit rates** of oligopolists is that oligopolists

   (a) are more efficient than average.

   (b) advertise more than average.

   (c) tend to avoid price competition.

   (d) pay lower-than-average wages.

   (e) pay a lower tax rate than smaller businesses.

12. State whether each of the following is a reason why the **prices** of oligopolists tend to be higher than they would be under competitive conditions.

   ____ (a) Oligopolists' production methods are less efficient.

   ____ (b) Oligopolists' advertising costs are higher.

   ____ (c) Competitive industries almost all pay the minimum wage.

   ____ (d) Oligopolists employ more people, and so have higher labor costs.

   ____ (e) Oligopolists' profits are subject to particularly high tax rates, which force up their prices.

   ____ (f) Oligopolists' profits are generally higher.

13. The prices of house brand or private label products in many supermarkets approximate the prices of similar goods under (competitive/ oligopolistic) market conditions while the prices of brand name products more closely match prices under (competitive/oligopolistic) market conditions.

14. Comparisons of the prices of brand name and private label products suggest that oligopolistic practices tend to raise consumer prices on the average by about _______ % above the level that would exist under competitive conditions.

15. List at least six criticisms which are made of bigness in business.

(a) ____

(b) ____

(c) ____

(d) ____

(e) ____

(f) ____

16. Write a description of the traditional view concerning the issue of bigness in business, and the appropriate government policy toward big business.

____

____

____

____

____

____

____

____

____

____

____

____

17. State whether each of the following is a reasonable argument in defence of bigness in business.

____ (a) The profits of big businesses (expressed as a rate of return on capital) are not higher than the profits of competitive industries.

____ (b) Oligopolists do not agree among themselves to raise prices and restrict output; rather, they compete vigorously on prices.

____ (c) Large corporations are more stable than smaller businesses, particularly with respect to maintaining employment during recessions.

____ (d) While abuses of big business' power (e.g., price-fixing) occurred in the past, these are now prevented by the anti-combines laws.

____ (e) Many criticisms of big businesses are vague and emotional rather than logical.

____ (f) Many oligopolistic corporations do not possess nearly the power to increase prices that their critics suggest.

____ (g) Big business tends to promote, rather than retard, technological progress.

____ (h) Oligopolists constantly strive to improve the quality of their products to the maximum extent possible.

____ (i) The reinvestment of the large profits of big business in research and development, technological change and capital investment raises productivity and thus society's standard of living.

18. State whether each of the following statements concerning the ability of oligopolists to raise prices is **TRUE** or **FALSE**.

____ (a) They have more ability to raise prices than do firms in "competitive" industries, but are limited by a variety of factors which often prevent them from raising prices and profits.

____ (b) They have no freedom to raise prices, as all prices are determined by the government.

____ (c) They possess the power to raise prices to any level they wish in order to maximize profits.

____ (d) They could band together in order to raise prices and maximize profits if it were not for the anti-combines laws, which outlaw and thus prevent such practices.

____ (e) They are usually unable to raise prices due to the fact that the demand for their products is nearly always very elastic.

19. Five factors which limit the ability of oligopolists to raise prices are:

(a) ____;

(b) ____;

(c) ____;

(d) ____;

(e) ____;

20. "Monopolistic (oligopolistic) corporations constitute a grave threat to the welfare of our society. The government should destroy them either by breaking them up into smaller units so as to increase competition, or by regulating them or by nationalizing them. Such action would greatly benefit the public."

Briefly explain how a representative of big business would reply to this statement.

____

____

____

____

____

____

____

____

____

____

21. The dilemma Canada faces in determining its competition policy is that if more restrictions are placed on the growth of big business, there is the risk that Canadian businesses will be ______ ________________ able to compete with foreign firms, whereas if government policy reduces restrictions on big business in order to avoid this problem, it creates the risk that consumers will be ____

____

____.

22. In determining an appropriate competitive policy for Canada, what factors create a dilemma for Canadian authorities?

(a) The profits of oligopolistic corporations in Canada are very much higher than in other countries, suggesting that price-fixing is a particularly serious problem in Canada.

(b) The fact that Canada's largest corporations are much smaller than their foreign counterparts places them at a competitive disadvantage in international trade.

(c) Industrial concentration in Canada is higher than in the United States and other countries.

(d) (a) and (b) together.

(e) (b) and (c) together.

23. It can be argued **not only** that the stronger laws against oligopolistic practices in general and mergers in particular would be beneficial to Canadians **but also** that such measures would be harmful to Canadians.

Explain the facts and the arguments underlying the views that stronger laws against bigness in business would be: (a) in the best interests of Canadians, and (b) against the best interest of Canadians.

24. The purpose of the Combines Investigations Act is to

(a) break up monopolies into small competing businesses.

(b) keep profit rates down to the average level.

(c) prevent take-overs of corporations by other corporations.

(d) prevent actions by businesses which unduly lessen competition and are thus detrimental to the consumer.

(e) all of the above.

25. State whether the Combines Investigation Act outlaws the following:

____ (a) One firm owning another firm in the same industry.

____ (b) Mergers of firms that would unduly reduce competition.

____ (c) Takeovers of firms by other firms.

____ (d) Four or fewer firms having 50% or more of an industry's sales.

____ (e) Price-fixing agreements among producers.

____ (f) Various restrictive trade practices which reduce competition unduly.

26. Which of the following is the most accurate description of the effectiveness of the Anti-Combines laws?

(a) They are totally ineffective. They do nothing to solve the problems that they are supposed to remedy.

(b) They have been very successful. They have accomplished most of their objectives.

(c) They are far from totally effective, mainly because they are hard to enforce, but it is likely that they serve to prevent some of the practices that they make illegal.

(d) While they have not been very successful to date, they would be much more effective if the fines they provided for were larger.

(e) They have been totally effective except in the area of mergers.

27. The Combines Investigation Act is least effective against

(a) price-fixing.

(b) predatory pricing.

(c) mergers.

(d) resale price maintenance.

28. State whether each of the following statements concerning attempts to reform the Combines Investigation Act is **TRUE** or **FALSE**.

____ (a) Legislators of the seventies sought stronger measures against mergers and anti-competitive measures.

____ (b) Historical proposals to reform the Combines Investigations Act have been based on the basic assumption that "big is not so bad."

____ (c) 1985 reform proposals require that banks, importers and Crown corporations be subject to combines legislation.

____ (d) Recent legislation focuses attention on anti-competitive behaviors and assumes "big is not so bad."

____ (e) A twelve-member Competition Tribunal consisting of judges, business and consumer experts is responsible for adjudicating offenses that unduly lessen competition.

29. Traditionally, Canadian trade policy has endeavored to ______________________________

____

____

30. During the 1980's, international competition facing Canada became ____________________ with particular reference to competition from __________ and ______________________.

31. Growing competition from the United States is expected to result from ________________

____

____.

32. The Competition Act allows firms to defend mergers on the grounds that the proposed merger would likely result in ______________________________ and thereby increase the ability of Canadian industry to ______________________________.

33. Other factors to be considered in reviewing proposed mergers include:

(a) ______________________________

____

(b) ______________________________

____

(c) ______________________________

____

(d) ______________________________

____

34. It is felt generally that the new Competition Act is much more effective than the previous Combines Investigation Act, particularly in the two specific categories of:

(a) ______________________________

(b) ______________________________

Chapter 13

LABOR MARKETS AND LABOR UNIONS

This chapter discusses the somewhat different situation of markets for labor. Labor markets can be compared to product markets, in which the degree of control which sellers have over prices varies from highly competitive to monopolistic situations. Similarly, in labor markets, sellers have varying degrees of control over wages, ranging from highly organized skilled trade unions and professional groups to extremely open and competitive markets such as those for non-union part-time workers. The basic tools of analysis for labor markets are the same as for product markets: supply, demand and elasticity.

This chapter deals with non-union labor markets, applying the same tools of supply, demand and elasticity, and examining the effects of government interference with markets, in the form of price supports (minimum wage laws).

Labor unions also are discussed, showing that the collective bargaining system in general works reasonably well and that not all labor unions — relatively few in fact — fit the stereotype that many people believe in.

General Learning Objective

Discuss the basic factors involved in the operation of labor markets for both union and non-union workers.

Specific Learning Objectives

		Self-Test Reference
1.	Describe the process of wage determination in the non-union sector of the labor market	# 1-3
2.	Identify factors leading to wage differentials for labor in the non-union sector	# 4
3.	Describe the impact of government wage legislation	# 5-7
4.	Define the basic development of labor unions	# 8-17
5.	Recognize alternatives for workers in joining or not joining unions	# 18-22

Self-Test Reference

6. Define the legal aspects of a union contract . . . . # 23-34

7. Identify forms of outside intervention in contract negotiations and labor disputes. . . . . # 35-40

Self-Test

1. In the **non**-union sector of the labor force, wages and salaries are basically determined by

____

ANSWER THE NEXT 3 QUESTIONS ON THE BASIS OF THE DIAGRAM IN QUESTION 4.

2. If the demand for fradistat formers is represented by the curve **D**, the hourly wage rate for fradistat formers will be $ __________________________.

3. If the demand for fradistat formers increases, as shown by the curve **D1**, the hourly wage rate will be $ ____________.

4. The market's adjustment to changes in demand will be smoother if the supply of labor is more inelastic. **TRUE** or **FALSE**? Explain your position and illustrate graphically.

____

____

____

____

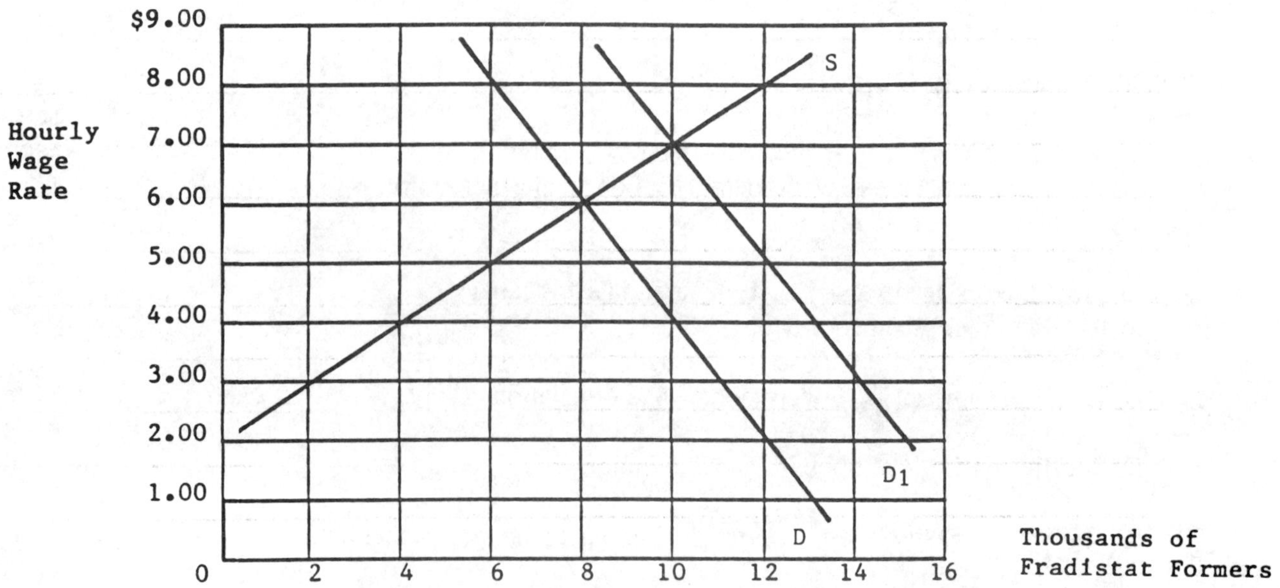

ANSWER THE NEXT QUESTION (#5) WITH REFERENCE TO THE DIAGRAM IN QUESTION 5.

5. If the government set a minimum wage of $8.00 per hour for fradistat formers and the demand for fradistat formers were represented by the curve **D**, the result would be

____

____.

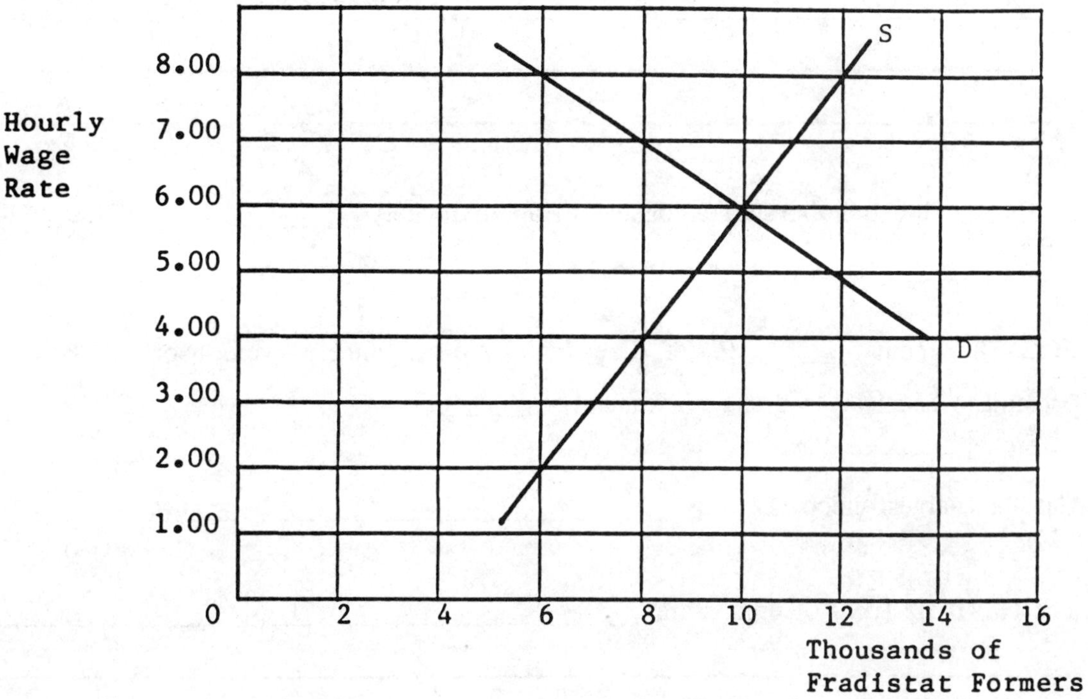

6. With respect to economics, briefly discuss the impact on labor markets of the imposition of minimum wage legislation.

____

____

____

____

____

____

____

____

____

____

7. In view of the economic impacts discussed above, explain why government would institute minimum wage legislation.

____

____

____

____

____

____

____

____

8. In 1985, union **membership** amounted to approximately __________ % of the civilian labor force.

9. In 1978, about ________% of Canada's union members were women. By 1988, this percentage had increased to approximately ________%.

10. Canada's largest union is ____.

11. The two basic types of unions are ____

____.

12. Historically, the first unions to emerge were ________________________________

because ____

____.

13. By 1985, over _______ % of government employees were unionized.

14. The three levels of union organization are:

(a) ____

(b) ____

(c) ____

15. In Canada, contract negotiations are generally undertaken by which level of union? ________

____

16. State whether each of the following types of employment is characterized by a relatively high degree of unionization.

____ (a) government employment

____ (b) manufacturing

____ (c) service industries

____ (d) construction

____ (e) transportation

____ (f) office employment

17. State the two main functions performed by union locals on behalf of their members.

(a) ____

(b) ____

18. The decision whether to join a labor union (i.e., form a union "local") is made by

____

____

19. At the Pungent Perfume Company, workers have the choice of whether or not to actually become members of the union, but all workers must pay union dues (which are deducted by payroll checkoff). The company has a(n) "__________________________".

20. Under a closed shop agreement, the employer agrees that ______________________

____

____.

21. The closed shop is most common in ______________________________________. unions.

22. Under an open shop

(a) only union members can be hired.

(b) workers may choose whether or not to join the union, but all must pay dues.

(c) workers have no job security.

(d) workers may choose whether or not to join the union and pay dues.

(e) it is a condition of employment that all workers join the union after a certain number of days.

23. The Precision Pencil Company can hire either union or non-union workers, but any non-union workers who are hired must join the union in 30 days or lose their jobs. The Precision Pencil Company has a(n)

(a) open shop

(b) Rand Formula

(c) closed shop

(d) union shop

(e) illegal agreement with its union.

24. Which of the four possible union security clauses places the union in the **strongest** position in dealing with the employer, and why? ______________________________

____

____

____

25. Which of the four possible union security clauses places the union in the **weakest** position in dealing with the employer, and why? ______________________________

____

____

____

26. If an employer violates the terms of its contract (collective agreement) with its union (for instance, in the disciplining of employees), the union is legally empowered to ______________

____

27. In Canada, a strike or lockout is legal

(a) any time there is dispute between a union and an employer.

(b) only after the contract has expired, the conciliation process has concluded and the cooling-off period required by the law has passed.

(c) as soon as the conciliation process has concluded.

(d) as soon as the existing contract (collective agreement) between the union and employer has expired.

(e) none of the above.

28. State whether each of the following statements regarding strikes is **TRUE** or **FALSE**.

____ (a) They are totally negative in character; they serve no useful purpose in our industrial relations system.

____ (b) They play an important role in our industrial relations system because the fear of a strike forces both the employer and the union to compromise in contract negotiations.

____ (c) Most employers would prefer a system in which strikes are outlawed and unresolved contract disputes are submitted to an arbitrator for a final decision.

____ (d) They impose very heavy economic costs on society in terms of lost output.

____ (e) Strikes by government employees constitute a more serious problem than strikes in the private sector.

29. The proportion of union-management contract negotiations that is settled by negotiation and without a strike is generally ________ %.

30. The percentage of total worker-hours worked in the Canadian economy that is lost due to strikes is in most years about ______________________________.

31. Which statement best describes the general attitudes of unions and management to a legal ban on all strikes?

(a) Both favor outlawing strikes because this would eliminate costly strikes.

(b) Employers generally favor such a move, but unions are reluctant to approve it.

(c) Unions generally favor such a move, but employers are reluctant to approve it.

(d) Both dislike such a move because it would require both of them to turn over to an arbitrator the right to decide issues of vital importance to them.

32. Which of the following best describes the nature and extent of labor unions' power over wages?

(a) It depends on the economic circumstances of the employer and the industry. In some cases, unions are able to increase wages substantially, while in others the extent of wage increases is severely limited by conditions in the market for the employer's product or by its ability to substitute capital for labor.

(b) It is very strong. Most unions are virtually able to dictate wages as well as other terms of employment to employers because if the employer does not agree to the union's demands, it will suffer a strike which would be even costlier than yielding to the union's demands.

(c) It is quite weak. Only a few unions have any significant effect on wages, which are decided almost completely by the economic forces of supply and demand, which the union cannot alter.

(d) It depends on the size of the union. Larger unions (i.e., with more members) are better able to get big wage increases because the larger the union, the stronger it will be in a strike. Smaller unions tend to be left behind.

(e) It depends on the size of the employer. Smaller businesses must pay higher wages than larger ones because they are less able to resist union demands.

33. Two factors which limit the ability of unions to increase wages are:

(a) ____

____;

(b) ____

____.

34. Three sources of the unusually high wages/wage increases won by some unions are:

(a) ____;

(b) ____;

(c) ____.

35. The best estimate of the overall effect of unions on wages is that, on average, unions have increased the wages of their members by about _____% above the levels that would have prevailed without unions.

36. Should the employer and the union fail to resolve their dispute themselves through the procedure referred to in the previous question, the dispute will finally be resolved by

____

____.

37. Compulsory conciliation refers to:

(a) the legal requirement that all unresolved grievances of workers (i.e., alleged violations of the collective agreement by the employer) be submitted to a referee for a final decision, to prevent strikes over them.

(b) a procedure in which, by law, government-appointed official(s) must attempt to help employers and unions avoid a strike by reaching a negotiated agreement before a strike occurs.

(c) a legal requirement that a government official from the Ministry of Labour must make final decisions on all disputes between unions and employers.

(d) a procedure in which a government-appointed official makes a binding decision concerning a contract dispute involving a group of essential workers who cannot legally strike.

(e) none of the above.

38. In public services which are considered to be essential, how are union-management disputes over contract negotiations resolved?

____

____

____

39. Two problems with the process referred to in the previous question are:

(a) ____

____;

(b) ____

____.

40. "Multinational employees should belong to an international union."

AGREE or DISAGREE?

Why? ____

Chapter 14

THE DISTRIBUTION OF INCOME AND EMPLOYMENT

This chapter more fully examines economic and social aspects of labor markets. Income distribution is a key issue, both on an occupational and a regional basis. The topic of poverty is also treated here.

The distribution of employment also is examined, including issues of pay equity, women in the work force, and changes in the nature of work as a result of technological and demand changes.

General Learning Objective

Examine the distribution of income in Canada with special attention to the problem of poverty, and observe the trends in employment resulting from changes in technology and demand.

Specific Learning Objectives

	Self-Test Reference
1. Recognize the wide differences in incomes among various occupational groups	# 1
2. Observe the pattern of distribution of incomes among different income groups over the past thirty years	# 2-4
3. Compare low income cut offs established by Statistics Canada with those established by the Canadian Council on Social Development.	# 5-6
4. Identify people living in poverty by (a) age (b) education (c) sex/family structure and (d) region	# 7-8
5. Measure the extent of poverty in Canada and observe the progress made in reducing it	# 9
6. Recognize the changing trends in the proportion of people employed in agriculture, manufacturing, services, and public administration	# 10-12
7. Examine the issue of male-female pay equity	# 13-16

		Self-Test Reference
8.	Examine the causes of the employment trends in the sectors identified above, from both the demand side and the supply side	# 17-20
9.	Appraise the effect of technological change on unemployment	# 21-22
10.	Consider future trends affecting the labor force and employment demands	# 23-24

Self-Test

1. State whether each of the following statements regarding occupational incomes during the early 1980's is **TRUE** or **FALSE**.

   ____ (a) On average, self-employed doctors and surgeons earned over twice the salaries paid to teachers and professors.

   ____ (b) Average incomes of farmers and fishermen were less than half those of self-employed engineers and architects.

   ____ (c) Provincial and municipal government employees' salaries averaged slightly higher than federal government employees.

   ____ (d) Self-employed entertainers and artists averaged among the top income earners of all professions.

2. In Canada, the top 20% of families receive roughly _______% of the total income, while the bottom 20% of families receive about ______% of total income.

3. Statistically, a family consisting of a married couple with one wage earner, children, and the husband being 35 years of age with a high school education, would most likely be in

   (a) the lowest income group.

   (b) the middle income group.

   (c) the highest income group.

   (d) a group not described by any of the above.

4. One way to measure the distribution of income is to record the shares of total income received by the highest-income 20% of families, the second-highest 20%, etc. down to the lowest 20%. According to this measure, the distribution of income in Canada over the past 30 years has

   (a) become considerably more equal.

   (b) not changed to a significant extent.

   (c) become considerably more unequal.

5. A widely-used definition of "poverty" in Canada based on Statistics Canada's low income cut-offs is

   (a) all families in the lowest 20% of income-earners.

   (b) all families in the lowest 10% of income-earners.

   (c) all families with a total income below $10 000 per year.

   (d) all families whose income is less than half the national average income for all families.

   (e) all families which spend more than 58.5% of their income on basic necessities (food, clothing and shelter).

6. Poverty lines established by the Canadian Council on Social Development differ from Statistics Canada's low-income cut-offs in that ______________________________

   ____.

7. List four groups among which poverty is relatively common.

   (a) ______________________________

   (b) ______________________________

   (c) ______________________________

   (d) ______________________________

8. Poverty in Canada is most severe in

   (a) British Columbia.

   (b) the Prairies.

   (c) Ontario.

(d) Quebec.

(e) the Atlantic provinces.

9. Between the early 1960's and the early 1980's, poverty in Canada

(a) showed a steady decline and is still continuing to drop.

(b) increased significantly, as unemployment became more serious.

(c) declined significantly until 1981, then showed an increase.

(d) decreased among family units, but rose among unattached individuals.

10. State whether each of the following describes trends in the distribution of employment in Canada.

____ (a) Employment in the service industries has been increasing faster than employment in the goods industries.

____ (b) Blue-collar production workers have comprised a declining percentage of the labor force.

____ (c) Agricultural employment has remained almost stable.

____ (d) White-collar employment has been increasing faster than blue-collar employment.

____ (e) Employment has been rising rapidly in the service-industry sector of the economy.

11. The changes in the labor force described in the preceding question have been largely caused by:

(a) ____

____;

(b) ____

____.

12. Largely as a result of the trends referred to in the previous two questions, union membership as a percentage of the labor force has in recent years tended to

____

____.

13. Studies indicate that women earn between _______ and _______% of what men earn for full-time work.

14. The difference between incomes of men and women is partly explained by economic factors such as ____,
and by productivity factors including __________, __________,and ________________.

15. The major gender factor explaining the male-female wage gap is referred to as __________
____

16. Approximately 77 percent of female employees work in five occupational groups:

(a) ____

(b) ____

(c) ____

(d) ____

(e) ____

17. In order to sustain their growth, unions are anxious to recruit ________________
________________ as union members.

18. The changes in demand for labor in the manufacturing and agricultural sectors has resulted from

(a) fewer agricultural and manufacturing goods being demanded by consumers.

(b) an increase in the demand for manufactured products, but a decrease in the demand for agricultural products.

(c) the extensive technological changes that have altered production methods in manufacturing and agriculture.

(d) all of the above.

19. As living standards increase, Canadians tend to

(a) spend more on services, thereby creating employment opportunities in service industries.

(b) increase consumption of food products, creating more jobs in agriculture.

(c) reduce their spending on manufactured goods.

(d) spend their increases in incomes proportionately on food products, manufactured goods, and services.

20. During the 1970's and up to the mid-1980's,

(a) the percentage of elderly people participating in the labor force rose substantially.

(b) there has been a continuing trend for a larger proportion of young Canadians in the labor force.

(c) the most dramatic development in the labor force was an increase in the participation rate by women.

(d) all groups have shown decreases in their participation rate in the labor force.

21. In the 1980's, it is forecast that the labor force will grow more ______________________ ______________________ than in the 1970's, that the proportion of women in the labor force will ____________, that the average age of workers will ____________, and that there will be ____________ of skilled workers.

22. The danger of jobs being lost as a result of technological changes is often offset by the following:

(a) ____

____;

(b) ____

____.

23. The (15-24) age group in the labor force had reached a high of ________% in 1979, but by 1989 had become ________%.

24. Through the 1990's, the female participation rate is expected to ______________________, while the male participation rate is expected to ______________________.

Chapter 15

GOVERNMENT AND THE ECONOMY

This chapter deals with various aspects of the role of government in the economy, describing a variety of government activities, aspects of government tax revenues and expenditures, recent deficits and the 1989 tax reform; including changes to marginal tax rates, tax credits as opposed to tax deductions and the new proposed sales tax (Goods and Services Tax).

For almost half a century, the growth of the role of government generally was regarded as beneficial, because it remedied economic problems and, thus, yielded favourable results. However, more recently, increases in government spending, taxation and borrowing came to be associated with the deteriorating performance of the economy. Thus serious concerns were raised over the extent of government involvement in the economy and the size of the federal deficit.

Although the years 1984-1988 saw minor reductions in the deficit, projections indicated substantial future increases in light of modest cuts in federal expenditures. Thus, by 1988, major efforts being identified to prevent excessive increases in the deficit, including selling off federal Crown corporations and instituting major tax reforms.

During the early part of the 1980's, there was a strong reliance on income tax as a source of federal government revenue but recently the federal sales tax has been growing in importance. The text examines both positive and negative impacts from the traditional federal sales tax.

The section on tax reform examines the 1988 changes in marginal tax rates, the system of tax credits, and the controversial Goods and Services Tax.

General Learning Objective

Identify the nature of government involvement in today's economy.

Specific Learning Objectives

		Self-Test Reference
1.	Explain the rationale for increased government spending over the past three decades	# 1-7
2.	Discuss the nature of fiscal arrangements in Canada	# 8-9
3.	Review the challenges confronting Canada's social welfare system	# 10-16
4.	Propose policy options for controlling federal expenditures	# 17-22
5.	Identify problems in federal spending reductions	# 23-26
6.	Appraise tax reform options	#27-36

Self-Test

1. Total spending (including transfer payments) by all levels of government in Canada has risen dramatically over the past three decades. From 1950 to 1980, total government spending (as a percentage of GDP) ________ from about ___% to about ___%.

2. Government involvement in the economy may be said to be limited to __________________, ______________________ and ____________________________; provided the regulator role and the many activities undertaken by __________________ are excluded.

3. Regulation may be defined as ____
____
____
____.

4. The three largest categories of government spending in Canada (for all three levels of government combined) are:

   (a) ____;

   (b) ____;

   (c) ____.

5. Which of the following is not an example of an income security program?

(a) Old Age and Blind Pensions

(b) Family Allowances

(c) Quebec Pension Plan

(d) Canada Savings Bond Interest

(e) Unemployment Insurance

6. The indexing of government transfer payments to individuals (such as family allowances, pensions, and unemployment insurance benefits) means that if the Consumer Price Index ________________, these benefits will ________________ proportionately.

7. State at least five reasons for the substantial growth in spending on income security, health care and education programs over the last few decades.

(a) ________________

(b) ________________

(c) ________________

(d) ________________

(e) ________________

8. By far the greatest portion of government expenditures is on ________________ programs.

9. State whether each of the following statements is **TRUE** or **FALSE**.

____ (a) The federal government lacks the taxing authority to raise sufficient revenues to finance all of its expenditures.

____ (b) Federal government spending has in recent decades expanded more rapidly than has spending by provincial and municipal governments.

____ (c) Generally, provincial governments tend to be the wealthiest of all three levels of government.

____ (d) City governments are very severely strained financially due to their extensive spending requirements and their very limited authority to levy taxes.

____ (e) The federal government is responsible for funding education, health and welfare programs throughout Canada.

____ (f) The federal government has shown an interest in reducing its expenditures on health care and education by limiting increases to the rate of increase in GNP.

10. Four basic criticisms of Canada's social welfare system are:

(a) ____;

(b) ____;

(c) ____;

(d) ____.

11. State whether each of the following statements regarding Canada's welfare system is **TRUE** or **FALSE.**

____ (a) If the bureaucracy supporting Canada's welfare system were eliminated, every Canadian household below the poverty line could potentially receive an annual subsidy in excess of an annual minimum wage income.

____ (b) The principle of universality ensures that all Canadians can share equally in the benefits accrued from Canada's health care programs.

____ (c) Generally, it encourages welfare recipients to seek work.

____ (d) Unemployment insurance contributes to high-unemployment and low-wage regions.

____ (e) An increase in the minimum wage rate can actually contribute to unemployment by encouraging labor-force drop-outs to seek work.

12. The major way in which our welfare system reduces the incentive of welfare recipients to work is that:

(a) welfare benefits are so high that many people actually gain greatly economically by quitting work and going on welfare.

(b) people on welfare are not permitted to seek work.

(c) welfare agencies and social workers encourage people to remain on welfare rather than to seek employment.

(d) there are no government agencies to help those on welfare to find employment.

(e) if a welfare recipient earns money by working, his/her welfare is reduced by so much that he/she has little economic incentive to work.

13. Ernie, an accountant, earns $30 000 per year, on which he pays income tax of $7000. If Ernie takes on extra work as a night school teacher, he will earn an **additional** $6000, on which he will pay **additional** income taxes of $1800. From this, we can conclude that Ernie's marginal tax rate is ______ %.

14. Generally speaking, high marginal tax rates tend to

(a) reduce the incentive to work.

(b) not affect the incentive to work.

(c) reduce the incentive to save and invest.

(d) (a) and (c) together.

(e) increase the incentive to work.

15. When all taxes are considered, Canada's tax system is quite progressive. **TRUE OR FALSE?**

Why? ____

____

____

16. Describe the net effect of government programs (including both taxes and government spending) on the distribution of income among Canadian families.

____

____

____

____

____

____

____

____

____

____

17. Canada's rising debt and its contributing deficits are a concern to many Canadians because:

(a) ____;

(b) ____;

(c) ____;

(d) ____

____

____.

18. State whether each of the following suggestions could serve as a possible means of reducing Canada's deficit.

____ (a) Target social expenditures to those who need them the most.

____ (b) Offer incentives to save, work and invest.

____ (c) Tax consumption.

____ (d) Implement a national guaranteed minimum income program.

____ (e) Increase eligibility requirements and reduce benefits.

19. State three major advantages which the Guaranteed Minimum Income is claimed to have over the present welfare system.

(a) ____

(b) ____

(c) ____

20. "The only really effective way to combat poverty in Canada is to increase taxes on the rich dramatically so as to provide the funds required for massive redistribution of income from the rich to the poor."

TRUE OR FALSE?

Why? ____

____

____

21. "We do not believe that the funds necessary to maintain and improve these programs cannot be found. The federal government did not need to spend more than $1 billion for the bank bail-out. It did not have to give more than $2 billion in capital gains exemptions and other tax breaks which favor the healthy and wealthy. It gave more than $1.6 billion in corporate income tax reductions and another $3.3 billion to increase defence spending by 35% by 1990-91. We believe a just and fair tax system would provide the money necessary, not only to maintain post-secondary education and health programs at present levels, but to provide more than enough to bring them up to the standard in many of the developed countries of this world."

David Orlikow, MP
Wpg. North
House of Commons Debate
June 12, 1986

AGREE or DISAGREE?

____

____

____

____

____

____

22. During the period 1984 to 1988, government spending (as a percentage of GDP) showed a(n) ____________ from ____% to ____%.

23. A major obstacle to proposed reductions in spending in the areas of pensions and unemployment insurance has been ______________________________

24. In the 1989 federal budget, tax increases outweighed spending cutbacks by a ratio of about ____________________.

25. In 1989, the federal government announced a proposed ________________ to replace the existing federal tax on manufactured goods.

26. The federal government entered the 1990's with budget deficits of about ______________ each year.

27. Governments can raise tax revenues (generally) by taxing ________________, ________________, and ________________.

28. Excessively high tax rates on business profits can reduce ______________________________ ______________________________.

29. The impact of a sales tax is particularly burdensome for ________-income people. Such taxes are ______________ taxes.

30. Property taxes are considered to be ______________ taxes.

31. In 1950, the personal income tax provided about __________% of all federal government revenues. By the 1980's, over ______% of federal revenues came from that source.

32. List the three major aspects of the 1989 federal government proposals for tax reforms.

(a) ______________________________

____

(b) ______________________________

____

(c) ______________________________

____

33. Discuss major advantages and disadvantages of federal sales taxes.

____

____

____

____

____

____

____

____

____

34. The objective of adopting the tax credit system was to ______________________________

____

35. The stated objective of the proposed Goods and Services Tax was ______________________

____

____

36. The following table illustrates several of the stages of production for an automobile. Based on a 7% GST (as proposed in 1989) fill in the blank under the Tax, Rebate, and Net Tax Columns.

Seller	**Buyer**	**Price**	**Tax**	**Rebate**	**Net Tax**
Iron Ore Producer	Steel Producer	$1000	___	___	___
Steel Producer	Car Manufacturer	5000	___	___	___
Car Manufacturer	Car Dealer	10 000	___	___	___
Car Dealer	Consumer	16 000	___	___	___

Chapter 16

THE POLITICS OF ECONOMICS

This chapter examines the relationship between politics and economics. Discussion focuses on different philosophies, which usually are described as "right-wing" or "left-wing" and how these philosophies apply to economic issues.

The main beliefs of both sides are described, indicating that right-wingers generally favor the operation of free markets, while left-wingers lack faith in free markets as a means of achieving prosperity.

Solutions to economic problems are presented, from both perspectives, with particular reference to business enterprise, profits, investment income, the distribution of income, social welfare, labor unions, and the role of government.

General Learning Objective

Distinguish between right-wing and left-wing philosophies as applied to specific economic issues.

Specific Learning Objectives

	Self-Test Reference
1. Understand the meaning of right-wing and left-wing as applied to economic issues	# 1-6
2. Recognize right-wing and left-wing solutions to economic problems	# 7-14
3. Recognize the accepted role of government under right-wing and left-wing philosophies	# 15-18
4. Describe changing trends in philosophies concerning economic issues	# 19-24

Self-Test

1. Right-wingers exhibit a strong belief in

(a) ______________________________;

(b) ______________________________;

(c) ______________________________.

2. Therefore, the best solution to economic problems is provided through

____

____

3. Economic efficiency is encouraged through the ______________________________ of the private sector.

4. Left-wingers maintain that the free market system is ______________________________

______________________________.

5. They argue that the benefits of economic prosperity basically will accrue to

______________________________.

6. To counteract this problem, left-wingers advocate ______________________________

____

______________________________.

7. A more collective approach to economic issues is stressed by the ______________________________ __________ wingers.

8. Profits are viewed as an incentive for efficiency by the ______________________________ wingers.

9. Relatively heavy taxation of profits is favored by ______________________________ wingers.

10. Right-wingers maintain that income from financial investments provides ________________
____
____
____.

11. The ________________ wingers consider that consumer sovereignty is an important factor in deciding what gets produced.

12. Left-wingers argue that incomes (do/do not) measure people's contribution to society.

13. Left-wingers believe government should redistribute incomes through the use of ____________
____ and ______________________________.

14. Labor unions generally find greater support among the ______________________________
wingers, because ____
____
____
____
____.

15. ____________________ wingers favor government policies to protect workers and consumers against ____.

16. A continued growth of government and policies to redistribute income and regulate business is considered by right wingers as a move toward ______________________________________.

17. A laissez-faire approach falls within the realm of the ______________________________ wingers.

18. Excessive government borrowing tends to ____________ interest rates, which ____________ business capital investment and __________ economic growth.

19. The long-term trend has been toward the ________________________________ wing position.

20. In Canada, from the mid-1960's to the mid-1970's, the role of government ________________
____.

21. By the mid-1980's federal policy in Canada had become more ___________________________
_______ wing in nature.

22. By the mid-1980's, the federal government in Canada was directing its efforts to control ____
_________________, while at the same time trying to improve _____________________________
____
____

23. Identify briefly the federal government's approach to economic policy during the mid-1980's and discuss the proposed impact of that policy.

____
____
____
____
____
____
____

24. How would provincial rightwingers and leftwingers likely respond to federal cutbacks in medicare and post-secondary education over the next few years?

____
____
____
____
____
____
____
____
____

Chapter 17

THE ECONOMICS AND POLITICS OF OIL

Chapter 17 presents a long story, but the background included is necessary in order to develop an understanding of the oil situation in Canada. A basic conceptual point in this chapter is that the supply of oil is not a **physical** concept (a continually depleting pool of oil reserves), as people tend to think, but rather an **economic** concept (the volume of oil offered for sale, which depends on the **price** of oil and the **technology** available). Thus the supply of oil can be influenced by factors such as trends in the world price of oil, technological changes and government policies, particularly policies relating to oil and taxation.

This chapter reviews oil-policy developments and responses for the past 25 years. It zeros in on the federal government's oil-policy objectives of the mid-70's and highlights the conflicts between these objectives of low prices, high tax revenues and security of supply. It then uses these policy choices as a framework for analyzing Canada's National Energy Program (NEP) of the early 80's, the subsequent policy changes made to it in 1981 and the eventual abandonment of the NEP in light of falling world oil prices in the mid-80's.

General Learning Objective

Discuss the major factors that influence the supply of oil available to Canadians.

Specific Learning Objectives

		Self-Test Reference
1.	State who sets the price of Canadian oil in Canada	# 1-2
2.	Explain the impact of changing world oil prices on the Canadian economy	# 3-7, # 14-16, # 22
3.	Analyze the federal government's policy responses to OPEC price increases of 1973	# 8-13
4.	Evaluate the effectiveness of Canada's controversial National Energy Policy of the early 1980's	# 17-21
5.	Outline the policy dilemma facing Canadian policy-makers in 1986 as world oil prices collapsed	# 23-26

Self-Test

1. In Canada, crude oil reserves located within the provinces are owned by

____.

2. State whether each of the following statements regarding the pricing of crude oil in Canada is **TRUE** or **FALSE.**

____ (a) Each provincial government decides the price of its own oil.

____ (b) The governments of the oil-producing provinces negotiate a uniform price for all to follow.

____ (c) The governments of the oil-producing provinces negotiate the price of oil with the federal government.

____ (d) If the governments of the oil-producing provinces and the federal government are unable to agree on the price of oil, the federal government has the authority to decide the price.

____ (e) The federal government decides the price of oil.

____ (f) The oil companies decide the price of oil.

3. During the 1980's, Canada produced approximately ______ % of its oil requirements and imported approximately ______ %.

4. Under the National Oil Policy (NOP) of 1961,

(a) some of Alberta's oil production was to be exported to the United States.

(b) the Canadian market west of Quebec was to use Alberta oil, which was more expensive than imports until 1973.

(c) (a) and (b).

(d) imports of oil were to be kept to an absolute minimum.

(e) Canadian oil prices were to be held below world prices.

5. State whether each of the following statements is **TRUE** or **FALSE**. In 1973-74, the world's major oil exporting nations (organized into the Organization of Petroleum Exporting Countries, or OPEC)

____ (a) announced that the price of their oil would in the future be linked directly ("indexed") to the Consumer Price Index, so that it would rise at the same pace as the Consumer Price Index.

____ (b) succeeded in nearly doubling the price of their oil.

____ (c) implemented the first of many planned major production cutbacks which would ensure that oil prices would rise steadily thereafter.

____ (d) reached an agreement to nearly quadruple the price of their oil.

____ (e) succeeded in restricting the sale of their oil to Europeans.

6. The international influence of OPEC on world oil markets was a concern to Canadian policy-makers because

(a) ____;

(b) ____

____;

(c) ____

____.

7. Provincial policy-makers argued that the economic benefits accrued from rising oil values should go to oil producers.

TRUE or **FALSE?**

Why? ____

____

8. Following OPEC's price increases of 1973-74, the Canadian government's oil-pricing policy was to

(a) keep Canadian oil prices far below world (OPEC) levels.

(b) raise Canadian oil prices gradually to world (OPEC) levels.

(c) raise Canadian oil prices to world (OPEC) levels immediately.

(d) increase federal taxes on oil, so that the revenue from higher oil prices would go to the federal government rather than to the oil industry.

(e) (b) and (d) together.

9. State whether each of the following statements is **TRUE** or **FALSE**.

In response to the increased price of imported oil after 1973, Canada's federal government

____ (a) raised federal taxes on oil consumers, to ensure that the funds from higher oil prices would be of benefit to all Canadians.

____ (b) began to phase out oil exports to the United States.

____ (c) extended the western oil pipeline to Montreal so as to use more Alberta oil (and less imported oil) in Eastern Canada.

____ (d) placed a tax on oil exports to the USA to bring the price of Canadian oil up to the world prices.

____ (e) raised taxes on oil, to encourage consumers to conserve oil.

10. Critics of the federal government's controversial oil policy of the mid-seventies claimed:

(a) ____;

(b) ____;

(c) ____.

11. State whether each of the following statements concerning the Athabasca Tar Sands is **TRUE** or **FALSE**.

____ (a) The Tar Sands contain 300 to 400 years' oil supply for Canada at 1980 rates of use.

____ (b) Plants to extract and process oil from the Tar Sands require tremendous capital investment--over $13 billion each in the early 1980's.

____ (c) Tar Sands oil is much more costly than "conventional" oil

____ (d) In the federal government's plans drawn up in the early 1980's, the Tar Sands represented an important element in Canada's future oil supplies.

____ (e) It was a certainty that the Tar Sands would represent an economical source of oil in the 1980's.

12. State the three basic objectives of government oil policy in Canada as Canada entered the 1980s.

    (a) ____

    (b) ____

    (c) ____

13. Explain the conflicts between the policy goals described in the previous question.

    ____

    ____

    ____

    ____

    ____

    ____

    ____

    ____

14. State whether each of the following statements is **TRUE** or **FALSE**. As a result of the situation described in the previous question,

    ____ (a) world oil prices increased dramatically in late 1973 and early 1974.

    ____ (b) the period from 1974 to 1978 was characterized by oil surpluses on world markets and slowly rising prices.

    ____ (c) the real price of oil remained constant after 1973, as oil prices rose at the same pace as the Consumer Price Index.

    ____ (d) the rest of the 1970's was characterized by oil shortages and rapidly rising prices in most years.

    ____ (e) real oil prices (that is, adjusted for inflation) actually fell from 1974 to 1978.

15. In the late 1970's, the federal government's policy regarding oil pricing was complicated by the fact that

    (a) there were supply interruptions due to political instability or war in the Middle East.

    (b) OPEC succeeded in 1979-80 in achieving a major increase in the price of its oil, making imported oil much more expensive.

(c) there was increasing political pressure on the government from the Canadian public to abandon its policy on oil prices.

(d) (a) and (b) together.

(e) (a), (b) and (c) together.

16. As a result of the development(s) described in the previous question

    (a) the Canadian government decided to move Canadian oil prices to world (OPEC) levels.

    (b) the cost of subsidizing imported oil so as to keep it artificially cheap became extremely high, adding to the government's massive budget deficits.

    (c) the Canadian government's oil-pricing policy had become unrealistic and unsustainable.

    (d) (a) and (b) together.

    (e) (b) and (c) together.

17. State whether each of the following was an aspect of the federal government's National Energy Program (NEP) passed in the fall of 1980.

    ____ (a) A large increase in federal government tax revenues from oil and gas.

    ____ (b) Increased Canadian ownership of the oil and gas industry.

    ____ (c) A shift in oil exploration away from areas under provincial jurisdiction and toward areas under federal jurisdiction.

    ____ (d) Rapid increases in the price of conventional Alberta crude oil over the 1981-85 period.

    ____ (e) Reduced dependence on imported oil supplies.

18. Under the NEP, according to federal calculations, the federal government's share of oil revenues would rise from ______ % to ______%, mainly at the expense of a reduced share of revenues for ____.

19. Under the NEP, Canadian ownership of the oil and gas industry was to change from _____ % in 1980 to _____ % in 1990.

20. State whether each of the following statements is **TRUE** or **FALSE**.

The security objectives of the NEP were to be achieved by

____ (a) offering incentives to substitute natural gas for oil in home heating.

____ (b) revisions to the taxation and incentive system for oil companies which would induce foreign-owned firms to sell shares to Canadians and to take on Canadian firms as partners.

____ (c) takeovers of oil and gas firms by Petro-Can, the federally owned oil company.

____ (d) offering grants to explore for oil in frontier or offshore areas under federal jurisdiction.

21. State whether each of the following was a feature of the September 1981 agreement on oil pricing and taxation reached by the Alberta and federal governments.

____ (a) It provided for much more rapid price increases than those set by the NEP.

____ (b) It increased Alberta's projected tax revenues over the term of the agreement.

____ (c) the rest of the 1970's was characterized by oil shortages and rapidly rising prices in most years.

22. State whether each of the following statements is **TRUE** or **FALSE**.

As world oil prices fell in the eighties,

____ (a) there was some uncertainty as to the future level of Canadian oil prices, since the price of Canadian oil was to be capped at 75% of the world price, which was itself uncertain.

____ (b) two important Tar Sands projects were cancelled as the result of low oil prices and high Canadian interest rates.

____ (c) Canadian oil self-sufficiency by 1990 was virtually assured.

____ (d) Canadian policy-makers were forced to rethink the provisions of the Alberta-Ottawa agreement of 1981.

____ (e) OPEC tried to support prices by cutting output but Saudi Arabia broke ranks and helped to keep oil prices low by increasing its output.

____ (f) the federal government chose to maintain essential NEP directives of grants and price controls and abandon its taxation initiatives.

____ (g) the Canadian oil industry's plans for major oil exploration and development were jeopardized.

23. The 1986 world oil-price collapse

(a) seriously undermined policy initiatives aimed at achieving oil self-sufficiency.

(b) benefited Canadian consumers by increasing their disposable income spent on consumer goods and services.

(c) was believed to be a Saudi Arabian plot to discipline members of OPEC.

(d) was possibly the result of a combined effort by OPEC nations to expand their market share of world oil sales.

(e) all of the above.

24. Canada's oil policy legacy of the past decade appears to have been

____

____

____

____

____.

25. Canadian drivers are probably no better or worse off than in the sixties, but probably worse off than they were in the seventies.

TRUE or **FALSE**?

Why? ____

____

____

____

____

____

____

____.

26. Petro-Can represents the most ambitious government enterprise ever undertaken in Canada. It is involved extensively in oil exploration and gasoline retailing. Was it worth it? Give reasons for your response.

Chapter 18

ENVIRONMENTAL ECONOMICS

Environment problems have been with us for a long time and pollution in particular is not a recent phenomenon. But during the late sixties and the early seventies, environmental awareness and concern about pollution was on the rise. Governments across Canada joined the crusade to 'save the environment' and initiated steps to try and protect it. The majority of politicians responded to our concerns by passing environmental legislation of one sort or another. Many provinces went one step further and created quasi-judicial agencies to fight and/or regulate polluters. But, environmental concerns took second place to the economic priorities of severe inflation in the late seventies and unemployment in the early eighties. Only of late has the environment emerged as a major public issue. Unfortunately, Canadians still seem to be preoccupied with who's to blame, rather than focusing on causes and remedies. There are still strong incentives to pollute and government has been reluctant to take any really serious action against polluters. Canadians want a cleaner environment. They may be ready to incur the costs of a clean-up. Many Canadians are trying to do something about protecting our environment. If we don't succeed nothing else will matter.

General Learning Objective

Explore the nature of environmental concerns confronting Canada today.

Specific Learning Objectives

	Self-Test Reference
1. Identify Canada's major environmental concerns	# 1
2. Examine the costs/benefits associated with pollution	# 2-6
3. Review environmental practices and incentives	# 7-12
4. Evaluate the alternatives for dealing with pollution	#13-15

Self-Test

1. State whether each of the following statements is **TRUE** or **FALSE**.

    ____ (a) The major environmental problem of the 1960's was acid rain.

    ____ (b) Canadians tend to blame industry rather than themselves for pollution.

    ____ (c) It pays to pollute.

    ____ (d) Pollution is more a matter of negligence than anything else.

2. Define

    (a) private costs ______________________________

    ____

    (b) social costs______________________________

    ____

3. The following is an example of a social cost.

    (a) wages, salaries, rents, dividends

    (b) leasehold improvements

    (c) sulphur dioxide emissions

    (d) interest payments on corporate debentures

4. A socially responsible producer will try to (minimize/maximize) their internal costs while trying to (minimize/maximize) their external costs.

5. An externality is defined as ______________________________

    ____

6. Which of the following are examples of externalities?

    ____ (a) loud "rock and roll" music

    ____ (b) industrial air pollution

____ (c) exhaust emissions from automobiles

____ (d) a new treatment for AIDS

____ (e) public school education

7. The government's role with regard to pollution is that of a ______________________________

____.

8. Explain why the government has been reluctant to take action against polluters.

____

____

____

____

____

____

____

____

9. "Fighting pollution will result in a poorer standard of living for Canadians." Discuss.

____

____

____

____

____

____

____

____

____

____

10. The trade off between environmentally friendly and harmful products may be illustrated by using ________________ ________________ curve.

11. The cost of reducing sulphur dioxide would cost the average Canadian about $20 annually. Would it be asking Canadians too much to give up the cost of a good dinner? Discuss.

____

____

____

____

____

____

____

____

12. As one industrialist put it, "it's simply too expensive to eliminate pollution, totally." Explain.

____

____

____

____

____

____

____

13. Cost/benefit analysis can help regulators to determine

(a) ____

(b) ____

(c) ____

14. State whether each of the following statements is **TRUE** or **FALSE**.

____ (a) 1% of Canada's labor force is employed in the environmental industry.

____ (b) Setting limits on emissions is the most effective way of dealing with polluters.

____ (c) Fines generally discourage polluters.

____ (d) A tax on polluters facing inelastic demand puts the burden of pollution clean-up on the consumer.

____ (e) Class action suits would be an effective means of curbing pollution.

____ (f) Individual lawsuits are too expensive and take too long to be effective.

____ (g) Subsidies (or tax cuts) for polluters are justified if they can save jobs as well as the environment.

____ (h) Recycling paper undermines employment in the pulp and paper industry.

____ (i) Plants consume carbon dioxide, the more carbon dioxide the more plants, the more plants the more oxygen, so we should not be overly concerned about increases in carbon dioxide emissions.

15. Generate a list of actions you can personally take to help reduce pollution.

____

____

____

____

____

____

____

____

Chapter 19

THE AGRICULTURAL SECTOR

This chapter applies the tools of supply, demand and elasticity which were developed in earlier chapters to an important economic and social problem. In doing so, it provides another example of economic policy trade-offs, not only between the interests of consumers and of producers, but also between the goals of policies (support of farm incomes) and their side-effects (such as crop surpluses and reduced efficiency).

General Learning Objective

Analyze the problems facing agricultural producers and consider a number of possible solutions.

Specific Learning Objectives

		Self-Test Reference
1.	Recognize the importance of Canada's agricultural sector	# 1-2
2.	Demonstrate the effect of the agricultural revolution on the Canadian economy	# 3-4
3.	Using demand and supply, illustrate the reason for low farm incomes, in the face of increasing supply	# 5-7
4.	Apply the concept of demand and supply inelasticity to explain why farm incomes tend to be unstable	#8-10
5.	State the purpose of the Canadian Wheat Board and the Agricultural Stabilization Board	# 11
6.	Apply each of the following to support and stabilize farm prices or incomes:	
	(a) Offers to purchase	# 12
	(b) Acreage restriction	# 13
	(c) Deficiency payments	# 14-16

Self-Test Reference

7. Evaluate the operation of a marketing board, using the criteria of
   (a) effect on prices
   (b) efficiency of production
   (c) control of output
   (d) equity of assistance provided . . . . # 17-19

8. Discuss the merits of government programs to support and stabilize agricultural incomes imposed by government . . . . # 20

9. Consider the economic advantages of using deficiency payments to provide agricultural assistance, as compared with the establishment of marketing boards . . . . # 21

10. Evaluate the effects of Free Trade and international competition on Canadian agricultural producers . . . . # 22-25

Self-Test

1. Canada's farming industry consists mainly of

   (a) medium sized corporations.

   (b) sole proprietors, who own the land they work.

   (c) partnerships of land owners and farm operators.

   (d) large incorporated farm businesses.

2. Agricultural production in Canada amounts to

   (a) 4% of our total output, generating 5% of our total employment.

   (b) 20% of our total output, generating 25% of our total employment.

   (c) an ever increasing share of our total output.

   (d) an insignificant share of our total output.

3. As a result of the Agricultural Revolution between the 1940's and the 1980's,

   (a) the number of farms in Canada has increased.

   (b) fewer people now live on farms.

(c) productivity on farms has increased.

(d) a lower proportion of Canada's labor force is now required on farms.

(e) (b), (c), (d) above.

4. The effects of the Agricultural Revolution on Canada's economy are generally considered to be

(a) unfavorable, as they have added to our unemployment problem.

(b) beneficial, in that they have allowed workers to be transferred from agricultural production to industrial production.

(c) neutral, in that they have benefited one sector of our economy, at the expense of another.

(d) of little consequence, since agricultural output is no longer an important part of our total output.

5. Which of the following describes the historical farm problem?

(a) Farm efficiency has been high, but farm prices and incomes have been low.

(b) Farm prices and incomes have been unstable, with a tendency to decline sharply periodically.

(c) Both (a) and (b) above.

(d) Low efficiency and high-cost-per-unit operations have caused profit margins to be narrow and farm incomes to be low.

(e) Because farm efficiency has steadily improved, profit margins and farm incomes have risen faster than those in other industries.

6. State whether each of the following has been a factor contributing to the problem(s) referred to in the previous question.

____ (a) Improved farm technology has made possible great increases in agricultural efficiency.

____ (b) Farming is a highly competitive industry.

____ (c) Because Canadian farms have been small by international standards, they have lagged behind foreign competitors in efficiency, and thus suffered from foreign competition.

____ (d) Both the supply of and demand for food tend to be relatively inelastic.

____ (e) Variations in weather conditions cause the supply of many types of food to fluctuate considerably from year to year.

ANSWER THE FOLLOWING FOUR QUESTIONS ON THE BASIS OF THE FOLLOWING GRAPH:

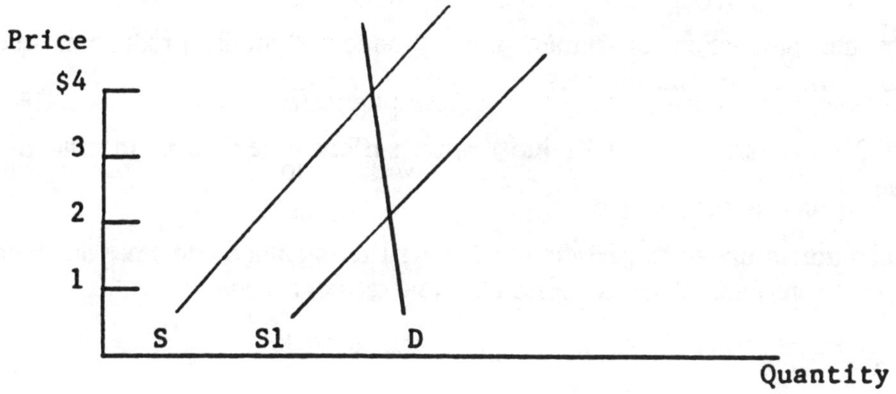

7. In the graph above, the change in supply represented by the shift from S to S1 would be caused by

(a) higher prices for wheat.

(b) a larger crop of wheat.

(c) a smaller crop of wheat.

(d) lower prices for wheat.

8. The change in supply from S to S1 would cause the price of wheat to change from $ ________ to $ __________ and cause farm incomes to ______________________________.
But if supply were to shift from S1 to S as a result of a major drought then some farm incomes would _______________.

9. This fluctuation in price is as large as it is because:

(a) demand is inelastic

(b) demand in elastic

(c) demand has decreased.

(d) demand has increased

(e) the demand for food is unusually stable

10. If the demand for wheat were more elastic, fluctuations in its price would be ______________________________.

11. The purpose of the Agricultural Stabilization Board (ASB) is to

(a) ensure than all farmers under its jurisdiction earn a reasonable profit.

(b) restrict the production of certain farm products through production quotas, and thus increase farm prices and incomes.

(c) ensure that no farmer under its jurisdiction suffers a decline in income from one year to another.

(d) prevent farmers under its jurisdiction from suffering major declines in their income when crop prices are particularly depressed by market conditions.

(e) all of the above.

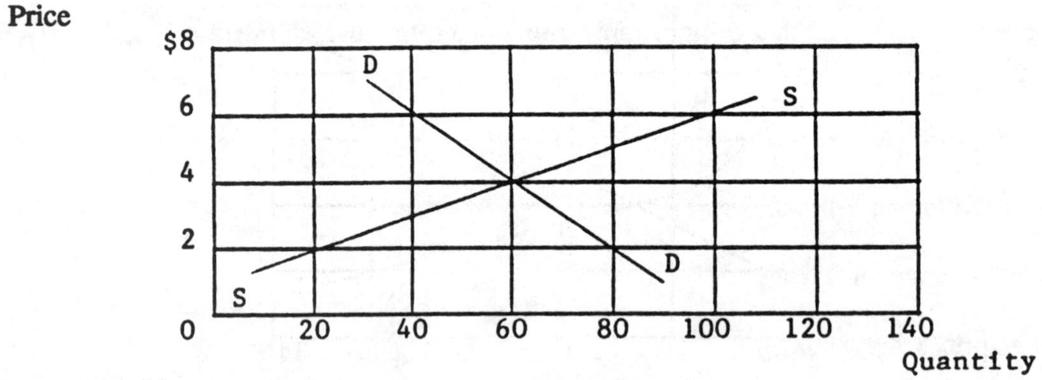

12. In the market represented by the above graph, if the government supports the price of product B at $6 by the means of offers to purchase, the result will be ______________________________

____

13. To avoid the situation described in the previous question, governments in some cases ______________________________

14. State whether each of the following accurately describes the operation of a system of deficiency payments.

____ (a) The government abandons all attempts to support farm incomes and lets them be determined freely in the marketplace, even if prices are deficient.

____ (b) The government does not buy surpluses or restrict farm output, but rather ensures through direct subsidies to farmers that they receive a predetermined price for their crops.

____ (c) The government sets up marketing boards which allocate quotas to individual farmers to ensure that prices are high enough to yield reasonable returns to the average farmer without generating surpluses of farm products.

____ (d) The government offers to buy farm products at predetermined prices and absorbs via these purchases any surpluses which may occur.

____ (e) The government guarantees farmers 90% of the average price over the past 5 years for their crops.

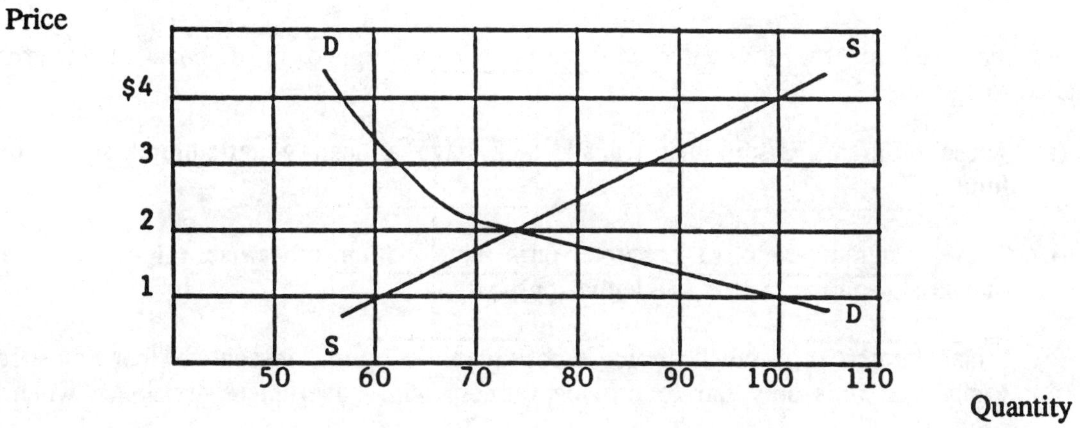

15. If a system of deficiency payments were applied to the product B market represented by the above graph, with a target price of $4, the output of product B will be ________ units and the market price will be $ _______ per unit.

16. Under the deficiency payments program described in the previous questions, the government's obligation would be to ____

____

____

17. The purpose of marketing boards is to ____

____

18. State whether each of the following is a criticism that has been made of marketing boards.

____ (a) They have failed to increase either farm prices or incomes.

____ (b) Their monopolistic power has resulted in excessively high prices.

____ (c) They limit the expansion of farms into larger, more efficient units.

____ (d) They have resulted in windfall profits for some producers.

____ (e) They keep small, inefficient farms in operation.

19. It is estimated that the practices of marketing boards cost Canadian consumers approximately $________________ per year.

20. State whether each of the following can reasonably be argued in defence of government assistance to farmers.

____ (a) These programs ensure that Canada will have a healthy agricultural sector in the future.

____ (b) These programs help to preserve farm land which otherwise might be sold for industrial, commercial or residential purposes.

____ (c) Since farmers are much more exposed to economic insecurity than most other Canadians, it is only fair to provide farmers with government assistance when it is needed.

____ (d) It is economically desirable to keep as large a proportion of the population as possible employed in the agricultural sector.

21. Under Free Trade which group has the most to lose?

(a) farmers

(b) marketing boards

(c) food processors

(d) consumers

(e) none of the above

22. What is the "international subsidy war" in agriculture all about?

____

____

____

____

23. As of 1986, the country subsidizing its producers the most is _______________.

24. If food shortages became a general concern in the future, which of the following would be the most logical way to provide assistance to farmers in those cases in which this was necessary?

(a) marketing boards

(b) acreage restriction

(c) deficiency payments

(d) offers to purchase

(e) any of the above — none would be more advantageous than the others

Explain the reason for your answer _______________

____

____

____

25. Propose an appropriate policy or group of policies for enhancing Canadian agriculture.

____

____

____

____

____

____

____

____

____

____

Chapter 20

THE SOVIET ECONOMY

The Soviet economy is a subject which students always find interesting, largely because of the myths and mysteries surrounding it and because of the differences between the Soviet economy and our own system. In addition to these fundamental and important differences, however, there are certain underlying similarities in both systems which many people find surprising, particularly the market forces that exist even in a centrally planned economy. Chapter 20 includes several examples of these, such as the use of wage differentials to attract workers into certain occupations, industries and regions and to provide incentives for work. The black markets for certain consumer goods are also examined, as are the high sales taxes placed on scarce goods to make them expensive; the parallel markets in which plant managers buy and sell materials and supplies outside of the law in order to fulfil their quotas; the "private plots" and free markets in agriculture; and the experiments with producers taking orders from retailers (and thus consumers); and plant managers being evaluated according to their profits. These examples underline the fact that economic problems are similar in all societies, that economics deals with human behaviour as expressed in decisions in the marketplace, and that these realities cannot simply be repealed by government edict. If a centrally planned system does not take basic market forces into consideration, they tend to circumvent its regulations. Thus, studying the Soviet economy is not only interesting, but also instructive regarding the basic nature of economic forces as expressed through markets.

By the mid 1970's, it was apparent to all that the Soviet economy faced enormous problems: stagnation, acute shortages of consumer goods, inefficient production methods, and low worker productivity to name a few. A new Soviet leadership launched major reform initiatives, collectively known as *perestroika*, or "restructuring," which if fully implemented will have a greater impact on the Soviet system than anything undertaken since the 1920's.

The success of the *perestroika* reforms is by no means assured. The bureaucracy, the conservative elements within the Communist Party, and the labor force are all resistant to changes which may affect their perceived privileges. Even the consumers represent a threat to *perestroika* in that they expect immediate results which cannot be realized, and have become impatient with leadership assurances that the future will be better.

General Learning Objective

Examine the Soviet Union's 70 year experiment with a Communist economic system, and indicate the direction in which current reforms are taking the country.

Specific Learning Objectives

		Self-Test Reference
1.	Identify the fundamental differences between a command economy and a market system	# 1-3
2.	Recognize four major problems associated with the Soviet economy.	# 4-14
3.	Identify the three areas in which basic reforms of the Soviet economy must be focused.	# 15
4.	Outline the major reforms undertaken by the Soviet government prior to *perestroika*.	# 16-17
5.	Distinguish the "extensive" growth rate in the USSR from its "intensive" growth since 1917.	# 18
6.	Recognize the five key aspects of *perestroika* and indicate the specific thrust of reform in each of these five areas.	# 19
7.	Identify three major obstacles to the success of *perestroika*.	# 20-23
8.	Evaluate the effectiveness of *perestroika* up to the early 1990's.	# 24-27

Self-Test

1. The command economy of the Soviet Union differs from the market system in two basic respects, which are

   (a) ______________________________

   ____

   (b) ______________________________

   ____

2. List four **basic** economic decisions that are made by the Soviet government.

   (a) ______________________________

   (b) ______________________________

   (c) ______________________________

   (d) ______________________________

3. Since the Bolshevik Revolution of 1917, economic growth in the Soviet Union has generally been __________ than in North America, mainly because ______________________________

____

____

4. Which of the following are characteristic of consumption in the USSR?

____ (a) Consumption is a relatively high priority of Soviet economic planners.

____ (b) There are waiting lists for many consumer goods.

____ (c) Many consumer goods are of low quality.

____ (d) The prices of consumer goods are directly related to (that is, based on) the costs of producing them.

____ (e) The current low levels of consumption per person are not viewed by the economic planners as a permanent characteristic of the Soviet economy.

5. The typical Soviet citizen's volume of consumption is approximately ____________ as large as that of a typical North American.

6. State whether each of the following statements concerning the pricing of consumer goods and services in the Soviet Union is **TRUE** or **FALSE**.

____ (a) Prices are directly related to costs of production (that is, cost plus a percentage).

____ (b) All consumer goods and services are subsidized by the government, which helps keep prices below costs of production.

____ (c) Essentials are taxed quite heavily to provide large revenues for the government, but non-essentials are priced according to their costs of production.

____ (d) All consumer goods and services are taxed heavily by the government.

____ (e) Essential goods and services are heavily subsidized to keep prices low.

____ (f) Non-essential and luxury consumer items are usually taxed heavily by the government, making them expensive.

7. How does worker productivity in the USSR compare with that of the U.S.?

____

____

8. How does the lack of incentives in the Soviet system affect

(a) Worker productivity ______________________________

____

(b) Efficiency of Soviet enterprise ______________________________

____

9. Two factors that cause Soviet capital equipment to be inadequate are:

(a) ______________________________

____

(b) ______________________________

____

10. The agricultural sector of the Soviet economy

(a) has persistently suffered from low productivity and thus represents a major failure of the Soviet planning system to meet its objectives.

(b) has advanced at about the same pace and to about the same productivity levels as the North American agricultural sector.

(c) represents a major success of the USSR's economic system as compared to North America's.

(d) has been the source of many problems for Soviet economic planners in the past but is now advancing quite rapidly.

11. State whether each of the following is a reason for the situation described in the previous question.

____ (a) Soviet farm workers do not have strong incentives to work well.

____ (b) Many Soviet state farms and collective farms are too vast in size to be managed effectively.

____ (c) Soviet planners have made agriculture one of the highest priority sectors of the economy due to its fundamental importance.

____ (d) The Soviet agricultural sector has relatively little capital equipment compared to other nations.

____ (e) Soviet agriculture suffers from a short growing season and a harsh climate.

12. State whether each of the following statements regarding the agricultural sector of the Soviet economy is **TRUE** or **FALSE**.

____ (a) While agricultural productivity is low, this presents no serious problems for the economy, as it can be offset by higher productivity in other sectors of the economy.

____ (b) Soviet economic planners must find a way to improve agricultural productivity if they are to succeed in raising consumer-goods production to its desired levels without sacrificing other priorities.

____ (c) Productivity in agriculture remains low despite the fact that the government has allocated to the agricultural sector approximately the same quantities of capital equipment as are used in North American agriculture.

____ (d) Productivity is high, partly because of heavy capital investment and partly because of economic incentives provided by the government for agricultural workers.

13. State whether each of the following statements concerning the Soviet economic planning system is **TRUE** or **FALSE**.

____ (a) It has tended to make significant errors as the economy has grown larger and more complex.

____ (b) It has difficulty correcting errors and adjusting to changing conditions, due to the inflexibility of the plans.

____ (c) It has suffered from inefficiency of production methods and a lack of incentives.

____ (d) It has often failed to produce complementary goods in sufficient quantities to match other products.

____ (e) It has an effective system for feedback from consumers to central economic planners.

____ (f) It has avoided overproduction and underproduction of consumer goods by effectively forecasting and responding to consumer demand.

14. Which of the following statements concerning the Soviet system whereby plant managers receive production quotas (targets) from the central economic planners is **incorrect**?

(a) It has proven to be an effective way of coordinating production in various industries.

(b) It has tended to result in low-quality products in many industries.

(c) It has resulted in plant managers distorting products in order to meet quotas.

(d) It has resulted in the persistent production of goods not considered appropriate by consumers.

15. Proposals for improving Soviet economic performance include (1) ______________________ ______________________, (2) ____, and (3) ______________________.

Briefly explain why reforms must be focused on each of these three areas:

____

____

____

____

____

____

16. Indicate whether each of the following statements is **TRUE** or **FALSE** concerning economic reforms introduced in the USSR prior to *perestroika.*

____ (a) Steps were taken to distribute incomes more equally, by reducing wage differentials between various occupations.

____ (b) Planning authorities were empowered to force workers to accept certain jobs for life.

____ (c) Factory managers were authorized to give merit raises and bonuses to workers.

____ (d) Western technology was acquired through direct purchase from the West with foreign currencies earned by exporting Soviet products.

____ (e) Attempts were made in the Kosygin era to give more decision making power to consumers.

____ (f) Central planners decreased the incentive for manufacturing firms to earn profits.

____ (g) Conservative elements within the Communist Party encouraged the introduction of "market oriented" reforms.

17. Which of the following is **incorrect**, concerning the operation of private plots of the Soviet Union's agricultural sector?

(a) They represent a small proportion (1 to 3%) of all Soviet agricultural land.

(b) They produce a large proportion (about 27%) of the total value of Soviet farm output.

(c) Their output is sold privately by farmers, in free markets and at market prices rather than at prices dictated by the government.

(d) Despite their capitalistic elements, they are encouraged by their government.

(e) Their output is sold at lower prices than the output of government-owned farms.

18. The rapid growth of the Soviet economy from 1917 to the 1960's is referred to as (extensive, intensive) growth. Low productivity, however, requires the USSR to achieve ____________ growth, which means ____

____

____

19. Indicate whether each of the following statements is **TRUE** or **FALSE** as it relates to the *perestroika* reforms:

____ (a) About half the staff in the planning bureaucracy were to have been removed by 1990.

____ (b) Up to 70% of factory output is to be produced according to customer orders.

____ (c) To facilitate production along market system lines, factories would continue to be heavily subsidized by the government.

____ (d) Some factories would be allowed to lease space to groups of workers, who would operate the plant and distribute the profits among themselves.

____ (e) Joint ventures between Soviet enterprises and foreign firms were to be forbidden.

____ (f) Establishment of small private business became legalized, in an effort to stimulate more efficient production of consumer goods.

____ (g) Emphasis was to be placed on the construction of new factories to replace older, inefficient ones.

20. What threat does *perestroika* pose for the planning bureaucracy in the Soviet Union?

____

____

____

21. Which of the following statements best reflects worker attitudes in the U.S.S.R.?

(a) Workers have shown great enthusiasm for accepting risks and responsibilities made possible by *perestroika.*

(b) Workers in the agricultural sector have been eager to lease land and operate in a market environment.

(c) Both industrial and farm workers have shown reluctance to become entrepreneurs, even where *perestroika* has made this possible.

(d) (a) and (b) above.

22. Faced with inefficient state enterprises and severe shortages of consumer goods, how has the Soviet government kept essential consumer goods prices from rising?

    (a) consumption taxes

    (b) elimination of profiteering

    (c) subsidies to state enterprises

    (d) massive imports of consumer goods.

23. In order to finance the means of keeping prices down (question 22), the Soviet government has ____,

    which in turn has lead to ____.

24. **TRUE** or **FALSE**? By 1990 the *perestroika* reforms

    ____ (a) had succeeded in transforming the USSR into a market oriented economy.

    ____ (b) caused most Soviet industry to produce according to consumer demand, instead of central planning quotas.

    ____ (c) caused prices to be determined in accordance with changing consumer demand conditions.

    ____ (d) caused major disruptions of the central planning system, without replacing it with a market system.

25. In what ways has the concept of *perestroika* been in conflict with established Soviet economic and political practices?

    ____

    ____

    ____

26. In a firm commitment to the concept of *perestroika*, the Soviet parliament approved legislation on September 24, 1990 authorizing its leaders to transform the USSR into a market economy within 18 months.

    What do you consider to be the major obstacles to the implementation of this plan?

    ____

    ____

27. (a) After experiencing more than three generations of a centrally planned command structure, which aspects of a market economy do you think would be most appealing to citizens of the USSR?

(b) In its transition to a market economy, what would you predict to be the most unpopular developments in the USSR over the next few years?

Chapter 21

THE OUTLOOK FOR CAPITALISM

This final chapter seeks to provide a broader perspective for some of the matters discussed in the text. The future of capitalism is the central issue: Will capitalism survive in its present form or flounder in a resource-poor and vastly overcrowded world? Or, alternatively, will capitalism gradually be transformed into some form of socialism? Although these are matters of speculation, events unfolding in the present may give us a few clues concerning the future of capitalism. During the decade of the 1960's and early 1970's, many people concluded that "creeping socialism" would eventually undermine capitalism, resulting in a transformation of our economic system into a socialist structure. Today, there is evidence of a renewed commitment to competition and the free market, with a declining role for government in economic decision making. Whether or not our economic system — whatever its form — can survive the Club of Rome's dire predictions of collapse and catastrophe before the year 2100 is a formidable question.

Within this overall framework we will consider Canada's past performance, review its present situation, and entertain some thoughts about its future directions and requirements. There is ample evidence that an economy which relies heavily on natural resource industries will no longer provide Canadians with the same high income levels and employment opportunities as it once did. In a rapidly changing world, Canada must first define and then pursue new directions in its economic endeavors, where the use of high technology and high productivity will allow it to compete effectively on world markets.

Canada possesses a number of advantages which could be exploited more fully in its future development. These include its wealth of mineral deposits, forest reserves, energy, and its proximity to a large and wealthy US market.

General Learning Objective

Develop an awareness of the problems and challenges facing the capitalist system in general, and Canada's economy in particular, both now and in the future.

Specific Learning Objectives

		Self-Test Reference
1.	Evaluate the optimistic view that technological progress will provide society with ever increasing prosperity	# 1-2
2.	Criticize the pessimistic view that society's economic systems will collapse under the pressure of increased demands on our finite resources	# 3-5
3.	Consider the widely held belief that government intervention in the market place will gradually but inevitably lead to socialism	# 6-8
4.	Assess the role that the federal government has traditionally played in Canada's economic development	# 9
5.	Examine the recent trends in world markets which have seriously affected Canada's resource industries	# 10
6.	Develop an approach by which government and industry may proceed to secure Canada's future prosperity	# 11-12

Self-Test

1. State whether each of the following is or is not an aspect of characteristic of the "optimistic view" of the future as described in Chapter 21.

 ____ (a) This view was most popular during the 1960's and early 1970's.

 ____ (b) Technological progress would create unprecedented levels of material prosperity.

 ____ (c) The division of the economic pie among groups and individuals would continue to be basically decided by incomes earned in the marketplace.

 ____ (d) The arts and recreational and leisure activities would flourish.

 ____ (e) Only a small proportion of the population would be needed for work.

2. It is now believed that the probability of this optimistic view of the future becoming reality in the twentieth century is:

 ____ (a) reasonably high. Although economic progress has slowed down in recent years, renewed progress is expected to make the optimistic view a reality before the end of the century.

 ____ (b) very low, because the assumption that productivity (output per person) would continue to increase rapidly has proved incorrect.

____ (c) very low, because these predictions assumed that vast amounts of capital investment would be available to the consumer-goods sector, which is not as realistic today.

____ (d) very low, because the optimistic view's assumptions of cheap and abundant energy and natural resources are no longer realistic.

____ (e) (b) and (c) and (d).

3. The pessimistic view of the future, as expressed in the Club of Rome's 1972 Report (*The Limits to Growth*) is that continued economic growth will lead to a catastrophe before the year 2100, due to a complete interaction of the following four factors:

(a) ______________________________

(b) ______________________________

(c) ______________________________

(d) ______________________________

4. Indicate whether each of the following statements is **TRUE** or **FALSE.** The probability of the pessimistic view of the future becoming reality is generally considered to be:

____ (a) low, because this assumes that trends of the recent past will continue indefinitely into the future.

____ (b) low, because this view ignores the capacity of the market to adapt to changing conditions.

____ (c) high only if past trends continue unchanged.

____ (d) high; *The Limits to Growth* illustrates effectively how economic growth will inevitable lead to collapse.

5. Indicate whether each of the following statements is **TRUE** or **FALSE.**

In a market system type of economy, as a particular natural resource becomes more scarce:

____ (a) business, in response to consumer demand, will continue to use up that resource steadily until it is depleted.

____ (b) its price will increase, creating incentives to economize on the use of that resource and find substitutes for it.

____ (c) increases in its price will provide incentives to find new supplies of that resource.

____ (d) recycling of that product will become more economical as its price rises.

6. The view that socialism will gradually replace capitalism as government intervention increases in the marketplace is supported by evidence such as ______________________________

____

____

____

7. The attempts by governments of most industrialized countries to improve productivity growth in the late 1970's and the 1980's has led to (more/less) reliance on the "market" approach.

8. Which of the following approaches have been used by the governments of the US, the UK, and Canada during the 1980's to enhance productivity?

____ (a) stricter government regulation of industry.

____ (b) promoting more competition among business firms.

____ (c) providing incentives for business investment.

____ (d) increased reliance on the private sector.

____ (e) improvements in social assistance and services to the public.

9. In the past, when Canada prospered from resource-based industry and an influx of foreign investment, the economic role of government was mainly one of ______________________

____

____

____

10. Developments during the 1980's that have affected Canada's resource industries include:

____ (a) greater competition from the under-developed countries for supplying raw materials.

____ (b) a strong world demand for timber and minerals, leading to higher prices.

____ (c) a growth in demand for products of high-tech and information industries.

____ (d) all of the above.

____ (e) (a) and (c) above.

11. Continued reliance on our natural resource industries to provide for much of Canada's employment and incomes in the 1990's and beyond is considered to be:

____ (a) desirable, due to our long tradition of being a supplier of raw materials to the world.

____ (b) a safe and secure policy for continuing strong economic development.

____ (c) inevitable, due to the immense wealth of our resources, and their value in foreign markets.

____ (d) a course of action which may result in Canada's failure to achieve its full economic potential.

____ (e) (a), (b) and (c) above.

12. Major advantages possessed by Canada which may be utilized in future economic development include ____

____

____

____

MACROECONOMICS

ANSWERS

Chapter 1

1. (d)

2. is not; it deals with the behavior of people, which cannot be scientifically analyzed or predicted.

3. False statements: 1, 3, 4, 5

4. (b)

5. false.

6. false. Most economists would probably be content with describing "what is" or analyzing the consequences of "what could be", leaving "what ought to be" to politicians. A discussion of positive, normative and empirical economics may follow.

7. matters pertaining to the economy as a whole (e.g. — recession, inflation, unemployment).

8. particular aspects of the economy (e.g. — big business, labor unions, rent control)

Chapter 2

1. all skills, along with the ability to do mental work.

2. it increases production per person (productivity), making higher living standards possible.

3. (d)

4. (d)

5. the development of new technology, which creates additional resources.

6. (a)

7. (a)

8. (c)

9. (d)

10. (e)

11. (a)

12. (b)

13. (c)

14. (d)

15. experience higher economic growth and prosper more

16. (b)

17. (b) 52
    (c) 18
    (d) 10
    (e) underutilized, or misused
    (f) it would shift outward
    (g) increase
    (h) manual:
    (4 x 8 x 15) + 70 + (10 x 25) = $800.
    Per unit: 800 + 25 = $32.
    mechanized:
    (2 x 8 x 15) + 70 + 290 + (10 x 25) = $850.
    Per unit: 850 + 25 = $34.
    (i) manual:
    (4 x 8 x 20) + 70 + (10 x 25) = $960.
    Per unit: 960 + 25 = $38.40
    mechanized:
    (2 x 8 x 20) + 70 + (10 x 25) + 290 = $930.
    (j) manual:
    $32. per unit.
    mechanized:
    790 + 25 = $31.60 per unit.
    (k) manual:
    $32. per unit.
    mechanized:
    900 + 25 = $36. per unit.
    (l) manual:
    $32. per unit.
    mechanized:
    (2 x 8 x 15) + 70 (10 x 50) + 340 = $1150.
    Per unit: 1150 + 50 = $23.
    (m) full employment of resources; the efficient allocation of resources; the type of technology used.

Chapter 3

1. the government or government economic planners.

2. (a) True (b) True (c) True (d) False (e) False (f) True

3. 1. Decentralization of economic decision-making.
   2. Introduction of limited elements of private enterprise.
   3. Increased financial incentives for employees and managers.

4. Possibly a transformation of the USSR's command economy into a market economy such as our own.

5. consumers as they make their spending decisions in the marketplace.

6. (d)

7. (d)

8. lowering the price of the product and the profits of the producers, thus reducing the incentive to produce that product.

9. producers, as they select the resource mix which will minimize production costs.

10. (a)

11. (a) iii (b) iv

12. (i) increase, because of the shortage of apartments.
    (ii) declines, because of the surplus of audio goods.
    (iii) might decline, since the producers will not have to offer the same wage incentives if the industry is declining.
    (iv) might decline, due to the surplus of analysts.
    (v) increased employment and incomes, as a result of the construction of new apartments.
    (vi) declines, because of the surplus.
    (vii) declines, because of the lower wheat prices.

13.

Type Of Economy	What To Produce	How To Produce	For Whom
Command System	c	h	d, f
Market System	g	a	b, e

14. (e)

15. (d)

16. (b)

17. (a) true (b) true (c) false (d) true (e) false (f) false (g) false (h) true

18. 4 or 5

19. (a) payments to shareholders as dividends.
    (b) retained to finance new investment in the business.

20. 6%

21. (a) true (b) true (c) false (d) true

22. (a) $5000.
    (b) $3750.
    (c) 8.33%
    (d) $1250. + $2750. + $1000. = $5000.
    (e) $35 000., 0

23. (a) false (b) false (c) true (d) true

24. 1.(a) more resources (e.g. land, labor, etc.) must be allocated, in order to increase cotton production.
    (b) resources will have to be diverted from these crops, causing a reduction in output.
    (c) with less feed, production of livestock will be lower.
    2.(a) more resources must be made available for cotton fabrics, in order to increase production.
    3.(a) more resources shifted to the production of blue jeans, which may result in fewer alternative garments.
    (b) less labor available for the production of woolens, resulting in a decrease in production.
    4. possibly more capital goods must be produced to facilitate blue jeans production, which may result in fewer capital goods available for other industries.

25. Governments (1) buy one quarter of all goods and services produced in Canada (2) produce goods and services (3) provide capital for some business enterprise (4) regulate business operations (5) act to redistribute income.

Chapter 4

1. the value of all final goods and services produced in a country during a year.

2. $260 000

3. (a) consumption (b) investment (c) government (d) net exports

4. (a) government (b) imports (c) investment (d) exports (e) investment (f) consumption (g) exports (h) investment

5. $220.

6. $30.

7. $430.

8. $522.

9. greater

10. prices that prevailed during the year in which GDP was measured

11. is calculated using prices that prevailed during the "base year."

12. price increases have exceeded the increases in real output.

13. underground economic activity, the standard of living, the quality of life.

14. (d)

15. (a) $345., $408. (billions)
(b) $550. billion
(c) 117.7
(d) 25.8, 34.4

16. the annual rate of increase in the general price level.

17. reference to the consumer price index: the annual increase in the CPI.

18. the average of the prices of goods and services bought by representative urban households.

19. 4.1%

20. 132.3

21. the number of unemployed people expressed as a percentage of the labor force.

22. 8.86%

23. The labor force increased at a faster rate than the increase in employment opportunities.

Chapter 5

1. (d)

2. the amount, and quality of capital equipment per worker (and therefore, the amount of capital investment undertaken by society)

3. (c)

4. (d)

5. (a)

6. (c)

7. lower, higher

8. (d)

9. Wealthy countries find it relatively easy to forego consumption (save) in order to invest and grow; poor countries cannot afford to give up present consumption in order to save and invest in capital goods which would facilitate economic growth.

10. (a) British enterprise paid low rates, forcing low consumption upon workers, and invested their profits back into their businesses.
(b) The Soviet state diverted resources away from the production of consumer goods (thus forcing the people to save), and used these resources to produce capital goods.

11. (a) Education and skill levels of the labor force.
(b) The level of managerial ability.
(c) Size of the market and scale of operations, which provides opportunities for increased specialization.
(d) Incentives in the economic system that promote efficiency.
(e) The state of the economy, i.e. rising production generates higher worker productivity.

12. 25

13. 25, 21.9
An increase in the average or marginal tax rate may reduce Carol's incentive to work extra time. She would likely save less with higher tax rates.

14. increased efficiency as a result of larger scale productive operations.

15. (d)

16. (b)

17. (d)

18. (d)

19. (d)

20. (a) The low levels of demand forced a reduction in the work forces in many plants, but not in proportion to the drop in output, thus resulting in decreased worker productivity.
(b) The addition of "baby boomers" caused the labor force to grow at a high rate, but this was not matched by an increase in capital investment, leaving workers on average with less capital to support their efficiency.
(c) High interest rate levels made borrowing very expensive, depressing business capital investment spending.
(d) The proportion of workers employed in the service industry increased, which are less suited to productivity-improving technological advances.
(e) Canadian manufacturers may have been slower to adopt the most up-to-date production technology.
(f) Foreign ownership may discourage research and development from taking place in Canadian branch plants.

21. the relationship between the level of total output and the cost per unit of producing that output.

22. graph

23. (a) true
(b) true
(c) false
(d) true
(e) true

24. (d)

25. (e)

26. (c)

27. (d)

Chapter 6

1. (a)

2. 60%

3. (d)

4. (a) the level of personal disposable income
(b) habit
(c) interest rates
(d) people's expectations about the economic future
(e) government tax incentive to promote saving.

5. rises, rises

6. 600

7. (b), (c), (d), (f), (g)

8. 9

9. (a) consumption
(b) saving and financial investment
(c) real investment
(d) saving and financial investment
(e) consumption
(f) real investment

10. 15—20

11. (e)

12. decrease

13. (a) personal savings
(b) business savings
(c) foreign savings

14. (c)

15. In the **short run**, investment causes resources to be shifted away from consumer goods production, leaving consumers with less. In the **long run**, since more capital goods facilitates greater production of all goods, economic prosperity will be enhanced.

Chapter 7

1. total spending on goods and services. The four components:
(1) consumption spending
(2) investment spending
(3) government spending
(4) net exports

2. consumption spending; investment spending

3. Both statements are incorrect:
(a) Since total income payments equal the value of production, aggregate demand is not necessarily insufficient.
(b) Aggregate demand will not be sufficient to purchase maximum output if not all incomes are spent.

4. (d)

5. (c)

6. the funds saved are invested in capital equipment which increases productivity.

7. down; paradox of thrift.

8. remain stable

9. fall

10. (e)

11. rise

12. (b)

13. (a) fall
(b) rise
(c) fall
(d) rise

14. (a) fall; be depressed
(b) rise; expand
(c) equal

15. (a) increase
(b) increase
(c) decrease
(d) increase
(e) increase
(f) increase

16. The inflation may have been avoided if aggregate supply had also increased (i.e. shifted to the right).

17. (a) false
(b) true
(c) true
(d) false
(e) true
(f) true

18. (a)

19. (e)

Chapter 8

1. (a) contraction (c) peak
   (b) expansion (d) trough

2. (b)

3. fluctuations in aggregate demand

4. (e)

5. (c)

6. (a)

7. the fraction of changes in income which is re-spent

8. imports, taxes, and savings.

9. 1.67

10. (b)

11. (b)

12. 1.6

13. (a) 1.5
    (b) Initial investment spending: $9 million
    Stage 1 of re-spending: $3 million
    Stage 2 of re-spending: $1 million
    Total change in income (end of stage 2): $13 million
    Total change in income (end of series): $13.5 million
    (c) $22.5 million

14. (d)

15. the economy must be at or near capacity output.

16. capital investment undertaken by business in response to increases in sales (which have brought production to near capacity levels) and which are expected to continue

17. keep rising

18. fall

19. $3 million; $9 million; $6 million

20. (e)

21. $160 million; $240 million.

22. (a) & (b):

YEAR	CAPITAL	INVESTMENT
1988	37.5	7.5
1989	50	12.5

    (c) $50 million; 0
    (d) 1988: expansion
    1989: expansion
    1990: recession

23.

	Investment	Change in Income
1988	$7.5	$15
1989	12.5	25
1990	0	0

24. (d)

25. (a) yes (d) yes
    (b) yes (e) no
    (c) yes

26. (a) yes (d) no
    (b) yes (e) yes
    (c) yes

27. (e)

28. (a) dropped from 90% at the start of 1980 to 70% at the end of 1982.
    (b) decreased by 3% in 1982
    (c) fell by 35% in 1982
    (d) declined to a level 17% lower than in 1981
    (e) declined by more than 3% in 1982, amounting to 362 000 lost jobs
    (f) rose to 13% of the labor force

29. (1) By forecasting the various components of aggregate demand, using past trends and likely future developments
    (2) By using leading economic indicators, which tend to rise or fall before the GDP shows any appreciable change

---

Chapter 9

1. (c)

2. balance their budgets, and avoid intervention in the economy

3. deficits; stimulating aggregate demand, output and employment

4. (e)

5. (d)

6. increase

7. (e)

8. depress

9. (b)

10. neutral

11. (a) no (e) no
    (b) yes (f) yes
    (c) no (g) yes
    (d) yes

12. (d)

13. Counter cyclical fiscal policy involves the use of government budget deficits to stimulate aggregate demand during a recession, and government budget surpluses to reduce aggregate demand during an inflationary period.

14. (a) yes (c) no
(b) no (d) yes

15. rise by $112 million

16. when the economy is in a slump, it may be possible for the government to stimulate it by a temporary budget deficit, after which the economy will recover on its own.

17. False. Job creation refers to a wider and more positive concept: the stimulation of the entire economy by government policies, which will result in the creation of jobs within the private sector.

18. (b)

19. severe inflation, as the extra money gets into circulation and gets spent, causing an increase in aggregate demand.

20. the overall debt of the federal government: the difference between the federal government's liabilities and its net recorded assets (mostly those assets which yield interest, profits, or dividends)

21. The National Debt is the total accumulation of federal government deficits, less any repayments made in periods when the federal budget is in a surplus position.

22. (a) yes (d) yes
(b) no (e) yes
(c) no

23. (a) false (g) true
(b) true (h) true
(c) false (i) false
(d) false (j) true
(e) true (k) true
(f) false

24. (a) false (e) false
(b) true (f) true
(c) false (g) true
(d) true

25. (b)

26. (1) rising interest rates, which make capital investment less predictable
(2) the "crowding out effect," where government borrowing leaves insufficient funds for private business borrowing

27. (a)

28. (d)
29. (d)

30. upward; increase; higher; increase; major; compound

31. (d)

32. (1) Interest payments (a major expenditure) **must** be made
(2) Social programs (also a major expenditure) are politically difficult to cut back

33. (c)

34. The impact on the deficit would initially be the same. However, the increase in government spending will be more expansionary than the tax cut (since people will save part of the tax cut) thus resulting in larger government revenues and a lower deficit

---

Chapter 10

1. it influences the level of aggregate demand.

2. recession; inflation

3. (a) medium of exchange
(b) a standard of value
(c) store of value

4. (a) a store of value
(b) medium of exchange
(c) a store of value
(d) medium of exchange
(e) a standard of value

5. (c)

6. portable, durable, divisible or relatively scarce.

7. (a) true (d) false
(b) true (e) true
(c) false

8. (a) true (d) true
(b) false (e) false
(c) false

9. (a) false (d) false
(b) true (e) false
(c) true

10. (d)

11. (a) neither (g) neither
(b) neither (h) money
(c) money (i) neither
(d) money (j) near money
(e) neither (k) neither
(f) money

12. 10, 90

13. (a) true (d) false
(b) true (e) true
(c) true

14. currency (notes and coins) outside the banks plus demand deposits.

15. (e)

16. deposits at trust and mortgage loan companies, credit unions and caisses populaires.

17. (a) $25 billion (c) $150 billion
(b) $105 billion

18. (e)

19. fall, rise, fall or rise, fall, rise.

20. bank deposits; the lending activities of the banking system.

21. (d)

22. $1.9 million

23. decrease

24. (b)

25. $2000; $18,000; willing; able; $1800; increase; $16,200; increased; $200,000.

26. (a) remains the same
(b) decreases
(c) remains the same
(d) remains the same
(e) increases
(f) increases

27. (d)

28. (d)

29. In good times banks lend more and increase the money supply which may result in too much money chasing too few goods, i.e. inflation.
In bad times banks lend less or call in loans and decrease the money supply which may result in lower consumption and higher unemployment.

30. If the money supply is expanded at a rate equal to the growth in Real GNP, then it should not contribute unduly to inflation or unemployment but may even lessen them.

Chapter 11

1. (d)

2. (a) true (e) true
(b) true (f) false
(c) true (g) false
(d) false

3. a privately-owned, financial intermediary chartered by an Act of Parliament.

4. 3% and 10%; 4%

5. 33% to 50%, deposits at the Bank of Canada

6. Treasury bills; very short term notes issued by the federal government; 4%

7. (c)

8. the federal government; to regulate the money supply and interest rates.

9.

Approach	Description
(a) Open market operations	buying and selling bonds on the open market.
(b) Bank Rate	changing the rate of interest at which chartered banks can borrow money from the central bank.
(c) Secondary reserve ratio	changing the proportion of total deposits which chartered banks are required to hold as very liquid short term assets.
(d) Moral suasion	attempting to persuade the chartered banks to follow the policy directions of the central bank.

10. open market operations

11. fall by $20 million; decline; rise decline by $20 million; remain the same.

12. (b)

13. tighter.

14. week; 1/4 of 1% above the average yield on 3 month treasury bills.

15. easy; increase; reduce.

16. buying; lowering; into

17. (d)

18. (b)

19. (b)

20. increasing the federal government's deposits (book entries) at the Bank of Canada.

21. increase; increase; remain the same; remain the same. Refer to figures 11-11&12.

22. (c)

23. (a) true
(b) true
(c) true
(d) true
(e) true

24. (a) true
(b) true
(c) false
(d) false
(e) true
(f) true
(g) false
(h) true
(i) true
(j) true
(k) true

Chapter 12

1. An increase in the general level of the prices of goods and services, including wages and salaries.

2. CPI

3. 12%; 6 years.

4. (a) true
(b) true
(c) true
(d) false
(e) false
(f) false
(g) true
(h) true

5. (c)

6. aggregate demand [C + I + G + (X - M)] exceeding the capacity of the economy to produce goods and services.

7. excess demand.

8. heavy government spending drives prices upward.

9. rising prices and rising unemployment.

10. increasing the money supply by printing money to finance its budget deficit. Students should illustrate a figure similar to 12-3 in the text.

11. (c)

12. (d)

13. more; employers are less resistant to union wage demands and consumers are less resistant to price increases.

14. less; sluggish demand makes price increases more difficult, forcing employers to resist union demands more strongly.

15. rise; 4%; students should illustrate a figure similar to 12-4 in the text.

16. (c)

17. increase

18. rise; want compensation for the erosion of their dollars due to inflation

19. (e)

20. unless the money supply is increased enough to maintain output and employment at the new higher price level, unemployment will rise.

21. increase; these policies increase aggregate demand.

22. excess aggregate demand.

23. (b)

24. rise

25. rise; the higher international value of the Canadian dollar tended to increase imports and reduce exports.

26. more; prevent the international value of the Canadian dollar from rising too far.

27. (e)

28. (a) rapid growth of the labor force, due to the postwar baby boom;
(b) growth of the labor force due to an increased number of women entering the labor force;
(c) the increasing level of voluntary unemployment.

29. stimulated aggregate demand.

30. (c)

31. (b)

32. an increase in unemployment.

33. Economists would probably refer to excess demand, unrealistic expectations, rising costs, emphasizing the consumer role in causing inflation. The public blame unions, government and big business. The difference in views is more of a discussion over who versus what.

34. Answers will vary. A reduction in diposable income could be anti-inflationary. However, if wage-earners demand higher incomes and if businesses do not pass along savings, then GST is likely to be inflationary. The service sector of our economy will be the hardest hit.

Chapter 13

1. excessive aggregate demand for goods and services; prices to rise due to demand-pull pressures.

2. cost-push inflation; secondary cause, or a contributing factor to inflation.

3. the expectation of future inflation; large wage and salary increases that add significantly to cost-push inflationary pressures.

4. (a)

5. restrict aggregate demand.

6. (a) yes (b) no (c) yes (d) yes (e) yes

7. slower; higher; reduced; higher

8. rise; lower aggregate demand will cause output to fall.

9. cause shortages of products by discouraging increased production.

10. (e)

11. more; cost-push pressures from wages would be more severe.

12. (a) true (b) false (c) false (d) false (e) false

13. selective apply only to prices and wages of large corporations and unions. General apply to all prices and wages.

14. (e)

15. (a)

16. (a) false (b) true (c) true (d) false (e) true (f) false (g) true (h) true (i) true (j) false (k) false (l) true

17. shortages of products (and layoffs) will result as controls cause firms to lose money; require monitoring by government.

18. (d)

19. Answers will vary.
    Basically, in times of galloping inflation with excessive price and wage increases, controls can be used as a short term measure to take off the excess pressures on wages and prices; while the government is incorporating long-term measures to build up the supply of goods and services.
    Controls are useful during war time to prevent excessive wage and price increases. After war time, when production of consumer goods resumes, controls can be removed.

20. (b)

21. (d)

22. (a) The statement is incorrect. High interest rates encourage consumer saving and discourage borrowing and spending, thus helping to remove excess demand pressures on the economy.
    (b) This statement is correct. Reducing the size of Canada's deficit and its national debt would contribute to lowering interest costs or cost-push inflation.

23. restraints on the expansion of the money supply.

24. (d)

25. (d)

26. prices to rise sufficiently to cover increases in production costs per unit.

27. (b)

28. (c)

29. (c)

30. (e)

31. Answers will vary. Student could mention: a dose of unemployment, self-discipline, improving productivity, less spending, more saving and investing and so on.

Chapter 14

1. 585 000

2. (a)

3. Yes, in the short run but in the long run if a firm is successful growth through increased sales can actually result in more employment.

4. (a) structural (c) frictional
   (b) structural (d) seasonal

5. unemployment rates are highest among young people (age 15-24) and in Quebec and the coastal regions of Canada.

6. (e)

7. (a)

8. (b)

9. (c)

10. is no longer

11. over half of the unemployed are not breadwinners, but represent a second or third income in a family. Also, better unemployment insurance benefits have increased the amount of voluntary unemployment.

12. 90% to 96% of the labor force being employed, depending upon how politicians care to define it at any one time. However, the norm is probably 96% — the remaining 4% accounting for the amount of frictional unemployment that will persist in the economy.

13. labor force of 19.2 million; employment of 17.4 million; unemployment rate of 9.4%.

14. **On the demand side** — increase government spending, incur budget deficits, reduce taxes, increase the availability of loans, lower interest rates.
    On the supply side - retrain and relocate unemployed workers, training allowances, control wages.

15. Supply side policies are less likely to promote inflation.

16. (c)

17. structural unemployment — made worse by a shift to a services producing economy, weaker world markets for Canadian exports, and perhaps Free Trade and the GST.

Chapter 15

1. (a) economic growth
   (b) full employment
   (c) stable prices

2. stable prices

3. the high levels of aggregate demand, which generate economic growth and full employment, also tend to generate inflation.

4. (b)

5. less;more.

6. (d)

7. pursue one economic goal through a course of action which will have a negative effect on the achievement of at least one other economic goal.

8. (b)

9. conflicting goals, that is, where the problems associated with each goal are not unacceptably severe.

10. (a) The "recognition lag," due to the time it takes for the authorities to recognize the existence of a particular economic problem.
    (b) The "policy lag," before the appropriate economic policies can be implemented.
    (c) The "impact lag," before these policies actually have an effect on the economy.

11. (a) true (d) false
    (b) false (e) true
    (c) true

12. (a) yes (d) yes
    (b) no (e) yes
    (c) yes

13. (a) yes (e) yes
    (b) yes (f) no
    (c) yes (g) yes
    (d) yes

14. decrease

15. (d)

16. (a) likely (d) likely
    (b) not likely (e) likely
    (c) likely

17. (a) likely (d) likely
    (b) not likely (e) likely
    (c) likely

18. (c)

19. severe inflation, slow economic growth, high unemployment, and weak business investment spending.

20. (b)

21. (d)

22. (a) 2% (10%-8%)
(b) —2.0% [2% —(10% x 4%)]

23. It makes bond issues unattractive, because of the high interest rates which the corporation would be committed to paying over the life of the bond issue.

24. depress

25. (a) the negative effects of inflation and taxation on the real after-tax financial position of many businesses;
(b) the fact that high interest rates attracted savings into interest-bearing investments such as bonds and mortgages, thus depressing the demand for (and price of) stocks generally.

26. (a) 3000
(b) overstates real profits by $1000
(c) the $1000 of extra "profits" will be needed merely to replace inventory at the new higher prices.

27. (b) - understating depreciation expense by $5000 per year
- overstating profits by $5000 per year

28. more

29. (d)

30. weak

31. (a) yes (e) no
(b) no (f) no
(c) yes (g) no
(d) yes (h) no

32. (e)

33. (a) depressed (c) depressed
(b) more rapid

34. (c)

35. (a)

36. Answers will vary.

Chapter 16

1. (c)

2. (b)

3. decreased, 40%, 22%, weaker, less

4. (b)

5. a higher standard of living.

6. (e)

7. (c), (b), (a), (d)

8. (a)

	Canadian Firm	Chinese Firm
Hourly costs	$90	$10
Hourly output	3000	200
Cost per unit	$90÷3000=$.03	$10÷200=$.05

(b) $ per unit
(c) technologically advanced capital equipment
(d) $100 000 in China
$60 000 in Canada

9. False, because technological advancement and higher productivity in many North American industries result in lower costs per unit of output despite the higher wage rates in North America.

10. False, efficient and competitive producers, such as agricultural and primary product industries (as well as some manufacturers) favour freer trade, which would allow them freer access to foreign markets.

11. (b)

12. (a) 120 000
(b) 80 000
(c) 120000 - 80 000 = 40 000
(d) zero, since free trade without tariffs is assumed.
(e) 105 000
(f) 95 000
(g) 105 000 - 95 000 = 10 000
(h) 10 000 x $10 = $100 000 per month
(i) — Consumers lose because they now pay a higher price and there is a reduction in the purchases of the product.
— Foreign suppliers lose since they have less sales to Canadians.
— Canadian importers suffer from the same plight as foreign suppliers (i.e., less sales and subsequently lower income).
— Government gains as a result of the $100 000 tariff revenues and the higher tax revenues from Canadian producers.The government is likely to lose some income tax revenues from the Canadian importers since their employment and profits decline.
— Canadian firms gain as a result of their improvement in sales.
(j) A subsidy of $10 per unit to producers is a better way of isolating the cost of protection and eliminating the other side effects of tariff protection.

13. other nations will retaliate by increasing their tariffs on Canadian products. Consequently, some jobs will be 'saved' in Canadian industries which receive increased tariff protection, while other jobs will be lost in industries which will suffer retaliatory tariff increases by foreign nations.

14. (b)

15. (a) no (e) no
(b) no (f) yes
(c) yes (g) no
(d) yes (h) no

16. (a) false (d) false
(b) true (e) true
(c) true

17. (b), (c), (d), (e)

18. (a) provide considerable advance notice of tariff reductions
(b) provide financial and/or technical assistance to help firms adjust to the new situation
(c) provide retraining and/or relocation assistance to help workers adjust to the new situation

19. (e)

20. true, false, true, false

21. (a) $12 000 (g) $11 000
(b) 90 000 (h) 120 000
(c) $10 000 (i) 78 000
(d) 140 000 (j) 42 000
(e) 70 000 (k) $1000 x 42 000 = $42 million
(f) 70 000

22. H Subsidy
D GATT
E Non-tariff barrier
G Tariff
A Import Quota
B Branch plant
C Comparative Advantage Theory
F Trading Bloc

Chapter 17

1. The manufacturing industry

2. larger, increased, less

3. building a subsidiary plant in Canada

4. (a) false (c) true
(b) true

5. (a) true (c) true
(b) false (d) true

6. (d)

7. higher, more

8. (c)

9. (b)

10. (a) Geographically close to the U.S.
(b) Similar language and culture
(c) An easy market to enter for American firms
(d) Skilled and low paid labor force
(e) A source of great natural resource wealth

11. mining and manufacturing

12. 36%, 23%, 37%, 29%

13. increase, increased

14. (a) false (d) true
(b) true (e) true
(c) true

15. (a) (i) foreign investors act in their own best interest not Canada's;
(ii) dividends and interest revenue leave Canada;
(iii) foreign branch plants are subject to foreign law;
(iv) a parent company may interfere with exports;
(v) research and development may for the most part be done by the parent;
(vi) key corporate officers may be non-Canadians;
(vii) branch plants may be expected to purchase supplies from U.S. parents.
(b) Responses may vary but (i) in 10 (a) is likely the major criticism. If foreign investors act in Canada's best interest the remainder follow.
(c) Responses may vary, perhaps (vi) in 10 (a). Responses vary by industry.

16. (a) true (d) false
(b) true (e) true
(c) true (f) true

17. (c)

18. (a) it applied only to some types of foreign investment
(b) it applied only to future (not established) foreign investment
(c) it approved most applications from foreign firms

19. the delays and uncertainties involved in the review process have likely discouraged foreign investment that might have been beneficial to Canada.

20. promoting foreign investment; publishing, oil and gas

21. (a) false, relatively **low** Canadian productivity
(b) false, generally **high** levels of tariffs
(c) false, **small** Canadian market
(d) true
(e) false, **a lack** of specialization in one or few products.

22. (a) Declining world export markets for Canadian resource products
(b) Increased foreign competition characterized by the development of global markets.
(c) Canadians had decreasing access to the American market as the United States moved toward more protectionism during the mid eighties.

23. 100 million people

24. (d)

25. (1) Canadian firms have to purchase their primary food products through Marketing Boards where prices are relatively high.
(2) There is strong competition from large American firms who benefit from their economies of scale

26. world product mandating

27. (a) niche markets
(c) specialize
(e) develop new products
(f) corporate re-structuring

28. I dumping
J Globalization
A Subsidies
G Disputes panel
F Duty remission
D Countervailing duty
E Direct Acquisition
H Indirect Acquisition
C Auto Pact
B Marketing Board

Chapter 18

1. the price of one currency in terms of a foreign currency.

2. $1.16482 Canadian

3. .522985 pounds

4. (a) increase
(b) decrease
(c) decrease
(d) increase
(e) decrease
(f) increase
(g) parts (a), (d) and (f) are appreciations, whereas (b), (c) and (e) are depreciations

5. (d)

6. rise or appreciate

7. (a) receipt (e) receipt
(b) payment (f) payment
(c) payment (g) payment
(d) payment (h) receipt

8. (a) surplus
(b) deficit
(c) depreciate; appreciate; demand;

9. (a) (i) false (iv) true
(ii) true (v) false
(iii) false
(b) deficit
(c) fall or depreciate
(d) Exporters, because our export goods and services are relatively cheaper as a result of the Canadian dollar depreciation.
(e) Importers and consumers of imported goods because these goods are now more expensive.

10. (a) Both of these factors involve payments to foreigners causing deficit tendencies in the current account.
(b) Tends to fall or depreciate as a result of (a).
(c) are now more expensive.
(d) (i) buy Canadian dollars on the foreign exchange market and/ or
(ii) increase Canadian interest rates relative to foreign rates to attract foreign currency, thereby increasing the demand for Canadian dollars.
(e) Managed float or dirty float.

11. (d)

12. (e)

13. (d)

14. increase

15. increase; less.

16. (c)

17. (a)

18. For expansionary monetary policy, increasing the money supply leads to lower Canadian interest rates. If American interest rates are unchanged there is likely to occur an outflow of money capital and a depreciating Canadian dollar. This means lower priced Canadian goods for foreigners and higher Canadian export sales. The increase in foreign demand resulting from the lower priced Canadian dollar complements the domestic expansion resulting from the monetary policy.

For fiscal policy, the opposite result is possible. An increase in government spending through deficit financing leads to higher Canadian interest rates and increased money capital inflows. The resulting appreciation of the Canadian dollar means reduced Canadian export sales. This goes against the intent of increasing aggregate demand through expansionary fiscal policy.

19. (a) Canadian pulp and paper companies are exporters and benefit from a depreciated Canadian dollar.
(b) as the dollar appreciates against foreign currencies, import prices decline.
(c) The bank is attempting to accomplish
  (i) An orderly market for the canadian dollar. The bank wishes to stabilize the currency to avoid wide swings in price.
  (ii) The avoidance of a renewal of Canadian price inflation caused by higher import prices and followed by concommitant wage increases.

20. (a) \$11 000 000
Since \$1 Canadian = 200 yen
1 yen = $\frac{1}{200}$ = \$.005
Thus, one imported auto costs
2.2 million x \$.005 = \$11 000
1000 cars cost 1000 x \$11 000 = \$11 million
(b) 15 714 286 (i.e. 1000 x 2.2. million x $\frac{1}{140}$
(c) increase; decrease; automatic adjustment mechanism

21. (a) true (d) true
(b) false (e) false
(c) true

22. (a) false (d) false
(b) true (e) false
(c) false

23. (a) false (c) true
(b) false (d) true

24. (a) no (d) yes
(b) yes (e) yes
(c) yes (f) no

25. (d)

26. selling Canadian dollars and buying foreign exchange

27. The Bank of Canada had to borrow to obtain the necessary Canadian dollars. The amount borrowed was \$5.2 billion in 1987 and \$12 billion in 1988.

28. Interest and dividends are a payment to investors for the service of using their money capital

29. (1) Heavy borrowing by governments in foreign countries
(2) Relatively high interest rates

30. (e)

Chapter 19

1. (b)

2. more

3. sells; buys.

4. (c)

5. stagnate; increase.

6. (e)

7. true, true, false, true

8. rise; sell; buy.

9. fall; buy; sell.

10. (d)

11. (c)

12. Economic conditions change over time. Some nations experience surpluses in their Balance of Payments pushing their exchange rates upward. Other nations have deficits causing their currencies to depreciate.

13. (a) yes (d) yes
(b) no (e) yes
(c) yes

14. fall; buy; sell

15. decrease; decline; devaluation

16. (a) no (b) no (c) yes (d) no (e) no

17. impose an "austerity program" in order to combat the causes of its Balance of Payments deficits.

18. depressing aggregate demand to combat inflation, which makes domestically produced products more competitive with foreign products.

19. create unemployment.

20. devalued

21. (a) false (b) true (c) true

22. (a) false (b) true (c) false (d) true (e) true

23. that fact that it was backed by gold (until 1968).

24. surpluses; increasing.

25. deficits; decreasing.

26. (a) yes (b) yes (c) yes (d) no (e) yes

27. The overvaluation of the US dollar, which was pegged at an unrealistically high level.

28. increased greatly, to the point where the volume of US dollars held by foreigners exceeded the USA's gold stock.

29. (d)

30. devalue; Japan and West Germany; revalue (i.e., increase their value relative to the US dollar).

31. opposed; they were concerned that their exports to the USA would fall, causing unemployment in their nations to rise.

32. a surtax on imports into the USA from foreign nations; revalue their currencies upward relative to the US dollar.

33. increase; reduce; reducing or eliminating.

34. (a)

35. devalued the US dollar (by 8 1/2%).

36. increase; decrease.

37. of the vast outflow of US dollars in payment for oil following the large oil-price increases by the Organization of Petroleum Exporting Countries (OPEC) in the fall of 1973.

38. US dollars on deposit in financial institutions outside of the United States.

39. OPEC price increases and the resulting outflow of American dollars from the United States.

40. decrease, shortages, rise, increasing, unregulated, poor, high, oil or other commodities.

lower, higher, poor.

41. (e)

42. (a) true (b) true (c) false (d) false (e) true

43. increase, decrease, depreciation, increase.

44. 5, 6, 4, 1, 3, 2, 7

45. (a) false (b) false (c) true (d) true (e) true

46. 1987, a different, declining in value, seven, buying

47. (a) no (b) yes (c) no (d) no (e) no

48. (a)

Chapter 20

1. (a) yes (b) yes (c) no (d) yes (e) yes (f) no (g) yes (h) no (i) yes

2. (a) improve productivity;
(b) make Canadian firms more competitive;
(c) create employment;
(d) enhance living standards.

3. Borrowers, less, borrowed.
lenders, more

4. the fear of renewed inflation

5. Raising taxes or reducing government spending could increase unemployment and send the economy back into another recession.

   Reducing the deficit was not popular with the public and didn't seem to be a public priority. Governments are not re-elected by making the decisions to increase taxes or reduce spending.

6. of the current high level of the deficit. The government had little room to initiate tax cuts or spending increases.

7. renewed inflation.
   depreciation, increase, Higher, cost push.

8. (a) yes (c) yes
   (b) no

9. Increasing amounts of foreign savings were required to finance the federal deficit. To attract this money capital, Canadian interest rates had to be maintained at relatively high levels especially against American rates.

10. (b)

11. List A: 1, 4, 5
    List B: 2, 3, 6, 7, 8

12. Freer trade is a response to the reality of economic internationalism — the fact that Canada must compete in global markets. As a result, Canadian firms must be more competitive and profitable. As most profits are retained by corporations to increase capital and improve technology, wealth is created.

13. As a result of the 7% GST, the Manufacturer's Sales Tax of 13% was eliminated. This lowered the cost of production for manufacturing firms making them more competitive internationally. The improved economic activity and resulting increase in employment and profits creates wealth for Canadians.

MICROECONOMICS

ANSWERS

Chapter 4

1. the study of the behavior of individual households, firms and markets.

2. the usefulness of that product.

3. (d)

4. determined by supply and demand, and are therefore not necessarily related to the usefulness of products.

5. what to produce; how to produce it; for whom to produce it.

6. (b)

7. (e)

8. (c)

9. competition among sellers, available information for consumers.

10. (a) competition gives consumers a choice of different products in the marketplace.

    (b) competition encourages producers to be as efficient as possible, and to keep prices as low as possible.

Chapter 5

1. (a) yes (c) yes
   (b) yes (d) yes

2. (a) It is easy to form.
   (b) It provides strong incentives for the owner-manager.

3. (a) Once profits exceed a certain level, the sole proprietorship pays higher tax rates than payable on corporation profits.
   (b) It does not have ready access to capital.
   (c) It often lacks managerial expertise.
   (d) Its owners have unlimited personal liability for the debts of the business.

4. disagreements among the partners.

5. (a) The ability to raise large amounts of capital.
   (b) The limited liability of its owners (shareholders).
   (c) The lower tax rates on profits above a certain level (as compared to sole proprietorships and partnerships).
   (d) The fact that a corporation is a separate legal entity from its shareholders, so that it continues to exist and function after the death of its owners.

6. sole proprietorship.

7. (a) Unacceptable (d) Unacceptable
   (b) Unacceptable (e) Acceptable
   (c) Acceptable

8. (a)

9. 40

10. (d)

11. serve as a vehicle to regenerate the economy;
    fill distribution voids in the economy;
    increase the range of available alternatives;
    provide an environment for technological innovation and entrepreneurship;
    provide outlets for the talents and energies of entrepreneurial and independent people;
    enhance the quality of community life;
    serve as agents of decentralization;
    provide contracting services to large businesses.

12. (a) financing problems,
    (b) grants,
    (c) government regulations and extensive paper-work,
    (d) difficulties attracting and retaining capable employees.

13. (a) loan guarantees,
    (b) grants,
    (c) counselling programs,
    (d) training and information
    (e) research and development aid.

14. an organization comprised of small businesses;
    lobby governments on behalf of small businesses.

15. corporations, raising large amounts of capital.

16. General Motors of Canada Ltd., 100, foreign.
Canadian Pacific Ltd., 100, Canadian.

17. it represents a potential threat to Canada's markets by restricting competition, raising prices and reducing output (jobs).

18. (d)

19. Power Corporation,
George Weston Ltd.,
Argus Corporation.

20. shareholders; top management, Board of Directors; less; expertise.

21. a government owned and operated enterprise accountable to Parliament through a cabinet minister. As public policy tools they tend to perform functions the private sector would not or could not.

22. (a) false (c) true
(b) false (d) true

23. (a) electrical generation and distribution,
(b) transportation and communications,
(c) energy and resources,
(d) manufacturing.

24. Canadian National Railways,
Petro-Canada
Canada Wheat Board.

25. Privatization is the process of selling off Crown corporations to the private sector, especially ones that are inefficient money losing enterprises.

26. Crown corporations are generally classified into one of three different categories, each with their defined role.

Type	Function	Example
(a) Departmental	Responsible for administrative, supervisory and/or regulatory government services.	Economic Council of Canada, UIC
(b) Agency	Responsible for management of trading or service operations on a quasi-commercial basis	Lotto Canada CDC, Canada Post
(c) Proprietary	Responsible for management of lending or financial operations, management of commercial or industrial operations.	FBDB

27. They have contributed enormously to the economic development and unity of the nation. They provide a useful transportation system for Canadians. In such a large, widespread country as Canada, the costs of operating such enterprises are so great that it is necessary for the government to subsidize their operations in order to provide a reasonable level of service to Canadians.

28. They include money-losing businesses that the government acquired or maintained mainly for political reasons-mainly to "save jobs." Many government enterprises pay above-market wages and/or operate inefficiently; losing money regularly and falling back on the taxpayers for subsidies. These subsidies have contributed to past federal deficits.

Chapter 6

1. (d)

2. quantity demanded falls.

3. a downward sloping demand curve.

4. a specific amount that consumers are willing to purchase at a specific price.

5. (Graphic illustration of demand curve.)

6. remains unchanged

7. (a) tastes and preferences: move in favor of the product.
(b) income: increase.
(c) population: increase.

8. shift to the right (increase).

9. shift to the left (decrease).

10. shift to the left (decrease).

11. shift to the left (decrease).

12. shift to the left (decrease).

13. A product is inelastic (not sensitive to price changes) if there are:
(a) no close substitutes;
(b) it is necessarily good;
(c) there is a physical limit on consumption.

14. price sensitive (or very sensitive to price changes).

15. (a) Ford Mustangs: many close substitutes available.
(b) Pepsi Cola: many close substitutes available.
(c) Crest: many close substitutes available.

16. (a) inelastic, it's the barbecue season, and there are not many close substitutes for barbecued steak.
(b) elastic, the Canadian wine acts as a substitute.

17. porterhouse steak
steak
beef
meat

18. **Total Revenue**
$500
540
560
560
540
(a) inelastic (c) unitary
(b) inelastic (d) elastic

19. Revenue rises, but we must know how the costs are affected before we can determine whether or not the firm is better off.

20. E = 20% + 10% = 2, elastic
reduce, 5% (i.e. % ΔP = Δ Q + E)
$19 (20 - 1).

21. (c)

22. 0; 1.9; .5; infinite; .5; 2.8.

23. elastic

24.

If Demand is	the E is	If Price	the TR will
	0		decrease
	greater than 1 & less than ∞		increase
unitary elastic			remains constant
		increases	
perfectly elastic			increase/ decrease

25. larger

Chapter 7

1. (c)

2. many firms
price takers
freedom of entry and exit

3. (a)

4. (a) few firms
(b) market power (price makers)

5. there is a lack of price competition.

6. (a) competitive
(b) non-competitive
(c) non-competitive
(d) competitive
(e) competitive
(f) non-competitive
(g) competitive

7. (c)

8. the quantity supplied increases.

9. (a) shift to the right (down).
(b) lower production costs,
more firms,
better technology.

10. (a) shift to the left (up).
(b) increased production costs,
fewer firms,
increased taxes.

11. decrease,
a shift to the left (up).

12. increase,
a shift to the right (down).

13. (a) Result in a relatively small change in the quantity supplied.
(b) The inability (insufficient time) to change the quantity supplied in response to a change in price.

14. (a) Result in a relatively large change in the quantity supplied.
(b) Sufficient time for the producer to make changes in the quantity supplied.

15. More elastic.
Given sufficient time, the producer can make major changes in the quantity supplied in response to a change in price.

16. (a) $4
(b) 25
(c) excess supply (15 units)
(d) excess demand (35 units)
(e) 1.5

17. (a) increase (d) increase
(b) no change (e) increase
(c) increase

18. Surplus of $10 billion. Shortage of $15 billion.

Chapter 8

1. increase; increase.

2. decrease; decrease.

3. decrease; increase.

4. increase; decrease.

5. (a)

6. (b)

7. (b)

8. (d)

9. (b)

10. No. The market clearing price in this market is indicated at 75 cents per unit. If producers charge $1.00 per unit, there will be unsold cauliflowers (excess supply). Since this is a perishable product, producers will have to lower their price back down towards the equilibrium level in order to sell off the existing quantity that was produced for this market.

11. Generally, the income position of the grain farmer has worsened rather than improved over the period in question.
Improved technology has resulted in greatly improved productivity and reduced manpower, as more efficient machinery has been introduced to the farming industry. The increased productivity has resulted in increasing supply of grain products. However, the industry supply curves remain relatively inelastic (particularly over the short term). This inelasticity, combined with increasing supply, has resulted in lower prices per unit. This decline in price is magnified when considering the market demand curve, which also is relatively inelastic. Thus, farm revenues have not increased significantly, while costs of production have had substantial increases (for fuel, fertilizers, insecticides, etc.) As a result, farm incomes have suffered.

12. $1.50

13. a surplus of 60 units (quantity supplied would be 80 units; quantity demanded would be 20 units).

14. a shortage of 40 units (quantity demanded would be 70 units; quantity supplied would be 30 units).

15. (a) ceiling -- the equilibrium price P1 is the maximum price.
(b)

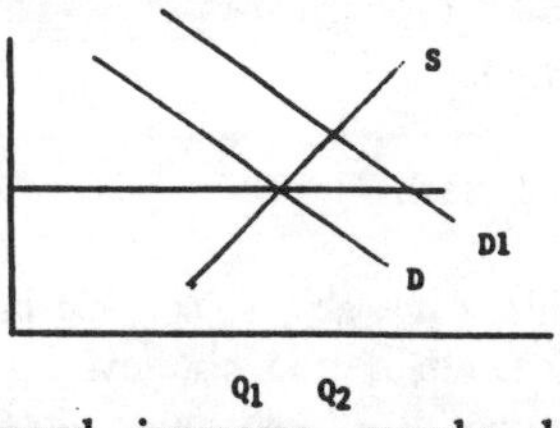

(c) Demand increases, supply does not since landlords are not motivated sufficiently to increase space and a shortage emerges.

Chapter 9

1. many small firms, easy to enter the industry and all firms sell identical products.

2. fall to zero

3. (a)

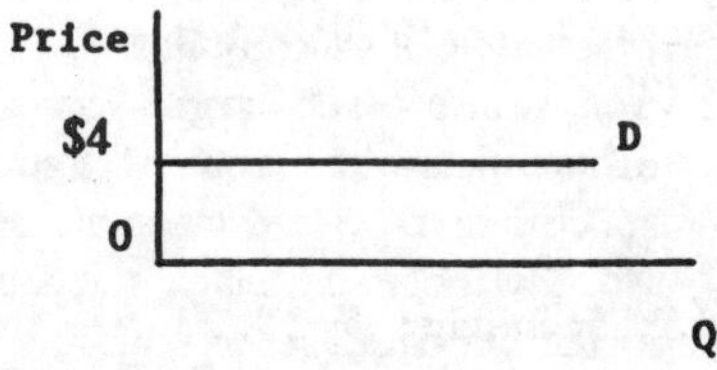

(b) (i) Price remains at $4
(ii) Produce and sell as much as possible
(c) Improve efficiency by reducing per unit production costs

4. (a) perfect competition
(b) Firm A $ 0
Firm B $ 1125
Firm C $ 6000
(c) Firm C is the largest and most efficient producer as indicated by the low production costs of $3 per unit.
(d) (i) $ 3
(ii) Firm A $ - 2000
Firm B $ - 1875
Firm C 0
(iii) Reduce costs of production, reduce costs and increase output, shut down
(iv) 2500
No, since this change in supply represents an insignificant contribution to total production. This is the primary reason why firms in perfect competition must accept the going market price.

5. (a) (iv) (it appears closest to perfect competition)
(b) many sellers,
an identical product,
each producer is small compared to the total industry output, each seller accepts the market price of $3.80.
(c)

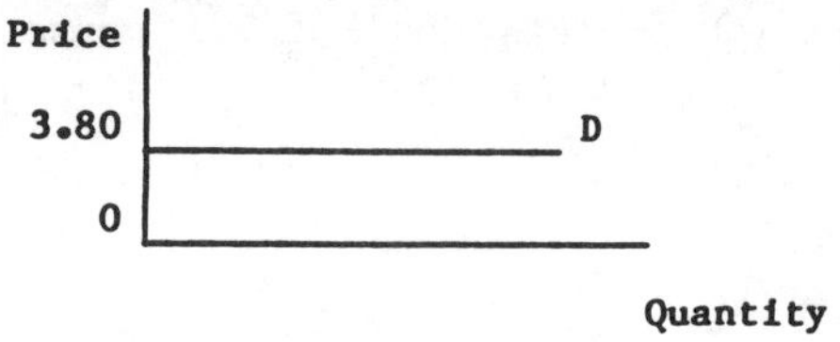

(d) Smith is not able to sell his product.
(e) No, Smith should not lower his price. He is able to sell all he can produce at the market price. Thus it is not necessary to lower the price since this only reduces profits.
(f) No, since he may sell as much as he wishes at the market price.

6. (a) many small firms
(b) easy to enter (and leave) the industry

7. the products of all sellers are not identical — each producer's product is in some (relatively small) way different from the products of the others.

8. (a) No, because large firms dominate in the production of automobiles
(b) Yes, since each stereo shop is able to differentiate its product through targeting specific markets and customer service.
(c) No. Bell Canada has a telephone monopoly in the Ontario-Quebec region.
(d) No, under regulation, where several large firms are granted the sole rights of specific routes. Yes, under de-regulation, as evidenced in the American market. In this latter case small companies have emerged, many with second-hand fleets concentrating on the short, high-traffic routes.
(e) Yes, since there are so many different restaurants catering to a wide range of tastes and clientele.
(f) No. Quebec Hydro has a monopoly on the production and distribution of Hydro power in Quebec.
(g) Yes. Florist shops are small firms offering a differentiated service.

9. (d)

10. (a) There is an incentive to practise product differentiation, that will emphasize the differences between your product and those of your competitors.
(b) There is also an incentive to increase the price of your product slightly, so as to take advantage of the inelasticity of demand created by this product differentiation. Whether this is in fact done will depend upon the degree of product differentiation and the decision of the producer, who may or may not wish to do so.

11. (e)

12. (a) (iii)
(b) inelastic
(c) Bob has created a 'niche' market where his loyal customers are unlikely to buy more baked goods if the price drops. Similarly, the customers are willing to pay a higher price, if necessary with little if any reduction in quantities purchased. Thus, when prices decline, total revenues decline and when prices rise total revenues rise.
(d) his unique products, the Belgian pastries and birthday cakes.

13. (c)

14. competitive

15. (f)

Chapter 10

1. there is only one seller of a particular good or service with no close substitutes.

2. the only logical way to organize an industry or a service is to have only one producer (e.g., hydro and telephone service).

3. (a) It can regulate the prices which the monopoly charges.
(b) It can take over ownership and operation of the monopoly.

4. (a)

Output	Monopolist ATC	Oligopolist ATC
100 000	$2.00	$3.00
600 000	1.67	3.00
1 800 000	1.11	2.22

(b) Average costs per unit decrease and output increases and the monopolist shows greater cost efficiencies compared to the oligopolists.
(c) natural monopoly.
(d) telephone services, hydroelectric power generation.

5. (e)

6. (a) Tendency to maximize production and sales to maximize profits.
(b) The price of the resource falls and the supply of the resource is depleted.
(c) The natural tendency of the monopolist is to charge a higher price which reduces quantity demanded. Also, the monopolist wants to be in business in the future and has incentive to invest in replenishing the inventory of timber.

7. (a)

8. four; 50.

9. (a) monopolistic
(b) oligopolistic
(c) perfectly competitive
(d) monopolistically competitive
(e) oligopolistic

10. (a) oligopoly
(b) (i) 3 large firms accounting for 100% of sales;
(ii) each specializes to meet the demands of a unique segment of the market;
(iii) little price competition since total sales decline for either price increases or price decreases.
(c) No, because at $1650, quantity sold is 1.6 million tons. Thus, total revenues are $2.64 billion. This is $360 million less than the revenues derived at $1500 per ton. Regal's competitors have maintained the old price and captured 400 000 tons of Regal's business.
(d) No. A 10% reduction in price means $1350 per ton. Sales increases to 2.1 million tons which means total revenues are $2.835 million. This is $165 million less than the $3 billion derived at $1500 per ton.

This time the steel competitors have reacted by lowering their prices making for an inelastic demand schedule for Regal.

(e) Price ($ Per Ton)

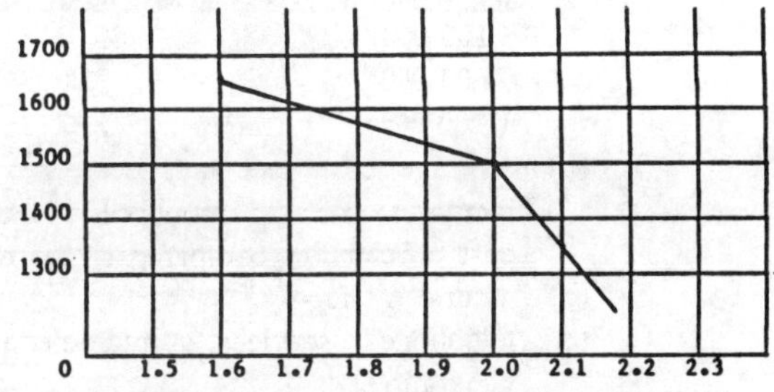

Quantity (Tons)

(f) elastic, inelastic

11. (a) the amount of capital required
(b) consumer acceptance/the cost of advertising
(c) patents
(d) government licences
(e) predatory pricing by the established firms
(f) mergers, in which established firms buy out newcomers

12. (a) false (c) false
(b) true (d) false

13. (d)

14. (c)

15. supply

16. (a) elasticity of demand (due to consumer resistance to higher prices, the availability of substitutes or foreign competition).
(b) lack of cooperation among the oligopolists (i.e., price cutting by some).
(c) fear of government action if price increases are considered excessive.
(d) the desire of the industry for growth (which may lead it to charge lower prices than it could charge).

17. (e)

18. (a) yes (d) no
(b) yes (e) yes
(c) yes

19. reducing prices; reducing output

20. The following were **not** factors in the disintegration of the power of the OPEC cartel.
— consumers switching from natural gas to oil (the reverse was true)
— OPEC had not agreed on price increases (OPEC had agreed on price increases but not on production quotas)
— non-OPEC members such as the United Kingdom, Mexico and Norway were reducing their supply of oil (these countries were increasing supply)
— OPEC was able to maintain its market share of the non-socialist oil market between 1979 and 1985 (their share fell to one-third of the market)

Chapter 11

1. (a) fixed (e) fixed
(b) fixed (f) fixed
(c) variable (g) variable
(d) variable

2. (c)

3. (c)

4. Law of Diminishing Returns

5. (a)

6. (a) average fixed cost per unit is high due to the low volume of output
(b) average variable cost per unit is high due to the Law of Diminishing Returns

7. (a)

8. (c)

9. (a) 20 (c) 15
(b) 17

10. (c)

11. (b)

12.

Employment	Average Output
1	20
2	20
3	30
4	37.5
5	32

(a) 150 tables, 4 employees
(b) fifth employee
(c) variable
(d)

(2)	(3)	(4)	(5)	(6)
0	600	0	600	600/0 = infinity
20	600	1500	2100	2100/20 = 105
40	600	3000	3600	90
90	600	4500	5100	56.67
150	600	6000	6600	44
160	600	7500	8100	50.63

(e)

Tables/ week	TR	TC	Profits
20	1100	2100	-1000
40	2200	3600	-1400
90	4950	5100	-150
150	8250	6600	1650
160	8800	8100	700

(f) 150 tables, 4 employees, $1650 per week
(g) Total losses exceeding total fixed costs which is both 20 and 40 tables in this example.

13. (a)

Labour	Daily Output	Total Fixed Costs	Total Variable Costs	Total Cost	Average Total Cost $	Mar-ginal Cost	Total Reve-nues	Profits	Marginal Revenues
0	0	50	0	50	—	—	—	—	—
1	1	50	80	130	130.00	80	75	(55)	75
2	3	50	180	230	76.67	26.67	225	(5)	75
3	7	50	320	370	52.86	35	525	155	75
4	9	50	420	470	52.22	50	675	205	75
5	10	50	500	550	55	80	750	200	75

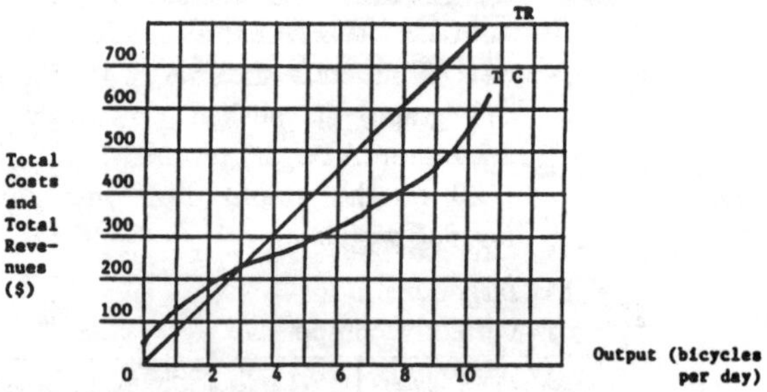

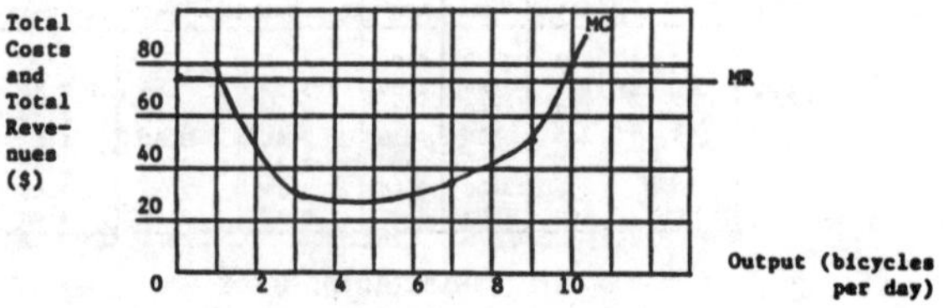

(b) Hire 4 people and produce and sell 9 bicycles per day.
Profits are $205 per day.
(c) According to the marginal cost/marginal revenue graph, the best profits occur at between 9 and 10 bicycles per day as this is where MC=MR. Since it is of no use to produce part of a bicycle we must choose either 9 or 10 as the optimum output.

If the firm hires one more person and produces 10 bicycles, the extra cost of this bicycle is $80, whereas the extra revenues derived from the sale are only $75. Thus, they are reducing their existing profits by $5 (i.e., profits fall from $205 to $200 per day if 10 bicycles are manufactured instead of 9).
(d) Shut down since the table below indicates that losses exceed total fixed costs at all levels of output.

Output	TR	TC	Profits
0	0	50	(50)
1	40	130	(90)
3	120	230	(110)
7	280	370	(90)
9	360	470	(110)
10	400	550	(150)

14. (a) 300

(b) $2400

Method 1

Profits per unit:	$30 — $22 = $8
Total profits:	$8 X 300 = $2400

Method 2

Total revenues:	300 X $30 = $9000
Total costs:	$22 X 300 = $6600
Total profits:	$9000 — $6600 = $2400

(c) Yes, because the demand curve is perfectly elastic. When extra profits are apparent, new firms enter the industry. Price (AR on the graph) is pushed downward until the minimum ATC is reached. At this point, ($20 on the graph) each firm makes only normal profits.

15. (a)

Units of Output Per Day	Fixed Costs	Vari-able Costs	Total Costs	Average Cost Per Unit	Average Revenue Per Unit	Marginal Cost Per Unit	Marginal Revenue Per Unit	Total Revenue
0	$300	$ 0	$300	–	–	–	–	–
300	300	850	1150	$ 3.83	$ 4.50	$ 2.83	$ 4.50	1350
600	300	1550	1850	3.08	4.00	2.33	3.50	2400
900	300	2050	2350	2.61	3.50	1.67	2.50	3150
1200	300	2500	2800	2.33	3.00	1.50	1.50	3600
1500	300	3100	3400	2.27	2.50	2.00	.50	3750
1800	300	4300	4600	2.56	2.00	4.00	-.50	3600

(b)

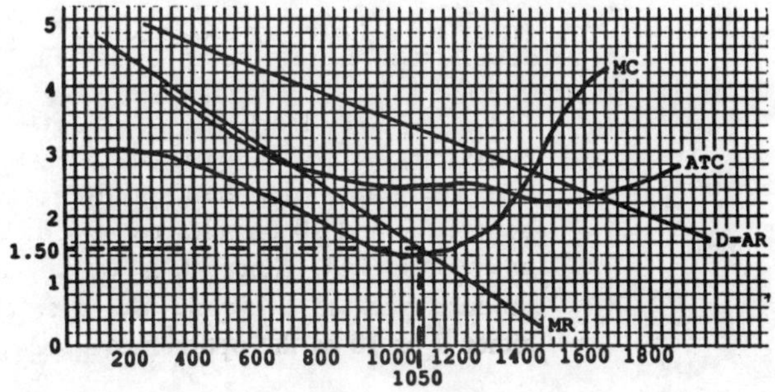

(c) 900 to 1200 units

(d) 1050 units

(e) $3412.50 — $2520 = $892.50

(f) No; demand is downward sloping and MR does not equal price.

16. (a) 300

(b) $11

(c) $8

(d) $900

(e) No, since it is facing a downward sloping demand schedule.

17. (a)

Quantity	Total Revenues
0	0
10	500
20	1000
30	1500
40	2000
50	2500

(b)

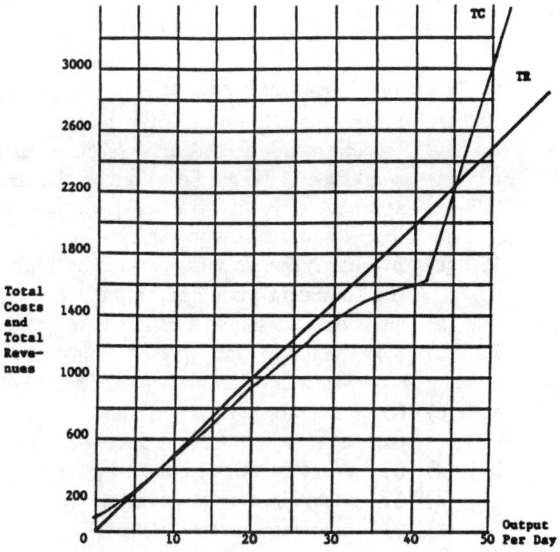

(c) 40 units

(d) 10; 10 and 46

(e) $100

18. (a)

Units of Output Per Day	Fixed Costs	Vari-able Costs	Total Costs	Total Revenue
0	$ 300	$ 0	$300	$ 0
200	300	900	1200	700
400	300	1600	1900	1400
600	300	2100	2400	2100
800	300	2400	2700	2800
1000	300	3100	3400	3500
1200	300	4300	4600	4200

(b)

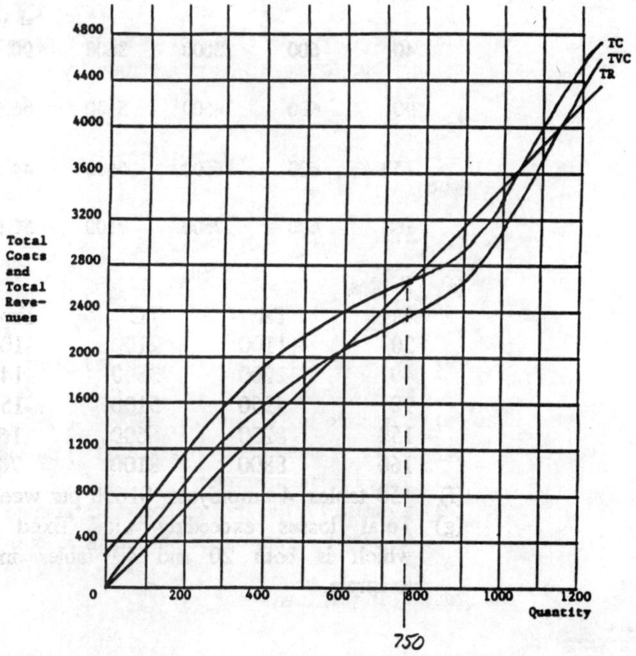

(c) 750
(d) 600
Below output levels of 750 units per day, total costs exceed total revenue; thus, output must exceed 750 units per day in order to break even. If output falls below 600 units, variable costs exceed total revenue, so that it would be less costly to close the business and have only the fixed costs to pay.

19. (a) (i) decrease output
(ii) maintain price and output
(b) (i) increase output and decrease price
(ii) maintain the present position since losses are less than total fixed costs
(c) (i) maintain current position
(ii) increase output and decrease price
(d) (i) decrease output increase price
(ii) maintain current position
(e) (i) maintain current position
(ii) maintain the current position if MR=MC. If MR<MC, reduce output and increase price.

Chapter 12

1. (a) Merger of Molson's and Carling O'Keefe breweries
(b) Purchase of Texaco by Imperial Oil
(c) Takeover of Wardair by Canadian Airlines International
(d) Dofasco's acquisition of Algoma Steel Corp.

2. about 600 per year, 1082.

3. (b)

4. the share (percentage) of an industry's sales held by the four largest firms in the industry.

5. (e)

6. true

7. (a) yes (d) yes
(b) yes (e) yes
(c) no

8. (a) a depressed economy (market) with lower stock prices
(b) attractive tax incentives
(c) weak Canadian legislation prohibiting mergers and takeovers
(d) a desire on the part of corporate management to beat out rumoured changes in federal law.

9. higher, lower, lower

10. one and one-half

11. (c)

12. (a) no (d) no
(b) yes (e) no
(c) no (f) yes

13. competitive, oligopolistic.

14. 25

15. (a) higher prices than under competitive conditions,
(b) lower output than under competitive conditions,
(c) lower product quality/planned obsolescence,
(d) slower rate of technological progress,
(e) competition to cost-push inflation,
(f) manipulation of consumers through advertising.

16. In sum, there is a tendency towards industrial concentration which restricts supply and raises prices and profits.

Price competition is replaced by advertising, superficial product differentiation and price-fixing.

The appropriate government policy called for is legislation aimed at preventing price-fixing and mergers and the formulation of any other measures that would reduce competition.

17. (a) no (f) yes
(b) no (g) yes
(c) yes (h) no
(d) no (i) yes
(e) yes

18. (a) true (d) false
(b) false (d) false
(c) false

19. (a) elasticity of demand (especially due to foreign competition);
(b) lack of cooperation among oligopolists;
(c) fear of government action, as price-fixing is illegal;
(d) desire for growth;
(e) desire for a good public image;
(f) countervailing power.

20. In general terms, a representative of big business would probably argue that big is not so bad. He may suggest that big business has benefited consumers, that criticisms are unfounded and inaccurate, that the power of big business is exaggerated and subject to limitations and that it is a source of significant economic benefits to the economy.

21. less; less protected against oligopolistic practices.

22. (e)

23. On average, Canadian top firms are smaller than their foreign counterparts. Industrial concentration in Canada is higher than comparable industries in the USA. In other words, Canadian firms large enough to threaten Canadian consumers are weak competitors internationally. Legislation aimed at restricting growth and concentration domestically to protect consumers could also prohibit Canadian firms from growing large enough to be internationally competitive. This in turn can threaten employment in Canada's already weak manufacturing sector. Policy makers are damned if they do and if they don't.

24. (d)

25. (a) no (b) yes (c) no (d) no (e) yes (f) yes

26. (c)

27. (c)

28. (a) true (b) false (c) true (d) true (e) false

29. promote development of Canadian manufacturing industries through tariffs, which protect Canadian manufacturers against foreign competition.

30. more intense, Japan and Southeast Asia.

31. the Canada-US Free Trade Agreement, 1989.

32. efficiency gains, compete internationally

33. (a) barriers to entry to the particular market

(b) the extent of foreign competition

(c) the effectiveness of the competition that would remain after the proposed merger.

(d) the availability of alternatives.

34. (a) mergers and acquisitions

(b) price fixing

Chapter 13

1. supply and demand for each particular job skill.

2. $6

3. $7

4. False: the more inelastic the supply, the steeper is the supply curve, and there will be a greater impact in the market given any change in demand.

5. an excess supply of 6 workers.

6. It creates imbalance (disequilibrium) in the market resulting in an excess supply (surplus) of labor at the artificially high price. The more elastic demand is the greater the surplus.

Therefore, job loss depends on the demand elasticities in the industries involved. For example: in tourism, the largest of minimum wage employers, demand is inelastic. People want personal service; despite increases in the minimum wage, hotel and restaurant business has increased. As long as **all** employers must pay the additional costs, the bulk of it can be passed on to the consumer.

Students can form their own summer companies and work on contract, thus avoiding the problem of wages. Their willingness and ability to paint houses, build fences, and so forth is not impeded by the minimum wage. Moreover, they are encouraged to be entrepreneurs, not just to think of finding someone to hire them.

Since there are employers who feel that the minimum wage keeps them from hiring more people, the question to ask is, does society want to encourage substantial employment in low wage areas? Perhaps people who are not able to command an adequate wage should be considering other activities such as staying in school, domestic work, and so forth.

7. To provide low-income earners with a more reasonable rate of pay, thus improving the degree of equity in the labor market.

8. 30

9. 28%, 35%

10. Canadian Union of Public Employees.

11. craft unions; industrial unions.

12. craft unions; the skills of such workers gave them the ability to resist employers' attempts to prevent them from unionizing.

13. 90

14. (a) local;
(b) national (international);
(c) federation.

15. local

16. (a) yes (d) yes
(b) yes (e) yes
(c) no (f) no

17. contract negotiation
contract administration

18. the individual worker.

19. agency shop.

20. he or she will hire only union members.

21. trade

22. (d)

23. (d)

24. Closed shop; unions can restrict the supply of labor and force wages up (by controlling the number of people who enter the union).

25. Open shop; problem of free riders — some workers may decide not to join and pay dues, but still derive the general benefits from union contract negotiations.

26. file a grievance against the employer.

27. (b)

28. (a) false (d) false
(b) true (e) false
(c) false

29. 90

30. one third of 1%

31. (d)

32. (a)

33. (a) bargaining power;
(b) status of the economy.

34. (a) inflation rates (cost of living);
(b) essential services;
(c) geographical imbalances.

35. 10-15

36. an arbitrator.

37. (b)

38. Contract negotiations take place as usual, including conciliation, but if no agreement is reached, the dispute goes to arbitration for a final decision

39. (a) strikes are not legal;
(b) no appeal after the arbitrator's decision.

40. Agree. On the basis of countervailing power, multinationals should be organized by international unions, national companies by national unions and regional or local organizations by locals or provincial federations.

Chapter 14

1. (a) true (c) false
(b) true (d) false

2. 39.5%, 6.2%

3. (b)

4. (b)

5. (e)

6. they do not vary with the size of the place of residence.

7. old, young, poorly educated, single parent families.

8. (e)

9. (c)

10. (a), (b), (d), (e)

11. (a) shifts in consumer demand, which have placed increasing emphasis on services;
(b) changes in production technology, which have altered industry's labor requirements.

12. grow much less rapidly than before the 1960's, and even decline in some years.

13. 62-67%

14. differences in hours worked
training, education, experience

15. occupational segregation

16. (a) clerical
(b) service
(c) sales
(d) medicine/health
(e) teaching

17. white-collar workers

18. (d)

19. (a)

20. (c)

21. slowly, increase, increase, shortages.

22. (a) rising productivity creates higher living standards, which increase demand for goods, thus creating jobs;
(b) rising productivity allows Canadian business to compete more effectively in foreign markets, thus creating additional jobs.

23. 27%, 19%

24. continue to increase
continue its gradual decline

Chapter 15

1. increase, 21% to about 42%

2. purchasing goods and services, redistributing income, and employing people;
Crown corporations

3. the imposition of constraints backed by government authority, that are intended to modify the economic behaviour of individuals in the private sector significantly.

4. (a) income security
(b) health care
(c) education

5. (d)

6. rises, rise

7. (a) Brought in Unemployment Insurance Program in 1942.
(b) Canada Pension, 1956.
(c) Child Tax Credit, 1978.
(d) Guaranteed Income Supplement, 1966.
(e) Hospital insurance and medicare programs were introduced.
(f) Indexing numerous welfare programs to keep pace with the CPI.
(g) Increasing inflation and unemployment.
(h) Increase in the number of tax expenditures

8. income security

9. (a) false (d) true
(b) false (e) false
(c) false (f) true

10. (a) too complex and inefficient
(b) inequitable
(c) generates disincentives or negative externalities.
(d) ineffective

11. all statements are true

12. (e)

13. 30%

14. (d)

15. False. The tax system is not nearly as progressive as is generally believed and is regressive for very low income people.

16. When all taxes are considered, the tax system does not redistribute income in the progressive way that is generally presumed. However, when government spending is considered, the net effect of government is to redistribute income from the upper-income third of families toward the others, especially the lowest-income third. On the other hand, the net effect of government programs is not as progressive as is generally believed beyond quite low income levels.

17. (a) they contribute to rising interest rates;
(b) they depress business investment spending;
(c) they threaten to undermine Canada's social welfare system;
(d) the interest payments on them are increasingly taking a larger portion of the government's budget.

18. (a) true (d) true
(b) true (e) true
(c) true

19. (a) It would be less costly to administer than other programs combined.
(b) It would provide people with an incentive to work.
(c) It would provide assistance to the working poor who are not eligible for welfare under present plans.

20. False. If all the income in 1981 in excess of $39 999 were redistributed to taxpayers with incomes of less than $40 000, each would have received $385.59. Besides, a few years of economic growth would do more for the poor.

21. Students should be directed to put forth economic arguments and reserve their political comments until they have explored Chapter 16.

22. decrease, 24%, 21.7%

23. fierce political resistance

24. 3 to 1

25. Goods and Services Tax

26. $20-22 billion

27. incomes, consumption spending, assets

28. incentives to invest and expand

29. lower, regressive

30. regressive

31. 25%, 50%

32. (a) reductions in the marginal tax rate on personal incomes
    (b) increase in tax credits for low-income earners
    (c) introduction of a broad-based federal consumption tax

33. **Advantages**
    - major source of tax revenue for government
    - may be applied at the manufacturer's level and be invisible at the retail level
    - can assist in deficit reduction

    Disadvantages
    - may be economically damaging to the nation
    - may become a discriminatory tax
    - may favour imports over domestically produced goods

34. to reduce the tax burden on low income Canadians.

35. to replace the Federal Sales Tax on manufactured goods with a more broadly-based consumption (sales) tax on a wide range of goods and services.

36.

Seller	Buyer	Price	Tax	Rebate	Net Tax
Iron Ore Prod.	Steel Prod.	$1 000	$70	$ —	$70
Steel Producer	Can Manu.	5 000	350	70	280
Car Manufacturer	Car Dealer	10 000	700	350	350
Car Dealer	Consumer	16 000	1 200	700	420
					1120

Chapter 16

1. (a) free enterprise
   (b) the market system;
   (c) individual responsibility for one's own economic fate.

2. the operation of free markets.

3. profit motive.

4. biased in favor of the powerful and wealthy.

5. rich and powerful.

6. an active role for government in the economy.

7. left

8. right

9. left

10. incentives for people to save and invest their capital in business enterprises, which provide employment and prosperity.

11. right

12. do not

13. taxes and transfer payments.

14. left; they see unions as organizations of workers to protect themselves against exploitation by employers.

15. Left, against business.

16. socialism

17. right

18. raise, discourages, slows.

19. left

20. grew very rapidly.

21. right

22. of budget deficits, incentives for investment by private business.

23. A shift to the right, less government spending, deregulation, and free trade.

24. Depending on whether or not a provincial government is in a have or have-not province, its prospects and its fiscal position could override

any political considerations. In other words, the economic situation may override philosophy. Right wingers, all things being equal, would likely support extra billing by doctors, and an increase in tuition fees.

Chapter 17

1. the provincial governments.

2. (a) false (b) false (c) true (d) true (e) false (f) false

3. 75; 25.

4. (c)

5. (a) false (b) false (c) false (d) true (e) false

6. (a) Canada's conventional oil supplies were predicted to last only 13 years;
   (b) an increase in domestic oil prices to world oil prices could result in windfall profits to Alberta and multinationals at the expense of Eastern consumers;
   (c) it put financial pressure on the federal government to subsidize have-not provinces under equalization payments.

7. False. Provincial governments, specifically Alberta, argued that economic rents should go to its citizens (legal owners).

8. (a)

9. (a) false (b) true (c) true (d) true (e) false

10. (a) it forced Westerners to subsidize Eastern consumers;
    (b) in encouraged consumption;
    (c) it discouraged exploration.

11. (a) true (b) true (c) true (d) true (e) false

12. (a) Holding Canadian oil prices well below world (OPEC) levels.
    (b) Development of Canadian oil sources so as to reduce Canada's dependence on imported oil.
    (c) High tax revenues for the federal government and for the governments of the oil-producing provinces.

13. If oil prices were kept low, governments could not receive the tax revenues they wanted and/or the oil industry could not receive the revenues it needed to develop Canadian oil supplies.

14. (a) true (b) true (c) false (d) false (e) true

15. (d)

16. (e)

17. (a) yes (b) yes (c) yes (d) yes (e) no

18. 10; 24; the oil industry.

19. 25; 50.

20. (a) true (b) true (c) true (d) true

21. (a) yes
    (b) yes
    (c) no, Canadian oil prices would be "capped" at 75% of "world" prices

22. (a) true (b) true (c) false (d) true (e) true (f) false (g) true

23. (e)

24. rising deficits and a National Debt higher than it might have otherwise been.

25. True. Apart from some regional variance in gasoline prices across Canada, Canadian drivers probably work no longer (in minutes) today than in the sixties but more than in the seventies when compared on an average or minimum wage basis. Recent price decreases (1986) may make Canadians marginally better off than in the sixties but probably no better than in the seventies. In other words, Canadians really don't have a lot to complain about.

26. Petro-Can has provided Canadians with a window on the industry. Many had hoped that through ownership Canadians might be better able to influence the behavior of other oil multinationals in the industry. Instead, Petro-Can has chosen to adopt oligopolistic behavior. Petro-Can has been

very reluctant to lower its prices at the pumps, acting in part as a price leader and keeping revenues up. Canadians continue to pay more than Americans for gasoline.

Chapter 18

1. (a) false (b) true (c) true (d) false

2. Private costs are costs paid by producers and included in the price paid by the consumer. Social costs are costs paid by society at large and not included in the price paid by the consumer.

3. (c)

4. minimize, minimize

5. An externality is an incidental cost or benefit derived from a product or service, e.g. goodwill.

6. all

7. watchdog, regulator

8. It has not been a priority; consumers (voters) don't want to pay for clean up; producers may shut down their operations.

9. If, by lower standard of living we mean a lower material standard of living, then yes! we will have to forgo consumption of some products, at least in the short run.

10. production possibilities

11. No, but why should all Canadians subsidize the operations of a few polluters. Polluters, on the other hand, argue that they either can't afford it or that they will be unable to compete in the marketplace.

12. Achieving the final 20% reduction in pollution may cost a polluter as much or more than it cost to cleanup or eliminate the first 80% of pollution.

13. set pollution control targets;
how to protect the environment
who should pay for abatement

14. (a) true (b) false (c) false (d) true (e) true (f) true (g) true (h) true (i) false

15. Answers will vary.

Chapter 19

1. (b)

2. (a)

3. (e)

4. (b)

5. (c)

6. (a) yes (b) yes (c) no (d) yes (e) yes

7. (b)

8. $4 to $2, fall, rise.

9. (a)

10. less

11. (d)

12. a surplus of 60 (quantity supplied=100, quantity demanded=40).

13. paid farmers not to grow some crops.

14. (a) no (b) yes (c) no (d) no (e) no

15. 100; $1

16. pay the farmers a subsidy of $3 for each unit sold at the market price of $1, to bring the price received by farmers up to the target price of $4.

17. restrict the output and increase the prices of farm products.

18. (a) no (b) yes (c) yes (d) yes (e) yes

19. $1 billion

20. (a) yes (b) yes (c) yes (d) no

21. (c)

22. Government subsidized export prices of agricultural products in an attempt to unload their surpluses onto world markets.

23. Japan.

24. (c), because this approach does not reduce the volume of food produced or put on the market, as the others do.

25. Answers will vary but any that will promote efficiency would seem appropriate from an economic perspective, strictly speaking.

Chapter 20

1. (a) state ownership of the production facilities, rather than private ownership;
   (b) economic decisions are made by central economic planners, rather than through markets.

2. (a) What to produce
   (b) How to produce it
   (c) For whom to produce it
   (d) The proportion of the economy's output to be devoted to consumption and to investment.

3. faster; Soviet economic planners emphasized production of capital goods, as opposed to consumer goods.

4. (a) no (b) yes (c) yes (d) no (e) yes

5. less than one-half

6. (a) false (b) false (c) false (d) false (e) true (f) true

7. Worker productivity in the USSR is estimated to be about half that of workers in the US.

8. (a) is diminished, since workers find that extra effort goes unrewarded.
   (b) is reduced, since good performance and higher output may lead to higher quotas in future years.

9. (a) More than one-half of the capital is badly outdated and obsolete
   (b) The use of computer technology is far behind that of the western countries

10. (a)

11. (a) yes (b) yes (c) no (d) yes (e) yes

12. (a) false (b) true (c) false (d) false

13. (a) true (b) true (c) true (d) true (e) false (f) false

14. (a)

15. (1) improvements in technology
    (2) stronger incentives for employees and managers
    (3) restructuring the economy into a market oriented system

    Reasons: (1) more modern technology is necessary to improve efficiency
    (2) stronger incentives will contribute to higher efficiency from workers and managers
    (3) this will allow the enterprises to produce in response to consumer demand, rather than according to quotas.

16. (a) false (b) false (c) true (d) true (e) true (f) false (g) false

17. (e)

18. extensive; intensive; the improvement in the quality of labor or capital used, resulting in better efficiency.

19. (a) true (b) true (c) false (d) true (e) false (f) true (g) false

20. The transformation of the Soviet economy to a market oriented system would mean that most of the planning bureaucracy would become redundant, resulting in a great reduction in its size and power.

21. (c)

22. (c)

23. resorted to printing money; a growing problem of inflation

24. (a) false (b) false (c) false (d) true

25. All political power and economic decision-making had previously been centralized. *Perestroika* has moved the economy towards a decentralized system, and politically, towards a more democratic society.

26. some obstacles to be considered:
(1) opposition from the bureaucracy
(2) lack of the necessary infrastructure for a market economy (eg. private banks, stockmarket, etc.)
(3) difficulties in transferring state enterprises to private ownership
(4) the inefficiencies and need for subsidies of many existing factories
(5) inexperience and unfamiliarity with the workings of a market system

27. (a) opportunities for entrepreneurship; more choice in the market place; a gradual improvement in living standards; better quality goods; growing confidence and optimism in their initiation to a system which has outperformed the Marxian model.
(b) rising unemployment; higher inflation as price controls and subsidies are lifted; rising inequalities in income distribution.

Chapter 21

1. (a) yes (b) yes (c) no (d) yes (e) yes

2. (e)

3. (a) resource depletion
(b) overpopulation
(c) pollution
(d) food shortages

4. (a) true (b) true (c) true (d) false

5. (a) false (b) true (c) true (d) true

6. regulation of business practices; rent controls; assistance to farmers; protection for corporations, consumers, workers; income redistribution; free or subsidized public services.

7. less

8. (a) no (b) yes (c) yes (d) yes (e) no

9. providing for a fair distribution of the nation's wealth.

10. (e)

11. (d)

12. natural resources such as forests and mineral reserves; energy; engineering and technological skills in certain areas; proximity to the US market.